MARKE BRANDS TO CHILDREN— ETHICALLY!

A compilation of strategies, thoughts, concepts and actions to help combine responsibility and effectiveness in marketing to children

Nic Jones

Strategic Book Publishing
New York, NewYork

Strategic Book Publishing
An imprint of AEG Publishing Group
845 Third Avenue, 6th Floor—#6016
New York, New York 10022
www.StrategicBookPublishing.com

ISBN: 978-1-60860-256-8

Printed in the United States of America

Dedicated to children, who deserve more from all of us, and to the vast majority of teachers, parents and child caregivers, for being so brilliant and yet so undervalued by our society.

Especially dedicated to the four teachers with whom I grew up.

About the Author

 Nic Jones has over 20 years of marketing experience, the majority of which have been spent working with children's brands.

He has worked with some of the most well-known children's brands in the world, including Warner Bros. (Looney Tunes, Harry Potter and Scooby Doo), Hasbro (Action Man, Playskool, MB Games) and Mattel (Barbie, Fisher Price, Hot Wheels), among many others.

Since 1996, Nic has run Jammy Rascals, a marketing company, which combines innovation and idea conceptualisation, with commercial brand positioning, consultancy, and product sales.

Nic has been published all over the world and wrote monthly articles for three years for *Toys n Playthings* magazine in the United Kingdom.

Nic lives and works in the United Kingdom.

Introduction

I have a passion for delivering great brands to children—brands that they will love. I also have a passion for communicating to young people in a manner that will engage them and encourage them to respond. And I am passionate about parents, caregivers and teachers trusting the brands they invest in, not just for their "educational" value but because they are engaging, they help communication and, ultimately, they are fun.

This book encapsulates those passions and aims to pass some of them on to you, the reader, so that you can set about your tasks with open, creative and ethical minds. After all, this is the mindset of the audience!

If you are interested in marketing to teens, pre-teens, juniors and infants, the words I have written should inspire you, at the very least, to respect your audience. Beyond that, I hope the book will motivate you to love this market, and to want to do what is right by the audience.

This is a book that tells readers how to market to children in a manner that is infinite in dimension and creative in structure, because—unlike with adults—no single set of rules applies across the board to children. Young human beings cannot be pigeonholed as simply as can grown-ups. They are not yet fixed into opinions that will dictate their behaviour; they are fickle and open-minded, so marketers should avoid setting strict rules in trying to understand them. Selling brands to children is an art.

I intend to guide you through the intricacies that make this audience so fascinating. Essentially, I have seen many marketing strategies fail because of a lack of specialized knowledge of this audience, as well as a lack of insight and market intelligence.

Most of us see youngsters through the eyes of an adult, of course. Instead, we need to start looking through the eyes of a child. What you're about to read can be considered a step on the road to enlightenment, in that I want to help open your eyes more widely to the children's market and its many foibles and twists. I encourage you to see the world as youths do. I don't want to enforce rules, though; in speaking to this market, rules are intended to be broken.

Throughout this book, when I talk about children, I am encompassing all ages, from infants through teens. Yet I fully acknowledge that there is a world of difference between a five-year-old and a 12-year-old, and between a boy and a girl. When delivering brands to children, you must always be acutely aware of which age group and gender you are talking to. This is a vital first step.

I also try throughout the book not to use the word "kids" when referring to children. Children do not see themselves as kids; in fact, they will often use the word "kids" as a put-down to those younger than themselves. Since children dislike the term, I am going to try to avoid the mistake that many, including myself, have made for many years.

Back to my passion. I love the fact that the children's market is not predictable. The fact that children are unpredictable should be embraced and celebrated. Enjoy the fact that one week will be different from the next.

While this book delivers answers, I don't want these solutions to be considered definitive. I want to challenge, and I expect to be challenged back. While I have said I don't want to impose rules, there are five axioms to which I adhere when planning strategies to deliver brands aimed at young people:

1. Treat them with respect.
2. Don't patronise.
3. See children through a child's eyes.
4. Accept that children change their minds—often!
5. Be ethical.

I will leave it to you to decide which of these you will follow, but I suggest that if you ignore the majority, you will not have a successful brand. And if by some chance you do find success, it will not last long.

Please bear in mind also that I am a product of my time. The media through which children take their lead constantly changes. The axioms, however, will still hold true through time.

Many of the words in this book were originally written for a number of media outlets, particularly for *Toys n Playthings Magazine,* for which I wrote a monthly article from September 2004 through August 2007.

The following pages offer my philosophies, formulated during 20 years spent listening to great marketing minds, working with some of the greatest brands of the 20th century, and watching and learning from children themselves. I hope my words will do them all justice.

And I hope these ideas point you in directions you hadn't thought of. I want to foster the understanding that with children, there are no absolutes. What matters is that you respect them, and that you are willing to go to great lengths to understand them.

Please enjoy this book as much as I have enjoyed working on it. Please feel free to contact me with comments and questions via my web site: www.jammyrascals.com.

Special Thanks

To Suze, merely for being special and who supported me when I first set out to work on my own in such a difficult industry.

To everyone with whom I have worked and argued over the years, and who have helped me become the person I am now.

To Simes, Mand and Bec, and to Terry and Joan, for letting me be me.

To Paige and Max for being the special children of my universe.

To Katie, my inspiration, best friend, fellow dog walker, and love; to whom I owe so much and whose contribution is so much more than can be detailed here.

Last but not least: Thanks to the children of the world. You have given me the most exhilarating run for my money, and I wouldn't swap it for anything.

Contents

1

Understanding Your Audience

As many who have studied the field of marketing already know, understanding a market is of paramount importance before launching a brand. With children, this is particularly critical because the margin for error is small. This is because children are fickle; they change their minds at the drop of a hat.

In order to get you in the right frame of mind, I'll begin by reiterating a comment from the book's introduction:

Let's Start by Calling Them Children

Kids don't like being called kids, so why do we refer to them as such?

I can't answer that, but I suspect that in the United Kingdom, it is part of our heritage to put children down. Being "seen and not heard" was a phrase I heard frequently as a child, and it is part of contemporary culture as well, even if modern mums wish to deny it. While other countries' cultures, of course, vary enormously from that in the United Kingdom, it is probably fair to say that wherever you go, children will use the local term for "kids" as a put-down.

The reason, I believe, is that children don't want to be young. They want to grow up and they want to be considered more mature than they are (the opposite of what men do when they turn 40!). Children in school refer to themselves as a set defined by their school year; being in a higher year earns a child unspoken respect from those in the years below. Those in higher school years get the best seats on the school bus, get to sit at the back of the hall at assembly, and generally use their status to position themselves in preferred school areas. Older children often describe those who are their junior as "kids"—not nice!

Ultimately, to be called a "kid" is to be called a subset of what young people usually are happy to accept as their human category: children.

Children call younger children kids because they recognise that they are not the same as they once were, and perceive themselves as "far more grown up" than a younger sibling, for example. Each age stage calls the one below "kids," and the term is used most definitely as an insult (except, of course, to the youngest subset: infants). Interestingly, children of all stages have a common name for those that can't argue back: babies. There is some respect in the children's jungle, after all.

Considering a child as a child is the first step toward being able to understand them, and possibly getting to know them better as consumers of brands. If you patronise them by calling them kids, you are just perpetuating the ultimate insult that children put upon one another, and you will be confirming to them that you don't know them and you don't respect them.

If you are sceptical, try to think of any long-term or classic brands containing the word "kids." If you can think of any, were they still around within five years of launch? If so, my guess is that the target audience was five-year-olds and younger.

And yet I acknowledge that, as with all axioms, there are some brands that are exceptions—not necessarily brands with the word "kids" in their names, but brands that have so earned the respect of children, they have earned the right to talk to them in their own language. I am thinking here about media owners, particularly worldwide television channels such as Cartoon Network, Disney and Nickelodeon. These are destination channels for children and they are considered style-leaders by children. As a result, these brands are not being patronising when they call their audience "kids." One needs to *earn* the right to refer to children as kids.

Unless you are absolutely confident about your relationship with your target audience, I suggest you begin your marketing strategy by thinking of and referring to them as children.

However, being respectful of how an audience wants to be addressed is only a beginning, as I discovered a few years ago when someone posed a simple question: "Explain to me," he requested, "exactly what it is you do, in words that a six-year-old would understand."

Wow . . . did he know what he did with that single sentence? He unwittingly unleashed a thought process that led me to not only appraise my business but to give due deference to the last part of his sentence: "in words that a six-year-old would understand."

The question seemed simple enough, and I was content to answer with words that an adult would understand: insight, intelligence, strategy, communications, etc. But it didn't take long to realise that I was doing what so many of us do when considering kids—we ignore them.

The solution isn't to simply translate big words into something easier to understand. That line of thinking leads straight into a common child-marketing trap: patronising the listener. What I needed to do was get inside the mind of the six-year-old and understand his or her motives. And my answer should be offered in words that fit into the world of the young audience.

Blimey, it was only a question! But the hand-wringing and soul-searching that resulted were good exercises. I think this is an approach the marketing field should consider when devising marketing and communications strategies.

Young people are a conundrum, an ever-evolving mass of hormones. There is no pigeon-holing. No science will dictate their behaviour, and it is the acceptance of this fact that is the first step toward enlightenment when it comes to marketing to children. Marketing to children requires time studying the form, so to speak. It is not just a case of using classic marketing techniques straight out of a lecture hall, or even those devised over years working on mass market, so-called "blue chip" accounts. It is also no longer enough to use the same tried and tested techniques year in and year out, as can be done with an adult audience.

When considering how to talk to a six-year-old, you need to weigh a number of factors that simply don't exist in the adult marketing world. For example, if you were talking to an adult about your business, you wouldn't as a rule need to give consideration to their age or their gender, or whether others of the same age are listening, or whether there are older people around. You wouldn't need to think about your surroundings or whether the other people listening were the friends or siblings of the person to whom you were directing your explanation—or the gender of any nearby friends and siblings.

But all of these are important when you have a conversation with a young person. It matters intensely to them that they do not stand out—that they do not look foolish and become the object of ridicule. Unless you know a child particularly well and have developed a trusting relationship, it isn't right to demean them, even ever so slightly; such a response would never be forgotten, or forgiven.

Can we honestly say that we take all factors into consideration when we plan to communicate our brands to teens, pre-teens, juniors, pre-schoolers and infants?

These audiences have many differences, some startling and others more subtle, but to a child these nuances are essential to their understanding of the world. They expect us to recognise this when we communicate with them. Failure to do so will lead to disengagement with us or our brands. In my opinion, we ignore these nuances at our own peril, and we do so more often than we should. I suppose the most effective way they let us know this is by not buying the product being marketed.

If I were to say there is a huge difference between a six-year-old and a nine-year-old, the response from many people would be a look that inferred I was being stupid (or rude, or patronising) for even making such an obvious statement. Yet how often is this simple mantra ignored when addressing young people?

When you want to sell products to children, you need to take a good look at these products and consider how a young consumer will look at them. This takes experience and insight, and, when this isn't quite enough, it takes market intelligence and research. The viability of your product range is at stake, so why not take some time over it?

With a viable product and a target consumer, the range has a chance of making it to retail. Success with the retailer is most often achieved with a promise of communication directly to the target audience.

This is where problems often start.

Too often, the communications let the range down. I believe this is because too little time is spent considering the strategy of how the range directly communicates with its true niche audience.

There is no valid excuse for this; it is simply a matter of getting to know consumers and then talking to them in a way they understand and enjoy; a case of paying respect to the nuances of children and being cognisant of the differences between a six-year-old girl, a nine-year-old boy and a tear-away teenager.

A lack of understanding exists regarding children's motives and the things that instigate them to seek certain brands. How would you reply if asked how you sell your products to young people? You would likely say that you sell to retail and they put the product on the shelf, and then the youths buy the product after seeing the ads.

Well, I disagree. In reality, you sell your products to the young audience directly, and you do that in the manner in which you communicate the brand, whether through television ads, online promotions or within the store. The responsibility is yours entirely, and I believe that more thought should be put into how you are creating and delivering your message. You must be entirely clear about your target, taking time to learn about them, and you must consider the context in which you contact them.

For example, if you have two ranges—one a collection and one a fashion doll—with identical basic target audiences, you might be tempted to think about the two together. However, these are completely different propositions to the audience, whose members will interact with these products in different ways and will externalise the merits of each to friends and family differently. For example, a collection is likely to consist of a large range, with each item priced at the cheaper end of the cost spectrum, giving a child the chance to "collect them all" whilst the fashion doll will likely be quite expensive, with accessories that fit into the cheaper market. It is clear, therefore, that the communication and audience context for the collection will be completely different than that for the fashion doll. This should be apparent in how you talk to the audience, and should be a component of your communication strategy.

Essentially, the whole thing comes back to a feeling of respect. If you give young people respect, you will get some back; with that, you can sell to them. Once respect is gained, your brand will have to work twice as hard to keep it, but that's another story.

So, back to the request that I explain my work in words a six-year-old would understand. After some time, my reply, worded as though speaking to a six-year-old, is this: "I show people how to sell things to young people like you!"

That's the nub of communicating your brands to children: You must be sure your understanding is as strong as possible. If it is not, the language, tone and context of your product, its packaging and its ultimate marketing campaigns may be too wide of the mark to make any impact. You also run the risk of frustrating or angering your audience in a way as to make it impossible to return.

Of course, the child of today is somewhat different from the child of decades ago. Media have opened up a world we didn't know existed when I was growing up in the 1970's.

Being a Child in 2008: Kids Getting Bolder Younger

Having scolded people for calling children "kids," I realise I have now fallen into this usage. However, the term's use here is important because for many years, marketers have been hounded by the mantra that our kids are getting older younger (KGOY). I first came across this supposition in the early 1990's, and it made sense to me at the time. However, 15 years on, the saying is still with us; surely our children should by now be going to university at 12, driving cars at 10 and learning to read in the womb. What I'm saying is that the true developmental facts don't bear out this myth.

If we take a good look at the literal meaning of KGOY, it doesn't stack up that youths can be considered "older" than those of a decade ago. Young people are the same now as when we were kids; they have the same concerns, growing pains, learning problems, playground politics, homework issues and parental pressures. They aspire to be older and more mature than their own age group, but so did adults of today when they were youths. It is fair to say that children today are no "older" than we were.

However, if you place KGOY into another context, it could make perfect sense. From a manufacturer's (and therefore sales and marketing) point of view, market forces have absolutely been affected by changes among the age group that purchases so-called "kids" products. So when talking about purchasing patterns, one is right to say that certain children's brands now appeal to six-year-olds, whereas previously they were sold to eight-year-olds. In the sense of positioning and selling brands, target markets have become younger; therefore, the universe of potential customers has become smaller.

So while development may not have changed, attitudes have. Children today have a deeper perception and understanding, a greater knowledge, of the world than those of a generation ago.

Why? Some say it is an issue of aspiration. Yet as has been discussed, children always have and will continue to look to older children for their influences.

The answer comes not in asking *why,* but *how.* How have children come to be more street- and worldly wise?

The solution lies in the media—the media they consume and its infiltration into their daily lives. The electronic media age has provided instant information to a generation willing to listen and understand. Each new generation is more media-savvy than the previous one. There is no fear of the unknown or of possibilities. This generation isn't getting older but *bolder.*

Our youth are grabbing possibilities far more quickly than their predecessors of a generation ago, and they are doing it earlier in their lives. I may only have added the letter "B" to the previous adage, but this single letter carries a heap of significance.

Let's look at the facts presented to us every day. The media is leading the way: Media targeted at young people has, in the last decade, provided children with instant information. Since the desktop computer arrived in the 1980's, each generation has subsequently become far more media-literate than the preceding generation, resulting in young people becoming more savvy younger and younger. They are leading the Internet generation and can be considered pioneers. They certainly are bold.

While researching a young audience, I asked seven- to 15-year-olds about their computing habits. I was astonished to discover that 100% of my group had access to a computer at home, and that they talked in a manner that suggested they also had control over the computer, with parents having little influence. I was expecting the children to be enthusiastic in their usage of the computer but didn't expect them to assume ownership, with parents essentially taking back seat.

Now, I don't want to suggest that children are running amok online without any control, because this wasn't the context of the research. What I learned, though, was that children are using the computer to communicate, play, learn and explore. I hope and expect that most online enquiries are perfectly innocent; the vast majority of children really are not interested in adult content. Youngsters are the pioneers; they are watching and listening and then passing along what they find. How else could Messenger, You Tube or My Space become as big as they are? Certainly adults wouldn't have recommended them.

Of course, the effects can be seen "offline" as well. All mobile communication innovations are driven by the teen generation and are passed down to tweens, juniors and those younger. The mobile generation is demanding and getting better-quality and quicker downloads, they are accessing information where and when they like and they are sharing this with similar-thinking individuals.

Which highlights another point: Social networking allows people to find like-minded individuals with whom they share common interests. For children, this is a marvellous way to "fit in." Such a mindset is of uppermost importance in a child's world, and social networking helps all children realise that there are many people just like themselves.

Having established that kids are now bolder than we were at their age, I also contend that this behaviour is starting at a much younger age than most would believe.

It is now a well established fact that mobile phones are owned by younger and younger people; it is not uncommon to see primary school children with phones. What hasn't been accepted is that the same age groups are now accessing their friends via the computer when they get home and that the home computer is *their* tool, one that they teach their parents how to use.

Crucially, I also suggest that parents of the very young are using the Internet to improve their child's media access and entertainment. Very young children tend to be extremely possessive of the characters they like and want exposure to them as often as possible, so the family home often has cable and satellite television, compact discs, and, as a result, numerous toys and gadgets assigned by licensing to their favourite characters. What the same home also has is the Internet and, through it, access to even more exposure; mum and child can simply sit in front of a computer and reach their favourite characters on-screen (just like a TV to a young child!). Even better, they find that they can now interact with the character; they can write a letter to him, for example, and get a reply. Their brands are now tangible in a way that simply was not possible a few years ago.

The result? Children become media-savvy incredibly quickly; first, alongside their parents, and not long afterward, on their own, prompted by schoolmates. As with all behavioural patterns in this market, use of mobile media will begin at younger and younger ages. So the brands struggling to reach them should be looking very closely at how brave this market has become in encompassing the new universe. Tradition has no place in a child's mind.

Young people, from teens to the very young, have no fear of technology and are leading the way into the digital frontier. We need to be just as bold in *our* understanding and communications.

Ok, so KGBY doesn't trip off the tongue as easily as KGOY. But it is apparent that KGBY is now a far more relevant barometer in gauging the behaviour and attitudes of today's children.

Kids are getting bolder younger. How bold are you?

2

Positioning Your Brand

When considering a marketing campaign, you first must look at all possibilities and come to grips with potential problems. With facts, you can move to a place of knowledge, where you can be comfortable with the positioning of your strategy.

I am a huge fan of planning and taking the time needed to address all issues involved. This chapter advocates long-term planning over short-term tactics—a mindset that is not prevalent in many industries anymore, especially those related to young people.

In understanding an audience and positioning a brand, it is paramount we remember who this audience's members are:

Begin with the Children's Point of View

I want to highlight the role played by children and their mums in your brands, and look at ways of getting more from their input.

It is not rocket science to say that a perfectly honed communications strategy should encompass everything about your brand: its positioning, its packaging, its promotional material, its advertising and its media communications strategies. Plans that encompass everything good about a brand and that recommend when and how to communicate these positive attributes should be successful. In reality, however, things are never this simple. There are many reasons—some beyond anyone's control—as to why strategies fail. But I want to highlight one often-ignored question: What do children themselves (and their mums) think?

Have you asked them or involved them in your brands? Have you, at any point during product development and the devising of tricky positioning and communications strategies, considered asking consumers for their opinions? Furthermore, are you prepared to act on such feedback?

Before you put pen to paper, decrying me for my naivety, allow me to explain my question. I am sure that many readers of this book carry out consumer research, and find that products that don't perform have to be changed or else will not see the light of day (at least, some of them won't). I also know that mums and children are asked their opinions regarding adverts—and possibly also asked about which programmes they watch.

So what am I getting at?

When you look at research carried out in the standard way—small focus groups, standard questions, and standard methods of asking the questions—you will get pretty much what you want. It is often said that if you don't know the outcome of the research, you shouldn't do it.

Is the point of research simply to back up one's own point of view?

Most children's products and the ensuing marketing—through packaging, on-shelf and advertising—are the result of adults' imagination. But how much sense does it make to produce "just what the kids want" based on the opinion of non-children? The safe option, and thus the least creative, least controversial and the least fun, is the simple option.

What I suggest is that when considering your options; try to take a kids-eye view at what you are portraying. Wouldn't it be better if your brands' positioning and communications were the result of a kids-eye view?

This entails more than just focus groups; this involves using child psychology and philosophy and interweaving it with "adult-oriented" research. Instead of suggesting ideas to children, why not let them give you the ideas? Let them lead you to the best solutions. Let their imaginations go and then let them tell you what they think. Children are always keen to help, but usually in a way that doesn't make them stand out from their group or make them feel foolish. Unfortunately, most research is the result of this kind of group.

So, when considering your new ranges, ask such questions as:

"How would children (or their mums) view this product?"
"How would they like to see it?"
"What would make a child enjoy this product?"

If you start from this point, it should change the way you conduct your ensuing research, and I guarantee it will change the information you receive—as well as your marketing (and sales) perceptions. You'll find your public relations budget is spent more efficiently, too.

The problem is, this could mean you must completely re-think your brand. Are you prepared to do so? I hope so, because the industry needs new ways of reaching its consumers and it needs to be more relevant.

Anyone involved in marketing to young people wants to spur the next big craze. A common perception is that marketers really can create a craze. Unfortunately, when talking about a market of teens and younger, this simply isn't so. We must think carefully before we assume we know what children want.

While children are all very different, and develop in different ays, a case can be made for positioning products into four overlapping categories:

Staple, Fad, Craze or Classic?

Is a product line a brand, or is a brand actually a line of products?

This is a pertinent question in the market today because, in many instances, licensing dictates that a range of categories are available under one umbrella, whether for a film, TV show or even a property that has been around for many years. Surely Disney, Barbie and Scrabble are brands. Movie releases are initially lines of product. But where exactly would *Star Wars* or even Harry Potter fit, now that they have been around for many years?

Most manufacturers refer to all of their ranges as brands, independent of whether they are producing a licensed category or their own new development. Such a statement is incongruous with the market where children are involved. Everything can't be a brand—or can it?

Children do not give a hoot as to whether or not they are playing with, wearing or even eating a brand. They are playing with a product they like—one that they may have asked for and, in most cases, certainly wanted—because it is fun. They are comfortable with and have an affinity for the property associated with said item; otherwise, mum wouldn't have bought it.

There needs to be another way—a way that allows the market to adapt to the fickleness of youth, coupled with the necessity for short-term gain against long-term asset-building. A way that allows everyone to claim they have a brand, no matter its history or future. A way that allows marketers to change the positioning of brands as they develop.

My instinct is to break the market into four categories:

Fad = short-term craze
Craze = long-term fad

Staple = "Every home must have one"—this can be a fad or a craze, or neither

Classic = one or more of the above; here to stay

Combined, the categories can be described using a very simple Venn diagram:

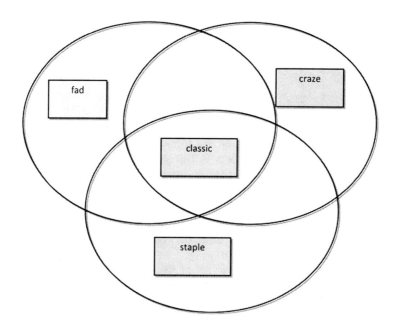

A fad is something that tends to come and go very quickly. A craze comes and goes, but generally lasts longer than the fad. A staple defines products that are essential. Finally, a classic is a brand that has been one or all of the first three, has long-term strategies, and has stood and will continue to stand the test of time.

Every market has its staples, and the children's markets are no different. These are brands that don't need to be hyped. Every now and again, a product will come along that can be defined as a staple but will develop into a fad and a craze; writing-implement variants such as gel pens spring to mind. The Yo-Yo is another staple that regularly comes back as a fad. Marbles are probably the most enduring staple, having been around for thousands of years and likely to be found in just about every home.

Children love a craze; they create them, after all. They don't like to admit anything they like is a fad. A fad, though, essentially is a craze that hasn't quite managed to take a longer-term hold on the collective psyche.

A classic (excuse the pun) example of a fad is the humble conker (horse chestnut). For a while, children are engrossed, collecting and cooking conkers to make them go hard, and fighting with them. Then get bored. All of this happens within days. Fads are like that; they take their lead from what's going on in children's lives at home and school. Fads are happening every day in schools throughout the country. Some last barely any time at all; others catch on and get passed along. Some go away and then return again (the conker). It is when the fad spreads beyond the school gates and gains some momentum that it can be considered . . .

. . . a craze! At this stage, the brand has withstood the first wave of cynicism and has enough going for it to have a much longer-term future. These brands will now have more confidence than fads, and will be able to talk directly to children. They also should be able to withstand having children talk back. Crazes may not have a finite time span, and could last for years. They may fizzle out and then come back, until eventually they move into the category of . . .

. . . a classic! All brands could aspire to sit in this category, but unfortunately, many fail. For some it is just not possible or even worthwhile. Many classic children's brands have been around for a long time. They have the advantage of age, of being from a time when immediacy and globalisation meant nothing. They had the advantage of time to mature into what they are now. Parents and children alike are comfortable with these brands and will in turn pass them down the generations. "Modern classics" are few and far between in the present-day children's market. Very few can claim to have moved on from the craze stage.

Brands can jump quickly from a fad to a craze and then become a staple in a relatively short space of time. However, there are no shortcuts to becoming a classic. In my opinion, a brand cannot be considered a classic without having been through one or more of the other categories. But upon achieving classic status, a brand has the luxury of being able to behave as if it were a fad, craze or staple, as long as it doesn't overstretch itself.

Marketers must consider a brand's foundation, whether that is a film, TV show, stand-alone product or an extension of a classic brand name. There is no shame in categorising a new brand as a fad, or stating a desire of becoming a craze.

You cannot force crazes onto children; they have to discover them for themselves. You can give the process a helping hand, but crazes don't develop overnight. If you are seeking to regenerate an old craze, you face the same hurdles as when introducing the original brand, because the market has moved on. In fact, the second time around is harder. These are only a few reasons why a small percentage of child brands have become classics. Based on the present short-term-thinking market, even fewer will do so in the future.

It is a shame that many brands aren't planned for the long term; those that are can become folklore. How often do you reminisce about what you did as a child—what music you liked, which fashions you wore and which toys you played with?

When you consider your next child-related launch, take a good look at where you think the brand or product in question will be in five years. Furthermore, will it ever be a craze, staple or classic?

Do Your Brands Have the "Craze" Factor?

I recommend that all children's marketers visit a museum of toys or childhood or something similar. In 2006, a very interesting exhibition from the Museum of Childhood—"Must-Have Toys"—toured the United Kingdom, showcasing favourite toy brands from the previous century. At first sight, the displays didn't appear to demonstrate much. But closer inspection revealed why certain brands have become part of the nation's psyche, and analysis of the elements that helped produce a successful children's brand became possible.

The Holy Grail of marketing is the establishment of a craze. Many believe that the bigger one's marketing budget for a product, the better the chance for creating a craze. But I can state with absolute certainty that marketing techniques alone are not enough. During many years spent observing children's behaviour and analyzing business practices, I have yet to see an example of anyone setting out to establish a craze and succeeding in doing so due to marketing alone.

Why not? Because a craze is created by *children,* not marketers. Crazes are not born; they evolve. This is why crazes seem to come out of nowhere, and take people by surprise.

Brands can be introduced to the audience and can capture imagination and even generate sales, but the ultimate arbiter of whether a brand will become a craze is the child. Whilst this is an accepted axiom of children's marketing, it appears that many marketers ignore this truth and forge ahead with campaigns designed specifically to start a craze.

An important question to consider when trying to sell products directly to children is this: How can you accurately position brands and adopt efficient strategies in these complex markets?

The solution is in the positioning, and marketers should look beyond a brand itself and focus on a child's perception of it. We want to know how children examine and categorize brands, and what happens from there that makes some products become a craze.

What most "craze hunters" fail to do when launching their brands is assess whether they are being realistic in their hopes and whether they actually have any chance at all of evolving into a craze. To review: A *fad* comes and goes quickly, leaving little impression in its wake. A *craze* is more established than a fad, and leaves a lasting impression on consumers. A *staple* is a product that most people have at home somewhere, and a *classic* is a brand that that has lived through any of the previous stages and has achieved timeless status.

The majority of children's brands fall into the category of fad, in that they are a hit for one or two years and then fade away. Conversely, Pokemon cards, when they first appeared on the market in the mid 1990's, were an example of a contemporary craze, similar to Chopper Bikes during the 1970's. Staples are products such as pens and pencils, chess sets and jigsaw puzzles. Classics include Barbie, Monopoly and Lego. In many homes, Lego is a staple—stemming from its turn as a craze back in the early 1970's.

By looking at the brands that make up the various categories, and by understanding their properties and unique traits, we can begin to learn how to realistically categorize new brands, and assess whether they possess the "craze factor."

It can be argued that if a product is of suitable quality and has high "play" factors, it has a great chance of becoming a craze. This is true, but there have been thousands of high-quality products over the years that have fallen short of this goal. So is it time to stop thinking in terms of "the next big craze" in marketing aspirations and plans? We may just have to be satisfied with the fact that a brand will be a fad, growing over time until it eventually becomes a craze, or even a classic. In fact, is it not better to be a classic, and revel in the long-term benefits?

A very good example of a modern-day craze is the Tamagotchi hand-held digital toy pet. Its manufacturer, Bandai, may argue that marketing made it a craze, but I believe there was far more to it than that, foremost being that it is an excellent and contagious product.

Strangely enough, some products already are considered a staple as soon as they are launched. For example, children have for years played in gardens building their own dens, pitching makeshift tents. So as various pop-up tents came on the market, they immediately became categorised as staples, enjoying immediate respect from the consumer, as did various products associated with them such as the Ready Bed, which is akin to the sleeping bag.

Being confident of a brand's traits can help set realistic aspirations—and tailor communication strategy—for a potential audience. How you talk to this audience is critical.

Positioning Your Brands—with an Eye on the Future

This is a good time to take a look at your brands and consider how they will communicate with their young target audience, as well as how they will continue to develop as the market changes in years to come. Tried and trusted methods of reaching young people don't necessarily hold sway in today's electronic, interactive world.

I offer a "back to basics" guide to strategies that won't leave you wallowing in the past and its misty eyed nostalgia. Children don't buy nostalgia; they are evolving, and we must adapt to their wavelength.

I hope to get you to think before you act and to consider all options before you embark on a child-targeted strategy.

The Consumer

Your key target consumer is the child, which may be stating the obvious but is actually important when put into context. It is easy in the children's market to mistake your intentions and to allow yourself to develop a range that you think is right for children but in fact is the result of a perceived gap in the market—such as a product that fulfils the wishes of a retailer.

The Law of the Land

If you want to produce materials for children, you must become familiar with the jurisdiction under which they will be promoted and sold. You need to be aware of laws pertaining to your product. The European Parliament now is looking closely at rules applying to advertising to children. While each member state has its own rules (some of which are extremely restrictive), a pan-European directive on the issue could become a reality. It is only a matter of time before governments in areas beyond Europe, such as Asia, Australasia, Japan and China, will look closely at how child-targeted industries conduct themselves, if they are not scrutinizing this field already.

Governments throughout the world seem to believe that children need to be protected from advertising. This ignores the huge effects of peer group pressure in homes and schools. Children are more influenced by others than they are by the media, though that is not to say that the media are not responsible for acting in the best interests of children.

One generally accepted rule is that products should not be promoted by trying to create "pester power" from a child onto a parent. The reasons are simple: Parents will resent you for doing this, and children will themselves feel pressured. Most importantly, it isn't ethical to push children into doing what you tell them to do so that you can make money. You should not encourage children to continuously ask their parents to purchase your product.

Rules to Live By

When addressing children, some simple rules apply:

- Children are not stupid.
- Children want to fit in; they don't want to stand out from others.
- Children will talk about your brand.
- Children will not be polite with their comments unless warranted.
- Children know you are advertising to them.
- Children are discerning, fickle consumers.
- Children know what licensing is.
- Children are lead by entertainment; they want to be entertained.
- Children are influenced in their product choices by peers first, older youths second, by the media third and by parents and teachers least of all (there are some age-group caveats, which I'll address later).
- Children dislike patronisation.
- Children can hear clearly.
- Children have opinions of their own.

There are, I'm sure, many more that readers can add, but I hope you get the point: Articulate and be "real" when talking to children. You need to consider who they are and what makes them tick. Positioning your brands correctly will be so much easier if you adhere to these truths.

Posi tioning

This is where things get very interesting, and not a little intricate. Once you have decided you want to reach a child audience, and when you have accepted the many rules pertaining to young consumers, you're ready to position your brand to them. But there are a few more rules to apply:

Gender: With children, there is an enormous difference between the sexes. This disparity doesn't really exist before age three, starts to reduce again in teen years, and is often blurred among adults. But with children between the ages of four and 13, the differences between boys and girls are clear and you need to be cognisant of this at every stage of development.

Age: As with gender, the difference between the ages is crucial. It is a fair generalisation that every child aspires to be older than he/she actually is. They want to behave like older children and be seen as being like older children. As previously discussed, there is no bigger put-down than being perceived as a "kid." It's stating the obvious that you cannot compare a six-year-old with a nine-year-old, but this is frequently ignored by manufacturers and marketers.

Here are some examples of how children can vary between the ages of 7 and 12:

Boys, Ages 7–8

This group have a tendency to be unsophisticated and very childlike, displaying a lack of concern surrounding most things. They take most things at face value.

Interests include sports (participating and watching), game consoles, playing with friends, watching television. Family relationships are positive and central, but sibling rivalry exists. Play is based on action, often simulating fighting. Brands are dominated by sports and heroes, based on current media trends. Pocket money is spent on small items such as sweets, games and toys.

Girls, Ages 7–8

Girls this age are teachers' and parents' delight—a happy, conscientious, family oriented group that shows few signs of "getting older younger."

Interests include television and playing with friends, with music and fashion beginning to show signs of influence. Girls this age spend a majority of their time with family, in particular with Mum. Sibling relationships provide lots of fun but also frustrations and hurt. Play becomes group-orientated, but toys are still present. Brands are dominated by programmes and music acts and heroes are based on current trends, girl fashion dolls. Pocket money purchases are small items such as sweets, games and toys.

Boys, Ages 9–10

This group is highly interested in "escapist" technology (computer games and TV), and is starting to show signs of independence and the beginnings of a more rebellious attitude.

Interests include sports (particularly soccer), playing with friends and watching TV. Most time is spent with family, although beginning to seek independence as well as seeking out favourite web sites and social network sites on the computer. Play becomes group-oriented; sports are a common bond, dominating brands and heroes. Pocket-money purchases are still relatively small: DVDs, console games and CDs.

Girls, Ages 9–10

This group begins displaying signs of more "adult" interests—enjoying music, clothes and makeup. Friends are important to this age group, which also takes conscientious approach to school.

Interests are based around friendship; TV is more influential than before, particularly live-action shows. Family relationships are still positive, although they are spending increased time with friends, and social networking through computer and mobile phone becoming far more prevalent. Play is centred on friends, as toys are left behind. Programme brands are important, as are music acts. Pocket money purchases include sweets, makeup, fashion accessories and CDs.

Boys, Ages 11–12

This group is less sociable than others; friends are important, but this age group is slightly oblivious to peer pressure.

For boys, the main transition from childish things to more grown-up habits and attitudes occurs in early teen years. Boys ages 11–12 are in limbo—still dependent on their parents and with some ambivalent attitudes toward peer group.

Interests are dominated by sports, games consoles and TV. Boys this age start to spend more time with friends than family, and the computer and mobile phone play key parts in their lives. Play is firmly replaced by TV, movies, sport and gaming. Brands are still dominated by sports clothing but peer and fashion pressures start to creep in. Pocket money continues to increase and is spent on DVDs, music, and console games and sports equipment.

Girls, Ages 11–12

This age group marks a difficult time, as girls are trying to find their own personalities but are anxious about friendships and very vulnerable to peer group pressure.

Interests are dominated by friends, becoming aware of makeup and fashion.TV is still important, but the computer and mobile phone are key components of communication. They are becoming more independent of family, and increasingly want to fit in with friends. Socialising takes the place of imaginative play and toys. Brands are dominated by trends in music and celebrity. Pocket money continues to increase, with more household tasks done to earn extra money. Money spent on CDs, DVDs, magazines, makeup.

Children define themselves and others by their gender and age. They aspire to be grown-up and expect to be treated in such a way. If you are blatant or plainly obvious with positioning a product, you might find yourself falling into the trap of generalisation (e.g., pink is for girls; blue is for boys), yet you should be aware of the effect of positioning on your consumer. Gender and age are crucial to the initial positioning; they are the key factors in the making or breaking of brands' strategies and plans.

Point of Difference

Once you've jumped on the merry-go-round that is the children's market, you will want to look at how your brand looks and how it will be perceived.

By using some of the above rules, correct colours and a suitable "look" should be selected for the product itself. What can't be controlled is the resulting on-shelf perception; that is up to your audience—the children. Children make decisions on the worthiness of brands, and they make these decisions in an instant.

Many worthy products have failed because marketers failed to gain standing within the child community. In many cases, this is because the product was let down by its positioning, or what it looked like. Here are a few rules that can improve the chance of successful positioning:

- Packaging is incredibly important, and must relate well to the product and its promotion campaign. Many children's brands are let down by their appearance on shelf and bear no relation to the marketing of the brand in other media. It is not unheard of for mums to enter stores looking for a particular product that has been communicated brilliantly, only to leave with another brand because the retail experience was so negative for the requested brand.
- Retail: Are you in the correct stores? It is tempting to allow your range to be sold to every retailer, which is understandable, but time should be taken to make sure that it is seen in the correct store for your

brand. Every effort should be made to make the brand experience in this store as magical as possible.

- Have you allowed yourself to be placed in the wrong category? Are you in the correct part of the store? You must be cognisant of what retailers' plans for your brand. Don't let your brand fail at the last hurdle.
- Are your promotions unique? Can they be seen among the clutter of competition?

If you are confident in your brands' positioning and that you are targeting the correct age and gender, you can be confident that you will produce the correct message, which can then be delivered at key in-store touch points. Having established your positioning, it is vital to consider how you want to communicate.

Branding Our Kids—without Being Patronising

Branding sounds painful—because it is!

"Branding" has its origins in the age-old ritual of placing hot irons against the rump of animals, demonstrating ownership. The ownership and the brand mark are forever.

Obviously, the word has become a metaphor for those who believe branding applies to all products, and that demonstrating and communicating in such a way will create instant gratification and a groundswell of popular support. Consumers will be *owned* by the mesmerising brand.

Brands for adults conform to the well-set regimen of their audience; they fit a lifestyle. Millions are spent researching, adapting, analysing, introducing and communicating these brands. The audience is receptive and can be manipulated; they are willing recipients of the brand owner's largesse. What is clear with adults is that once a brand is accepted, it is hard to shake off; it's comfortable and comforting. This makes targeting and message reinforcement more simple. Brand communication ultimately becomes more cost-efficient.

Children's brands have no rules. They don't conform. Money is spent researching or communicating in an attempt to cajole children into adopting a brand. However, they might accept a brand one week and disregard it the next. For children, comfort comes from the family home, not a brand name. Therefore, targeting and message-delivery become more crucial. Miscommunication is easy.

Children's brands seldom are given sufficient time, effort and budget compared to adult brands. Many children's brands follow a formula that has been tried and tested over many years and, therefore, is seen as being a correct, infallible method. These brands, the thinking goes, will sell because they always have. They are safe; they conform.

But whom, exactly, do they conform to?

Children? I don't think so.

Their mums? Well yes, to a certain degree.

The manufacturers and retailers? Most certainly.

Therein lies the rub. The very people who need to profit from the marketplace are the ones holding it back. Creativity, risk-taking and research and development are being sacrificed at the high altar of margin and profitability.

It is easier to jump on bandwagons, follow others, repeat the same thing year in and year out or take on licenses that are fads or likely to become fads simply because Hollywood has spent a fortune producing a film, or because a television company has an established cartoon series. The market is a sucker for the simple solution. Someone else is doing the selling of the property; someone else is responsible for the development and marketing of the property. If it doesn't work, blame the studio or the licensor. Many marketers do not have the inclination to take any risk in any shape or form. We are not going to develop new products.

This attitude takes away the drive to encourage creativity and entrepreneurship. There's no need for these because our work is done for us; we have the products tooled, designed and developed. All we need to do is put the requisite licensed character sticker on it and, presto, a line of toys, yoghurts, T-shirts or chocolate bars has been developed in conjunction with the licensor. Now all we need to do is show the range to the retailer and listen for the cash register to begin ringing.

It is a dizzy merry-go-round, and very few appear capable of getting off. Yet, at no stage in this scenario has consideration been given to the end user. Too many assumptions have been made about children: "They watch the film, therefore . . ." or "They enjoy the TV show, therefore . . ." As a result, the consumer actually is turning away from the market at depressingly high rates at an alarmingly early age.

I believe it is possible that in the near future, the toy market will exist only in preschool form. Mums and grand-mums are willing to spend money on preschool children, who are still at an impressionable age, an age during which parents hold sway and nurture has its strongest pull.

It is no surprise that the growth of the electronic game market has mirrored the decline of the toy market in terms of age of use. It is also a sad fact that the electronic game market stole creativity and risk-taking. This market was prepared to invest in research, development and communication to the end-user, resulting in games that, in themselves, have become enormously popular licenses. However, the electronic games market no longer is a key driver to the younger audience; it has caught the same bug as has the traditional toy market, operating under the assumption that licensing is the way to make money from the young audience. Nobody is prepared to take a risk in this market anymore.

What has happened to the attitude toward the key consumer? Why have these consumers been ignored?

Children move on very quickly. Having products put in front of them and being told that these are "cool" does not sway them. They can see that the latest film toy range is designed to make money, and that the range itself is the same as the one for a film they watched last year, but with a different character. They know that the advertisements they see are selling to them; they know that giveaways form part of a promotion, or a way of getting them into a burger joint. They are commercially aware at the same time that they are fickle, cynical and easily pressured by their peers. They like to think they are far older than they are, but they are still learning to communicate. They do not look upon the outside world as a big, scary place. The Internet has brought the world to them and they are soaking up the knowledge this brings.

Children are not stupid.

So why do we treat them like they are? Why do we patronise them?

We deliver to them goods they don't want. We make promises we can't keep. We treat them like second-class citizens. We expect them to enjoy what we tell them to. We ignore their values, attitudes and beliefs. We keep things away from them that we fear will hurt their sensibilities, only to find that those very things become staple in the playground. Sometimes, we are overbearing and overprotective.

Within the home, some of these tendencies make sense. But when we use the same attitudes in the methods we choose to communicate to children in the marketplace, we should not be surprised that we don't get the desired response. Children find these efforts childish and ultimately dismiss them at an early age in favour of communicators that pay them more respect.

Take a long look at the creative output within the children's market, such as TV commercials. It won't take long to spot the poor quality of these commercials and channels of communication. Why do ads all look the same? Why do we make the same ads for different regions without regard to their cultures? Why are we always trying to achieve so much with so little?

Almost without exception, TV ads targeted at children look awful and are unremarkable in their creativity and imagination. They make assumptions regarding the way children look and behave, and what they read, watch and do. They are not based on the world as it is today, leaving many children feeling detached from these ads.

It is no coincidence that fashion brands such as Nike and markets such as computer games are leaps and bounds ahead of others in the consciousness of today's children because they appeal to children of all ages, either directly or through aspiration. The way these messages are communicated are key drivers in their "street cred." They appeal to a multitude of environments; they translate seamlessly into the language of the target audience.

To regain respect and credibility, be more creative and more imaginative. Ultimately, to bring children back to the market, you have to keep them engaged be attentive to the simple child's command: "Don't patronise me."

I am of the firm belief that if you put a child into an alien environment, no matter their age, they will adapt to their surroundings. Parents often congratulate themselves on how well they nurtured their own children; my assertion is that parents actually have little influence in what sort of human being a child becomes. Disagree? Read on!

Targeting Children—Placing Things in Context

Arrgghhh, nobody's listening!
This isn't a lament as to the lack of change in the children's market, but a challenge to your positioning.

The problem with listening, I suppose, is that it depends on how a message is delivered: how you say it, the intended recipient, and how loud the message is. In other words, it all depends on the context.

It doesn't take a psychologist to explain that a message's influence depends on the context into which it is being delivered. But when it comes to children, psychologists appear to have quite a bit to say—such as the idea that children play a larger than recognized role in their own upbringings, influencing the way in which their parents nurture them.

Children behave differently when they are at home. We can't assume that the attitudes to which they are exposed outside the home are the same ones espoused at home. Children's behavioural patterns and attitudes vary according to the environments in which they find themselves, or place themselves. A child who may be quiet at home may be confident in the school classroom but also shy on the school bus. It's all in the context. Marketers must acknowledge this in the way we address our audience. It may seem natural to patronise kids (right use of the word here!) within the home (as is the case with most TV adverts), but it is not right to be patronising in youths' own environment.

What different contexts exist and which should be considered in the way a message is conveyed?

The list is endless, but here are a few:

- The home
- The bedroom
- School bus
- The playground
- The classroom
- Sports teams—in school and out of school
- Cub Scouts/Brownies
- On holiday
- Having friends for tea/sleepover
- Going to friends' homes

In each of these contexts, we might see a difference in behaviour and the methods of communication and interaction, depending on a child's comfort, shyness, newness, general confidence and other factors. Some are more perceptible than others, but each in its own way is important to the development of children and therefore the way they view what is being offered to them, and—critically—by whom.

Furthermore, and most frightening for the brand owner, is that children can and do flit from one context to the next as nimbly as a multi-lingual speaker changes effortlessly from French to German to English.

This should be where marketers come in. We are in the business of offering brands to this audience and we should be able to offer what it wants. But are we taking enough time to study the consumer and the varying contexts into which our brands will be introduced?

More than 90 percent of commercial messages aimed at children are seen within the home, and more than 95 percent of those messages will be seen by their target on TV.

As we have discussed, TV commercials targeted at children treat them like kids, which is OK if the child is acting in a way that adults want kids to act. So the childish advert, with childish noises and sound-track coupled with the patronising voiceover, might work when children are watching TV alongside their mums and dads; some would say they work better on the parents than the children! In this case though, the youthful target would be behaving in the context of the family environ-ment, as just the sort of "ideal" child their parents have nurtured. It would therefore seem, in this picture of domestic bliss, that we have created the perfect advertising scenario. But in this day and age, things are more complicated.

The key problem is that this environment is seldom seen within the contemporary home. Children are encouraged to be independent from an early age; they are given TVs, computers, video games, mobile phones and other tools that allow children to freely express themselves. It is rare for children to watch TV alongside their parents today, so they will not react to adverts as would have been expected historically.

Most children will take their opinions out of the home and into the playground and beyond. This is where the real decisions are made. This is where youngsters behave in the way that gives them the greatest credibility—where they want to fit, be liked, be competitive and, most importantly, where they learn to live their lives.

I hear the cries from marketing managers: "We have focus groups; we talk to children; they like the way we communicate with them."

This may be so, but in what environment? What is the context in which the group is being held? Usually, there will be at least one peer present who will dictate the context of the research being conducted. A grownup involved with the marketing effort (the invigilator) will be present, as well. There also is likely to be a parent or parent of a friend present. If no parent is present, then the group will come under the influence of the strongest (child) personality in the room, who in turn is behaving out of context, due to the presence of the invigilator.

There is no escaping the fact that when targeting young audiences, you need to take a serious look at how the message is conveyed. Marketers need to look at the context in which a message is received, and how that will subsequently be discussed within peer groups and in various environments. Very simply, marketers need to understand children as children—not as a concept of what they expect children to be.

Ultimately, marketers should examine the context into which their brand fits most comfortably—the home-with-parents scenario; the playground; the home-but-alone. Such a brand audit is the base of a successful marketing strategy and a more efficient communication campaign. With such research, positioning and targeting will be spot on.

No matter which context a brand is placed, marketers will almost certainly be talking to children during leisure time. Some brands endeavour to reach children by working in schools with the curriculum, but most brands try to develop an image as "entertainment" for a child. But what is meant by entertainment?

In an effort to get to the heart of this elusive question, I worked alongside a client and child psychologist, Dr. Amanda Gummer, seeking specifics of what it is that children and their mums call entertainment. We conducted a great deal of research, and ended up being entertained our-selves by what we learned!

Now That's What I Call Entertainment!

What is entertainment?

Here's my definition: Entertainment is something that enlivens the emotions within us. It can make us smile, laugh and cry, but most of all, entertainment is something provided by a third party. Of course, this party can take many forms: the media we consume, the music we listen to, the football teams we follow. It can occur through direct human interaction or through the use of props such as toys and games.

Humans have become dependent on entertainment—addicted to its allure, looking for a daily fix. Has it made us lazy, fattened on the comforts offered by others? Maybe. It certainly has spawned billion-dollar dollar industries dedicated to keeping us in a state of contentment; keeping us entertained.

The knock-on effect, it could be said is that people largely have be-come lazy in the production and consumption of food, accustomed to over-salted, over-sugared, processed products. We want quick fixes, are addicted to caffeine and, in general, crave a way of life that makes it easy for us to get back quickly to our fix of entertainment.

There's definitely an opportunity here for marketers. If one can cap-ture the values of entertainment and bottle them in a product, a runaway success will be born.

What are these values? Dr. Gummer and I embarked on an effort to ascertain what similarities and differences exist across audiences in the values associated with being entertained, from pre-schoolers though teens, their parents, grandparents and their caregivers or teachers. We wanted to project forward in an effort to find strategies that would appeal to various age groups, and we had some interesting results.

There are six key values associated with entertainment, each of which carries a varying weight depending on the audience.

First, unsurprisingly, *fun* is the key value that all audiences agreed upon. Kids particularly want to laugh, and parents and caregivers want to see children laughing. Something that is not fun gets dropped onto the "boring" pile very quickly.

Second, audiences value brands that are *educational* and/or *chal-lenging*. When parents talk about education, they are not talking about schooling per se; they mean creativity and imagination. Kids enjoy a chal-lenge, as there is a great sense of achievement upon completion.

Third is *familiarity.* More than ever, children want to feel safe and mums want to know their children are safe. Parents today are wistful about the fact that their offspring don't have the opportunity to play outdoors with impunity, as they could when they were young. They love brands that encapsulate this value.

Fourth is *versatility.* Children become bored if a product is repetitive. This is especially true of young kids; they want the challenge of learning the range of a product's capabilities. This value is important to caregivers because they want brands that can help develop imagination.

Fifth is *sociability.* Children want to have friends to play with and brands they can share. Caregivers like social game-play because the interaction helps children learn how to develop friendships as well as cognitive skills.

Last but not least is *environmental.* The ethics of a brand are important to mums and children alike, especially older ones who are more likely to understand the issues around recycling and waste. A positive environmental product is one that lasts longer than others.

When developing new entertainment brands, great consideration should be given to the end user and understanding what they want out of the form of entertainment provided—whether through TV programming, books and magazines, computers and web sites, toys and games, even food. Incorporating these values will positively affect a marketer's relationships with customers, whether licensors, retailers or consumers.

Let's now take a good look at new products and test them for the values they eschew and consider them in relation to the age of your target market in each case.

For pre-schoolers, imagination and simplicity are key. Children of this age love "peek-a-boo"-type game play. They like small pieces, because they are from a small world themselves (obviously, care is needed to make sure they do not swallow them) and they love to talk about things over and over again; repetition is a positive for them. Interestingly, preschoolers of different genders begin to behave in different ways.

For infants and juniors, their scope is enlarging, and segmentation between genders widens as they get older. For the youngest, "small world" is still relevant, but they are starting to take steps into the world around them. Role-play, imagination and fantasy play important roles, as do collecting and swapping, which also help develop sociability. As they reach ages 10 and 11, children are beginning to find some play themes such as fantasy a little childish.

Teenagers were a revelation to us. As most adults know, teens are particularly cynical of grownups, and the "whatever" attitude is their universal language. But when you talk to teens about being an eight- to 12-year-old, they are extremely lucid—probably because this age is still quite a fresh memory. It was not so much their attitude toward one another and the world around them that we sought, but their opinions about what is right and wrong for younger "kids" (as teens call them). They have a very interesting perspective on the sort of brands that engage younger siblings and others. I strongly recommend conversing with the teen audience should you be thinking of developing a brand targeted at the under-11 age group.

As for parents and caregivers they want to see imagination, positive child development, and, unsurprisingly, they want value for money. This doesn't mean cheap, as all parents are willing to spend a reasonable sum for the right range, brand or product providing it delivers value.

3

Being Ethical

So far, this book has covered positioning children's brands as an instructional guide, with some thought-provoking messages on patronising approaches, consideration of context and the definition of "entertainment" to a child.

But there is an elephant in the room and we cannot ignore him any longer: the ethics of marketing to children. I contend that you can be ethical while marketing to children, and I want to explain my rationale for saying so.

Over the last 10 years, advertisers in the United Kingdom and around the world have come under increasing fire as a result of social and political pressures surrounding obesity and the advertising of food and drink to young people. The result has been the drafting and imposition of a raft of rules that have severely hampered efforts to communicate brands in this arena.

I can't help but think that the food industry had this coming and were the architects of their own downfall, and I believe it won't be long before regulators turn their attention to other ethical issues that, so far, have not affected the children's industries. However I also feel that you can put into place practices that would mitigates any regulations and how they affect your business.

As a marketer, are you wholly satisfied that your messages targeting children are absolutely ethical?

I imagine most marketers feel that their approaches are spot-on—whiter than white—whether their products are being judged on being entertaining, educational, environmentally friendly, safe or providing value for money.

But let's be honest: Are you just in this for the money? Are you hoping to make a product for one price and sell it at a handsome profit? Are you advertising your products directly to a vulnerable consumer?

Which comes first—your product's ethics or the product's business plan?

I don't think I have to scrabble around for the answer. But that is why you are in business, after all. Someone has good ideas and a plan is made to take a product to market. It is reasonable to want to exploit a market position and gain maximum value out of an idea. This is the world in which we live, and if everyone else is doing it, why shouldn't you?

However, I believe we all have to start behaving better. We need to have morals; we need to get ethical.

For too long, many of the world's largest corporations have been providing products and services to children and their families without caring too much about the consequences of their actions. It is naïve to blame children and parents alone for *wanting* products that are either unhealthy or a downright rip-off. While I put some responsibility upon parents, I believe it is largely the fault of the fast-food industry that families love fast-food hamburgers, because of the way the products are produced, packaged and marketed.

For many years the culprits were happy to produce products that were dietary disasters—high in fat, sugar and salt. However, this isn't necessarily the whole problem, as one of these burgers every now and then is pretty harmless as part of a sensible diet. The main problem arose through the irresponsible way the companies communicated their products. Parents were seduced and children thought eating such food to be normal and the fast food companies took no responsibility in their role in helping families with their diets. They encouraged over consumption and were happy to allow pester power to feed their bottom line. Whilst they may argue, fairly in my opinion, that the fault is not entirely theirs it is also extremely fair to say that they were not behaving ethically.

"Pester power" got a bad reputation not because it worked on consumers, but because it was put into use by manufacturers and retailers. Children throughout history have asked for things, but today, parents are made to feel guilty or pressured into conforming to what others do or purchase.

There had been no attempt to educate the public—just a rush to make a buck. Nobody stopped to think about brand quality, food ingredients or the information contained in marketing efforts.

I compare the children's food market to the cigarette market. For years, cigarette manufacturers ignored the addictive nature of their product and the evidence that it was harming users' health to the point of killing them. Instead, they sought legal loopholes that could be used to sidestep regulations. Instead of assuming a mature and responsible attitude and providing necessary information to consumers, they were driven by profits.

If cigarette manufacturers tried to advertise to children, there would be a huge uproar, rightly, because of the unhealthy nature of the products, and the fact that to target children would be downright unethical. The argument that these companies used was that it wasn't entirely the fault of their products that the consumers were asthmatic, riddled with cancer and generally unfit and overweight, but that their lifestyle played a role. The way I see it, cigarette manufacturers may not be completely culpable, but they did contribute to problems and therefore should be held responsible.

It is simply not right to say that because fat-, sugar- and salt-laden foods and sugar-packed drinks have been around for a long time, manufacturers and marketers of unhealthy food are blameless. It is true that demand for "junk food" is high, and that consumers don't exercise enough. The food industry does share in the collective responsibility to public health, and therefore needs to change. When a child gets thirsty, for example, the industry should advocate the drinking of water, first, above one of their products.

The grocery division of children's marketing ignored the obvious for a long time, lobbying hard for years to be allowed to promote food and drinks that, if not incorporated into an otherwise controlled, healthy diet, could have a catastrophic effect on the health of the nation.

In the United Kingdom the market was pulled, kicking and screaming, into accepting a stringent set of rules. But one can't help but feel the industry is still looking for ways around these rules rather than improving the nutritional value of products being marketed.

The food and drink industries seem unwilling to acknowledge that if they had acted ethically in the past, they wouldn't be in a pickle now. An ethical plan going forward could end up *increasing* their business.

So, how can marketers "get" ethical? The answer is simple: Put children first, and do the right thing. Think about children at every point in a product's development, and make children's wellbeing the ultimate goal.

I suggest a few steps to move in this direction. First, take a good look at your products and how they were conceived and manufactured, packaged and marketed. Why are they on the market? How do they benefit children and parents? Research has shown that parents today are quite wistful about the lives of their children today in that children seem to have to grow up more quickly than their parents. They believe education has become far too intense from a very early age. Parents want children to have some fun time; they want education but also imagination and creativity. Parents want products that they can trust, that are safe (practically and environmentally), that promote left and right brain activity and, most of all, that are fun. Step forward, toy and entertainment industries!

Second, let's evaluate the way we communicate our products to our audience. It goes without saying that products should not be marketed if they are unsafe, have little play or monetary value or contain contaminants or illegal chemicals. Children today care about the environment, about other children around the world and about their own place in this world. It should also go without saying that marketers should not mislead an audience. Be honest about a brand; don't dress it up to be something it is not.

No child-targeted brand or industry, especially the toy industry, can sit on its hands and adopt a "holier than thou" attitude toward the maligned food industry. Ethics go way beyond the health of the nation. We only need to look at the fuss over recycling, carbon footprints, global warming, energy waste and the fashion industry's alleged mistreatment of staff in their factories, especially in recent years, to see where the pressure is mounting. Any industry that has as close a bond to its young audience as the toy industry is going to come under close scrutiny regarding its environmentally friendly and ethical credentials and, ultimately, the business practices used to promote and sell brands to children. Children often are the first to call upon us to help save the world for their future, and that of their own children. I say it is now time for the toy industry and all industries that market to youth to look in the mirror and ask if they are doing "the right thing."

Change in the marketplace, as always, will be lead by consumer demand. Today, many retailers have been queuing up to supply "Fair Trade" and organic products because customers want them. Retailers have started looking closely at the source, manufacture and chemical make-up of every item in order to appease an ever-inquisitive audience—an audience that wants to be more informed and is increasingly concerned about the "human effect" on the planet. How long will it be before everyone starts to question the carbon footprint of every single product purchased? Some may say this will take decades; I say it will occur with a few years. Being ethical engenders the most precious commodity a child can bestow—trust.

Now I can hear the scepticism brewing. "Come off it, Nic," you might be thinking. "These changes you are suggesting are seismic; they would wipe us out." But the importance of doing the right thing can not be overstated. Would you rather be at the forefront of change, or a follower of enforced regulation—like the food industry? Which position do you suppose will gain consumers' respect?

In doing the right thing, you will be taking the high ground; you will not be trying to evade issues and find ways around regulations. Instead, you will be embracing the need for change in an ever-changing marketplace. You will be able to look a child in the eye and say that you are doing your best to safeguard the future. What a nice position to be in.

And it *would* be a nice position—if everyone adopted this stance when considering the children's market. But I'm not so naïve, and I accept that with the good guys come the bad. It would be great if we could make sure that we are the majority!

If nothing is done, the toy industry and others connected to children could be in for more regulation, and each time it will get more stringent.

Traffic Lights for Toys and Games?

Having kept a close eye on the debate over obesity and the role the government believes manufacturers and retailers play in contributing to youngsters' health, I started thinking about how packaging that is being enforced on the food industry could be applied to the toy, computer games and entertainment industries. While these ideas are intended to be tongue-in-cheek, they carry a positive intent from which we can learn.

One of the results of increased attention to childhood obesity is the emergence in various forms of a "traffic light" system on packaged, processed food so that consumers know if a certain product causes artery blockage. Consumers need assistance in analyzing products' nutrients so that children can be served a healthy, balanced diet.

Within some retail outlets in the United Kingdom, we now have a system that issues a red light for high salt, sugar or fat content and a green light for low levels of the same. Despite its many weaknesses, this system is a step in the right direction.

What if other child industries adopted the same strategy? Would some toys be deemed "worthy" and be given a virtual green light? Would some toys be labelled "bad," and have an advertising ban slapped on them?

How would an industry such as toys react to seeing red lights on some products and green on others? How would consumers react?

A toy's *educational value* is one aspect that would be evaluated. Most manufacturers with a product deemed educational in any way make this the most visible claim on packaging and in promotions and advertising. Not surprisingly, parents probably are willing to pay more for a toy with a high educational value. How would they feel if a product in a certain age range had no "green lights" in this category?

Age range, too, could be evaluated. If a mum now buys a toy that shows an age range "3+" for a five-year-old, the child will naturally be put out a little, as they are five—and, obviously, too old for this product. Even though this was not intended to be the case, these guidelines may have become a negative. Age group traffic lights can be used to be with more specificity. For example, a green light could go to the age group most likely suited to a product (say, age's three to five). Amber, perhaps, could be for ages that will get enjoyment from the toy (six to eight), and red would give it a maximum age (nine and older). Would consumers appreciate such knowledge? I think so.

A third possible aspect to be evaluated is *fun.* How is fun judged? One person's idea of fun is not the same as another's. But how many products make it to market without any research regarding play value and their ability to entertain? How many licensed products have sacrificed fun at the altar of profit? This does the industry no good.

Longevity is another key element. Let's face it: Most products don't hold a child's attention beyond Christmas Day, let alone for the months to come and beyond. Red lights would help set realistic expectations for whether a child's interest will last beyond the holiday lunch.

Safety, too, could be subject to these evaluations. Such a system already exists with CE marks and international product safety regulations, but can it be improved? A red light could be used to warn about flashing lights, which would help those mums who have children prone to epilepsy. This need not be a negative, as it involves, simply, honesty. Again, it removes some degree of worry for a consumer.

My point is, marketing has reached a point where honesty certainly *isn't* the best policy. We all accentuate the positives of brands and products, and expect that media campaigns will outweigh any negatives or, dare I say, gloss over the inefficiencies. This is ever so slightly underhanded.

We have a chance in the youth market today to change the perception, to change how the consumer sees those who promote their brands to children. Cynicism toward manufacturers of processed food had already been on the rise when that industry found itself at the forefront of media criticism, and it is with a certain amount of inevitability that the toy market and other child-related industries will feel the chill wind by association.

Ultimately, we have the opportunity to treat the public with respect, take the high ground and regain some respect back. This is an opportunity too good to miss. If marketers take the end-user a little more seriously, we will produce brands that benefit this world.

Is the Time Right for "Positive Pester Power"?

The words "pester power" have been synonymous with children's marketing for many years and it is fair to say that the saying has been blamed for many "ills" within children's lifestyles such as making children obese, heightening family poverty, contributing to failing educational and social standards. Some say, furthermore, that pester power reduces parents to feeling so guilty that they simply have to say yes to their offspring's demands.

The result, unsurprisingly, is that pester power is a banished notion or tactic in children's marketing circles. Those who still pursue this strategy become akin to social pariahs.

Before I knew better, I gave my company the name Pesterpower. Blimey, why that seemed like a good idea, I don't know! I changed the name to Jammy Rascals a few years ago, which is testament to the fact that we in the children's marketing industry thought "pester power" was our own little secret; we were naïve in thinking consumers wouldn't be repulsed, and reject this ethos.

In my own defence, I have always been on the side of children. I believed and preached that pester power was about empowerment—about seeing children as valued contributors to society whose opinions counted. I am still an advocate of children as valued consumers; I've just "rebranded" my message!

These days, marketers steer away from techniques aimed at persuading children to persuade others to make purchases. That's not say it doesn't happen, but most have changed their ways.

At a children's marketing conference in 2006, the marketing director of a large food company in the United Kingdom that makes salty snacks said that everybody should be doing everything they possibly can to improve children's health, and that everyone should ask how their products can be improved in regard to children's health. This particular company has done so; it has reduced salt and changed the oil in which its products are fried. I may not agree with them when they say they don't target advertising at children, but I admire them for doing their bit.

Regarding pester power and the obesity debate, junk food restaurants, salty snack manufacturers and the toy industry seem to shoulder the burden. It hardly seems fair to bracket all toy companies into one, especially as 99% of toys can hardly be accused of causing children to eat too much. However, the toy and entertainment industries should share a collective responsibility to their consumers. The industry, after all, is just as culpable of sending out conflicting, confusing messages as are food giants. As they grow, children are asked to be more mature; why shouldn't children ask the same from the markets that target them?

The three mentioned "culprits" spend millions of pounds each year on advertising. Why not look at *how* the children view these efforts, rather than just seek the simplistic research of consumer scores for an advert or in a taste test. How cool would it be for children to participate and take ownership in a product that is being marketed to them?

Children lack the experience or education to carry through product development. But what if they were given the tools to succeed? I can't think of a better way to empower them.

These tools already exist; and I call them, collectively, "positive pester power." Children may not be able to grasp details of the manufacturing process, but they do possess opinions, lifestyles and attributes. Most importantly, they do have standards—standards set by their own social communities in the home, on the computer and in the playground. These standards vary from culture to culture, but *fitting in* and *contributing to so-*

ciety are overriding. The computer is adding extra dimensions to their own sense of community as well as their sense of belonging and their sense of injustice. Children have an affinity for one another, and they want the adult world to care about the same sorts of things that children care about. They want adults to demonstrate through their actions that they understand what children want, and that children are being listened to. The way we react to this will have far-reaching effects on the longevity or brevity of brands' popularity.

Children's sense of compassion can be harnessed as energy for ethical children's marketing, and it is this energy that is behind the concept of positive pester power.

Most companies have their own charity, in the form of a foundation, a partnership, or a favourite non-profit group to which they donate. Many companies work very hard and give back to their communities. These are different efforts than those I advocate.

Every year in the United Kingdom, a "Fair Trade Fortnight" has been held during which consumers are encouraged to purchase products bearing the Fair Trade label denoting that farmers have received a fair return for their produce. I don't know of anyone opposed to this idea, but do you know its biggest champions? Yes, children. They have been the force behind the movement. In some cases, their schools have been highlighted, demonstrating their contact with the Third World children whom they are helping. This is a cause that is being driven by children. Any child asking persistently for a Fair Trade product in the shopping basket cannot be considered a pest. Children have been a strong force behind campaigns such as this, as they want to have an impact on their peers across the globe and gain a sympathetic hearing from parents. This is a prime example of positive pester power, and there are plenty of others. World Wildlife Federation is understood by children to be working toward improvement of the planet. Such causes are exactly the brands children want to buy into.

Remember: This isn't about companies donating money to these causes, which they should do anyway. It is about adopting the policies advocated by these organisations, and becoming aligned with their aspirations. Can companies become carbon neutral? Can they source all components from Fair Trade cooperatives? Maybe, maybe not, but how many have tried? Such an undertaking requires change and leadership, and those that move in this direction should be able to tell people about these efforts—as long as they further the associated cause, such as WWF's mission. If such companies sell more products as a result of kids asking for them because they are tied to these positive-image organizations, more power to them.

I have always believed that one can be ethical *and* market products to children; these are not mutually exclusive goals. But what about advertising to children? Is it right? Should stringent rules be adopted? I think we should look at this field from this perspective: Ban advertising *to* children; but keep advertising *for* children.

Ban Advertising to Children; Keep Advertising for Children!

The debate on advertising to children has been raging for ages. We read about it in trade magazines and newspapers. We listen to debates on the topic by "bodies" that purport to represent us. There have been many well-meaning schemes proposed to "educate" children about the pitfalls and dangers of advertising, but to no real avail. There have been many attempts at self-governance, yet little seems to have changed.

While most people believe change in this field is needed, the marketplace still wants to advertise to children. The result is inertia. And the children's industries simply hope that the topic will somehow go away.

The truth is, the topic will not disappear. Children and adults alike have had enough of exploitive advertising campaigns.

I don't know why certain adverts make it onto TV. I am left wondering who researches these ads and allows them to be produced and broadcast. Is there any rationale for allowing adverts for products that contain high levels of sugar, fat or salt? These are unethical, patronising and formulaic, and leave me squirming with embarrassment.

As mentioned, picking on and admonishing the food industry is easy, though they are not alone. These industries certainly have spent too much time directing advertising *at* kids; they advertise *to* children. These ads tell children what, in the opinion of the brand owner, they should do and how they should behave. Basically, advertisers believe they know best and think they can pass this on to their youthful audience.

This may be true if a child is three years old or younger, but the approach is patronising to older children. Nearly all communications in the children's market patronise the audience, and where the target is particularly young, they tend to patronise the mums as well. More time should be spent thinking about the audience and communicating properly before millions of pounds are spent bringing products to market.

If we are to continue to advertise *to* children, then I am all for banning it.

It is time to show respect for the target market, and the way to start is to begin to understand these consumers better rather than seeing them merely as buyers. It is time to start developing advertising *for* children.

Any psychologist will tell you that children grow up with many influences and are not bound by convention. I would go so far as to say that all children are born non-conformist and that a cynical world subdues this attitude. These days, though, education is delivered so as to discourage debate; the world delivers facts and demands acceptance.

Answer this question frankly: Would you talk face to face to children in the same way as is portrayed in your adverts?

I doubt it.

Children should be talked to as non-conformists. See them for who they are, understand their aspirations, try to understand how they grow and develop within and outside of the family group, in school and elsewhere. By doing so, you will start to take a look at your own products, and the marketing thereof, from a child's-eye point of view.

One doesn't need to become a child psychologist, but it might not hurt to consult with one—or with an experienced teacher, for starters. These professionals know how to speak as well as listen to children and actually hear what they are saying.

My recommended solution is to take the opportunity to change the aims of your research. You will transform the results and ergo the whole dynamic of your market positioning. The best way to change the way you research is to find a company that consults with a child psychologist or uses teachers in the facilitation process. Changing this approach will help you begin advertising *for,* rather than *to,* your target audience.

4

Communicating with Children

The first half of this book discussed the philosophy and context into which you will be placing your brands, and offered thoughts on the ethics of the market. Now it is time to look at how you communicate your range to children and their families.

Key to communicating to this audience is to accept that children can be difficult to reach. But there are many ways to communicate with them.

Communicating into the Future

It is worth repeating this point made in Chapter 1:

Many worthy products have failed because they failed to gain standing among children. In many cases, this is because the product was let down by positioning in the marketplace.

The rules to remember:

- Packaging is incredibly important, as poor packaging can be the downfall of a product.
- Retail: Are you in the correct stores?
- On-shelf: Have you allowed yourself to be placed in the wrong category? Are you in the correct part of the store?
- Point-of-sale: Are your promotions unique? Can they be seen among the clutter of competition?

If you are confident in your brand's positioning, and that you are targeting the correct age and gender, you can be confident of producing the correct message, which then can be delivered at key in-store touch points.

The four point-of-difference considerations in positioning (packaging, retail, on-shelf and point-of-sale) are vital to how a brand is communicated. It would be tragic to move through the many stages of a brand's growth only to fall at the final hurdle because communication at the point of purchase doesn't rise to the level of the rest of the strategy. Much care must be taken at this point of the strategy, and you must be ready to tell the consumer who you are, what you do and where they can find you.

Targeting. As mentioned earlier, targeting is not as simple as telling children about the range. It is a matter of maximising communications coverage of your brand to its key target. If your target is of pre-school age, you may wish to target the mums. But there are many instances when you may wish to target an older children's audience in order to establish some "cool" credentials among the true, younger audience. This works because children want to be considered older than they actually are. It is known as "aspirational" marketing, where the goal is for consumers to create their own demand, largely through mimicry of older children or even adults. Mobile phones are a good example of this. Acknowledging this dynamic is important when considering your communications strategy.

Timing, of course, is vital. If your product is part of a film licensing programme, should it be promoted when the film is launched or when the DVD comes out? Or when the film moves to television? There are many considerations. Should your promotions be tied to certain festivals? Does the weather have a bearing on purchases of your product?

Placement, too, is key. Where will your highest sales be? Are you tied into one retail deal? Will your campaign to be national or regional?

And then, *how* do you intend to communicate your brand? Should you use advertising, public relations or both? What communications choices would suit your brand launch?

The debate over the use of advertising against other forms of promotion is becoming more relevant as growth and fragmentation of media outlets for children continues. As audiences fragment, reaching children en masse is difficult. Brands now need to be clever in how they find their audience and communicate with them. They need to forge an "active relationship" with children, through which dialogue and, eventually, trust can be built. This is done through integrated communications planning, and involves no longer just the concepts of advertising versus public relations, but the idea of how one can best build a relationship with a specific audience and further to engage and interact with them in a way that allows them to "touch" the brand.

The Internet

The Internet provides prime opportunity to engage with children. All children who have access to the Internet use it. It has become the most important tool for inter-child communication and is an ever evolving universe. It is likely that you will never harness the full power of this medium for your brands, as children are always one step ahead. But you can go a long way toward establishing great credibility.

Look at your products' sites, improve them and make sure they are engaging. Consider creating a site that has nothing to do with your product but is particularly relevant to the age group you are targeting; you'll learn a lot about them, providing they like your site. Spend some time online and get "with it" on social networking, "Second-Life," blogging and Twittering.

(I apologise if when you read this I seem out of date. When I wrote this, these were cutting-edge digital communications tools!)

TV

I advise that marketers go beyond the TV advert and get involved with television stations and their programming. Television stations are multi-media outlets, often with magazines and web sites, for example. They are also full of highly creative people. You must look at the likes of sponsorships, promotions, involvement with station activities and other opportunities.

Publishing

Marketers should consider publishing something themselves—a magazine, book, CD Rom, DVD or even just a pamphlet—and then consider how it should be distributed.

Programming/Films

Marketers should become involved in production, when possible—either through product placement, sponsorship, or, perhaps funding of a production. It is possible to produce a short animated piece, or even just a single animated character, which can then be used to front a brand in communications.

Events

All kinds of events should be considered, such as in theatres and stores. The strategy can create the story, and the brand can be built around the "events."

Mobile Technology

The worldwide growth in use of mobile phones has lead to a proliferation of communication methods—ringtones, wallpaper, SMS messaging and more. The biggest growth in sales of phones in recent years has been to those under age 12. Consider how your brand can co-exist with this medium, as it is a key communication tool for young people. Apart from the download opportunities that it delivers, there is also a requirement for content. How can your brand fit in here?

Interact ivity

This growing method of communication links into television, the Internet and mobile technology. It is a true "tactile" addition to the communication.

Music

Young people love and spend time and money on music. How can you establish your brands' credentials within the music industry?

Product Placement

Brands can be worked into television shows, on the Web or in films. What better endorsement?

Packaging and Brand Design

This, essentially, is advertising at the point of purchase. Marketers want the purchaser to pick up a product, feel confident about it and buy it, so packaging should be carefully considered.

Retail Presence

In-store "magic" is a major part of the communication; it is the last touch point prior to purchase.

Details of this overview will change depending on your plan. For instance, if you want to have national distribution in major multiple retailers, some choices are taken out of your hands. Most major retailers will only stock ranges if there is a promise of big marketing spending, predominantly on TV.

If you have a large marketing budget, TV would be part of your communications plan. But if you are working with a medium- or small-sized budget, you will want to seek maximum awareness for your brands in the best way possible, and you'll need to understand exactly how TV advertising works. The currency of TV advertising is the *GRP*, or *gross rating point*.

The TV Plan

The GRP is the percentage of a particular target audience viewing a TV programme into which an advertisement has been placed.

Most retail buyers will ask how many GRPs a manufacturer is buying to support a range. The GRP is used as a barometer for just about every manufacturer-retailer deal. Some equate a high GRP with a great deal of advertising and loads of consumer sales, meaning a retailer should have plenty in stock.

But the real picture is rarely so simple.

Retailers use GRPs to decide stock lists, and manufacturers use GRPs to persuade consumers to purchase these goods. Yet many people within marketing don't actually know what a GRP is.

During the past 10 years, I have asked many retail buyers, manufacturers, brand owners, people in sales and marketing, licensors, licensees and others in the field this very question. I was astounded to discover that the vast majority did not know the answer, and half of those who did could manage only part of the definition.

So does GRP even matter?

You bet it does.

When buying TV ad time, you are buying a commodity owned by TV companies. The target audience is children and you want as many of them as possible to see your advert.

The key to communications success is not the amount of GRPs purchased, but the impact of the communication, the number of people it has reached and the frequency of the message.

Critical components, then, are:

- Creativity of the commercial message.
- Percentage of total target audience that see the message; this is called *coverage.*
- The number of times the covered audience has been exposed to the message, or *frequency.*

Coverage and frequency are the true arbiters of an advertising campaign's success, especially in today's multimedia environment. The purchase of 400 GRP could reach 40 percent of the true target or it could reach 80 percent. So pronouncing high GRPs as a campaign prerequisite is meaningless, and misrepresents the true worth of ad campaigns.

Would you prefer to know that the expected exposure for a product will be 400 GRPs in a four-week TV campaign, or that the whole communication package will reach 7 million children, who will see the campaign five or six times through sources such as TV programmes, films, the Web, direct mail, sponsorship, licensing alliances, events, plus traditional advertising?

Such a mix amounts to a better-planned multimedia campaign than the mere sum of GRPs.

Because youths are so fickle, marketing to them is best seen as an art rather than a science. Those who try to make it into a science (and I've worked with many who have) tend to leave the industry, finding it frustrating to be unable to "pigeonhole" the target market. Once you accept that you can't predict children's behaviour, and that *they* decide whether your brand becomes a craze, you have this market cracked!

The purchase of GRPs is a simple trade. Media agencies buy them from inventory owned by TV stations, on behalf of clients. Historically, children's industries have sold product into retail by promising a great deal of TV station GRPs to promote the range. GRPs don't guarantee higher consumer sales, but they have historically engendered an upward curve of sales at key periods, and therefore are held in high esteem by retailers.

This appears to be changing, however.

The following chart shows the effect of purchasing GRPs during two periods—one during the early to mid-1990s, when I was a TV planner and buyer for Hasbro and Mattel, and one based on campaigns during 2004. The chart is for typical campaigns bought on a typical child-targeted schedule—part terrestrial, part satellite. I call this chart "The Coverage Conundrum."

Kids TV Coverage build

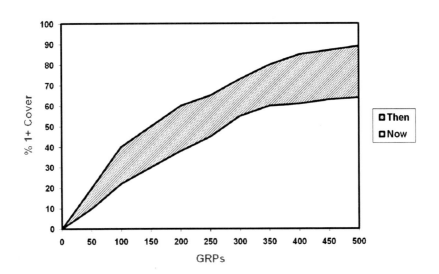

If we concentrate on the top line first, we see a growth of coverage alongside the mass of GRPs. The purchase of 100 GRPs would gain somewhere in the region of 40 percent coverage; the purchase of more would increase coverage accordingly, finally levelling out at the 400–500 GRP mark. It was not uncommon to achieve levels above 85 percent on the bigger spending campaigns.

The second line is typical of what can be achieved today. The purchase of 100 GRPs will only reach, in most cases, nearly 20–25 percent of the audience. Less than a quarter of the market will see an advert by a low-spending brand, or one purchased in small bursts. It is rare for those buying standard kids' campaigns to achieve a reach above 65 percent.

There are many factors affecting the change that has taken place over this past decade. Satellite TV, for example, has a much different audience universe. Fragmentation has significantly reduced average viewing audiences.

Now, it is important to note that 65 percent is a good figure, equivalent to about 3.5 million four- to nine-year-olds in the United Kingdom, but it is a good 20 percentage points below what was possible 10 or even five years ago. I reckon that most campaigns can reach optimum coverage of 60–65% at the 300 GRP level; so why buy any more?

A significant opportunity presents itself here. Buying GRPs helps to reach a large proportion of children. Below I present the same chart with a couple of additions, representing places to which you can look for improvement in your brand communications:

Kids TV Coverage build

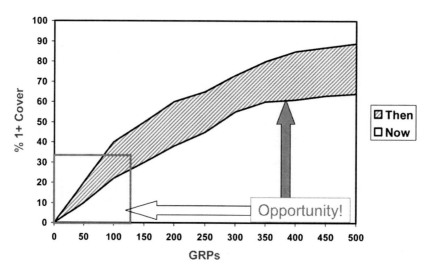

Marketers are wise to look closely at their marketing spends and deploy percentages of budget into areas that will increase a campaign's impact. At the low level of GRPs, represented by the small box, there is a case for not spending any money on TV, while at the higher level of GRPs there is a clear case for saving and redeploying your money after reaching the 300 rating.

Brand communication in the children's market involves far more than placing an advert in front of the audience. Children are even more media savvy than adults, and they have plenty of opportunity to view temptations—most often, away from a TV screen. What they want and respond to are brands that they can "touch and feel," and with which they can interact.

While TV advertising has been the mainstay in the past, if you want to make your brand as tangible as possible, you will want to incorporate a web site strategy, an online strategy, mobile content, promotions, events, sponsorship, targeted public relations, retail strategy and a tailored brand strategy.

This holistic approach will end up saving money, allowing funds to be redeployed effectively and efficiently.

Children's Tv Stations—It's a Love Love Love Thing

I have been accused over the years of being anti-media owners, but nothing could be further from the truth. In fact, I can't live without children's TV stations.

I don't mean to denigrate TV stations when I say that children's communications must move on from its single-minded worship of the GRP. I simply believe that communications strategies should celebrate the diversity now available, particularly through the multimedia platforms that have sprung from children's TV.

TV channels that specialise in reaching children offer a wealth of knowledge to marketers. They have extensive research on children and their habits, and they also have gone the extra mile to understand your needs and how they can bring you closer to your target market. They want to be seen as partners and I believe more marketers should treat them this way.

Children-targeted TV stations recognise that children have many other media influences in their lives; they have multimedia capacity and know how to use it. They know that children as an audience have diversified, and they want to offer you much more than the sale of a simple GRP.

I treat children's TV stations as partners in the business of extending my brands' "active" relationship with their audience. Maybe it's time you do the same. Make it a priority to develop a relationship with the media owners.

Content Is King

It bears repeating that brands gain far more coverage, and are better understood by consumers, when they engage the audience in an active relationship.

Licensing is one way to do this. Essentially, a licensed product is the result of an entertainment format that has gained exposure to its audience through TV, cinema, publishing, sports events and more. In this way, a licensed product has established a relationship with its users. I wouldn't go so far to say that this relationship is two-way, born of mutual respect and trust. Licenses are, ultimately, the result of someone's imagination—a highly creative imagination, yes, but an imagination nevertheless. Someone somewhere thought up a character or story that appeals to young minds, and possibly those of their parents, and then transformed this creativity into a book, film or TV show. The imagination's output finds its way to our screens and into the minds of the participants. But I believe that never once in this journey has the ensuing product been the result of a relationship with children.

It has often been said that TV shows such as Blue's Clues or Teletubbies are the result of extensive research into the needs of children of a tender age, and are based on the cognitive aptitudes of this age. Even if those programmes have got it right in terms of output—and it is undeniable that there is an engagement here—would you say the resulting licensed brands have an *active relationship* with viewers?

Yet children watch the shows. That is why licensing works.

Children watch and enjoy, and then may go to a Web site to find out more about a character. They get to love that character. They don't, however, fall in love with the manufactured products that exist with the character likeness on it.

It is the *content* that is king, not the resultant toy, gift or item of clothing. Being the medium itself, rather than its offshoot, is critical to being a strong brand and to establishing the active relationship so desired.

The relationship is getting lost. Just being a license is not the solution. Brands, including those that do not use licenses, need to look for ways to communicate in engaging, inspiring and active ways. A 30-second TV advertisement isn't enough to prompt a product's flight off the shelves.

Young viewers or readers are most likely to engage with things in front of their eyes. They are adept at discerning programming or written articles from advertising, promotions and sponsorship. Those who call for protection of children from commercialism should note that children are even more likely to dismiss approaches from advertisers than are their parents. Children are smart; they know their way around and learn from each other. Why else are they the ones helping adults with new technologies rather than the other way around?

So, you might be asking, how does my product become the content? The more crucial question is: How do you establish an active relationship with the target audience?

Most essential is subtlety and the method and context of the communication. Your plan is for the message to appear to be part of the whole and so to feel a natural part of the children's world and this can be achieved within all of the media environments or disciplines we mentioned previously—public relations, the Internet, television, and events etc.

In today's world, everything that touches a child's senses can be perceived as media, and is therefore a brand-building opportunity. Why not appeal to all the senses? Just remember that *content* is king.

The next step is considering the period during which you will market your brands.

At least 60% of sales in the children's market occur during the Christmas season. Here's a tool to help you stand out among the competition.

The holiday season is supposed to be a happy time of year, yet when it comes around, I feel the stress building among sales and marketing gurus. In truth, it becomes a nightmarish time of the year. Budgets have been committed, products are on shelves, and all are poised, ready for the rush.

It doesn't appear that the industry is having much fun at this point, so who is?

Well, the children. They have their TV programmes, which they watch avidly, and they have TV commercials, which, of course, they watch a lot less avidly. One of their favourite brands may pop up in front of them, and they may or may not spot it, and they may put it on the holiday wish list.

But what if they don't notice it—or they do, but they ignore it? Who is to blame? The communication method? The product? The price?

Lets' take a look at the most-blamed culprit: TV advertising. We put much pressure on this medium as the lead tool for the business of buying, selling and marketing in the toy market.

According to audience research company, BARB, in the United Kingdom in 2006, nearly 300 toy and computer game products were advertised during the month of November. Advertisers bought more than 35,000 GRPs, which equated to nearly 150,000 advertisement spots, giving a per-product average of 116 GRPs and 500 spots. No wonder so many products don't achieve their hoped-for prominence.

How difficult is it to achieve a decent share when advertising at Christmas? Only those who can significantly improve upon average numbers and command high audience coverage can confidently state that they are having any fun at all. (And in today's world, I doubt even they are!)

The answer can't be simply buying loads of spots on TV, because in such a case, small-spending brands wouldn't stand a chance of selling anything. Small spenders who put all their funds into the TV pot are taking a tremendous gamble if they choose to advertise at the same time as everyone else.

The most obvious solution to the November conundrum is to simply move advertising to another period. Unfortunately again for small spenders, they will find that the big fish are also swimming in this pool. Back in the early 1990s, advertising was first moved to begin in August in order to give a push to the Argos catalogue sales and also try to find a way onto the all-important wish list. This would be followed up by small bursts in October and November to act as reminders and maybe gain some new customers. The key was always to be at the top of the wish list when mum went shopping. This strategy had some success for a while, but it wasn't long before everyone followed suit. Retailers got wise to it and then began to expect it.

The 1990s was also the period of the early Christmas. People planned a long way in advance and shops had all the gear out before the kids had even gone back to school. Of course, this no longer holds true. The trend now is for Christmas to come later and later to retail. Consumers are wise to the waiting game. They know that shops will start to roll out promotions in December, and that it would be foolish of them to buy presents in November when they can get more for their money a few weeks later.

When planning the media strategy, picking the right time to advertise is going to get harder and so is any idea of gaining brand stand-out.

So why are TV buying strategies still the same?

Brand owners need to be looking for more innovative ways to reach their audience and should be more flexible in their willingness to turn to new communication channels and methods.

We have seen already that children are quite easy to reach on many different media platforms. They are, of course, heavy viewers of TV and leading proponents of cable and satellite, digital and interactive TV. They are heavy users of the Internet, they play computer games, they read magazines, they love the cinema, they are members of clubs, they collect things, they eat junk food but are aware of the obesity debate, they are safe in the family unit, they enjoy their friends but can change them whenever they want; the list is endless.

You may be forgiven in thinking that some of these are not media platforms, but that depends on your view of a media opportunity. Each of the above is a potential audience touch point, and in looking to the future we can treat each and every one of these as a communications opportunity and therefore a media platform. They are part of a children's communication chain and the key to standing out is the successful management of this chain.

Again, in the children's markets, it is not a case of whether to use TV but how to use TV. How does each campaign affect and/or dovetail with other channels of communication such as Web sites, partnerships with retailers, licensors and licensees, public relations and other avenues? How does your communications plan work with sales strategy and apply to business strategy?

In thinking this way, we open ourselves to the possibility of gaining standout through multiple channels rather than hoping for a bit of luck with just one channel at the same time as everyone else. In achieving the cross-platform strategy, we can coordinate all communications and achieve a consistency of message. Just take care that this message is not patronising. Children respond well to positive and challenging messages. They enjoy gaining knowledge and, most of all, they enjoy having fun.

Let's give them what they want.

Perception Deception: Making a £50k Budget Look like £200k

In most cases of targeting brands to young audiences, campaigns have much smaller budgets than those in the "adult" marketing world. Therefore, every campaign needs to work at punching above its weight in terms of exposure and awareness gained. No matter the budget, marketing activity is crucial. In generating the correct perception, you can make a limited spend seem like one that is four or five times its actual size.

Marketing will, in the vast majority of industries, play second fiddle to sales. I see sales and marketing as one and the same; both are about taking a brand to market. If you see them on the same footing, you will reap benefits; too often, sales and marketing sit in separate "silos" within large organisations, rather than working together.

Put simply, marketing is the application of the right product to the right person for the right price in the right place and all at the right time.

Many times I have heard managing directors say, for various reasons, that they don't do any marketing. Of course, they actually do quite a lot; what else, after all, are company logos, web sites, trade organisations, e-mails, business cards and packaging?

And while marketing ultimately is about the promotion of a company and brands, and its product sales, it is also about perception. You don't simply promote sales; you create a corporate image and promote it to three key audiences: The trade, the consumer and your own staff. Each should be treated with respect. Marketing is about how people see you, so it should go without saying that this needs to be positive.

To exemplify the way that different people form different perceptions, I use the case of dress code in golf clubs. Many people are familiar with the pictures in golf clubhouses of acceptable dress on a golf course in the summer.

Basically, golf clubs want patrons to dress tidily. To many people in the golf world, this sort of notice is a positive affirmation of the game and its traditions. Yet to others, it is heavy-handedness; to those who are not interested in the game, it is another example of the snobbery and stuffiness with which they associate the game.

So, when it comes to creating a positive perception, it's all about the strategy. It is about getting everyone on board internally and using them to get everyone on board externally. It might require change, which can be painful, but it should also lead to enlightenment—to empowered staff making positive decisions with great results.

There are many brands that have changed their approaches over the years, and some that can't do any wrong no matter what. In the early 1990's, when Nickelodeon launched in the United Kingdom, it was not well-received by children. Nickelodeon had to work very hard to turn the perception around to the positive image it enjoys today. A classic children's marketing example in the United Kingdom was a well-known fruit drink, which delivered a positive spin on a product that was actually heavily sugar-based. Unfortunately for the brand, consumers found them out and the perception was seen to be a deception, resulting in huge loss of trust. This still stands as a lesson to all children's marketers on the dangers of not behaving ethically. Brands such as Cartoon Network and Disney have always promoted a positive image, with no deception and no misinterpretation of delivery.

There are five steps toward positive perception: Analysis, evaluation, synthesis, strategy and implementation. Break down and look at what you have, put it back together again with a clear plan in mind, and, finally, deliver it to your audiences.

Once you have the strategy, you need to communicate it. When looking for what can be achieved over and above a budget in terms of value, coverage and efficiency, you should look at things you do anyway—things that cost little or nothing—and also how you can extract extra value from media communications.

If you would like to make a £50k budget work like a £200k budget, you should first look at what you do as a matter of course. What does your product's packaging say? You should look at how the brand looks at retail, and how this can be improved. When did you last look at your own catalogues? When did you critique your positioning? And how about taking a good look at your trade show stands—how are they decorated and manned? To many, this is the only company showcase; make it a positive one!

Next, take a look at what is free. First and foremost, *you* are. You and your staff can promote your company better than anyone and can raise a product's profile, highlight brands and more. You can speak at conferences, write letters to journals, join trade organisations and network furiously. If you have a positive story to tell, let people know.

Finally, how to advertise your brands without breaking the bank? Promotion isn't just about how many GRPs you can gain. Many brands don't have budgets large enough to go on TV, but that doesn't mean they can't have TV exposure through PR or media owner relationships. If you have a low budget, look internally at your web sites and their links to media partners, licensors or other licensees. Look at trade magazines as more than just a venue in which to place an ad. On the public relations front, consider how much of it you can do yourself with placements, or with competitions in magazines or on Web sites. You could consider a promotion linked to children's magazines or TV channels' Web sites. If you fancy digital exposure, try starting your own viral campaign. This can be as simple as sending out an e-mail. Take a look at Google Adwords, and then set it up for your brands. Look for partnerships: Who out there can you work with to co-operatively promote one another's brands?

If you take some time on strategy, you can apply many of these techniques to give the impression that your company and brands are ubiquitous. You will have completed your own "perception deception."

5

Delivering Great Brands
to Children

It is apparent in many industries that retail has become king. Retailers set the agenda. At Christmastime, major retailers often see child-targeted products, as supplements or add-on presents to the major purchase. Small products have long since disappeared from being the first item on a child's wish list, so retailers essentially are correct in their market assessment.

Whilst it may appear that retailers will always be in control, I feel that children's industries have an opportunity to change themselves to lead the market into the future by setting long-term strategies for products that will fetch higher prices at retail—strategies that seek alternative sales channels, and look to establish new categories and develop partnerships with new technologies. In this atmosphere, the innovative will survive; creativity will have its day again.

I believe we should always start planning by getting back to being the creative instigator of new trends, leading the market and being less focused on licensing. We need to change the way we communicate with our audience.

Planning

Plan every penny to be spent. Scrutinize all marketing and communication costs. Have a plan you can communicate to your agencies. Get them on board with your targets. How can they help you achieve these goals? Wring everything you can from every cent spent.

Agencies

Make all of your agencies accountable; make them fit the strategic vision. Pay them for delivery of your plan. Most media agencies already provide an accountable service in buying, but can you say the same for your research and event organisers and public relations agencies? Are PR agencies worth monthly retainers? What are they delivering day to day? It is preferable to pay such agencies to provide public relations when you want it, as defined by a strategic plan.

Listen—and Motivate

Take advice where you can get it, both internally and externally. Achieve buy-in for your plan from everyone. Motivate everyone to help build your brand and to sell it to the trade and the consumer.

Media Owners

Look at multi-platform communications and how media owners can be involved with your brand. This isn't the job of your media or PR agencies, as they do not have your market knowledge. It is *your* job, or the job of your communications strategist. There should be conversations about partnerships, sponsorships, competitions, promotions, Internet strategy, and, most important, how these will be delivered to the retailer. Media owners understand your market and have partnerships with retailers; above all else, they also have an intimate relationship with your ultimate consumer—the children and their mums. This resource is underused at present, probably because of time constraints. It is worthwhile to budget time and expertise to this exercise, as the rewards will far outweigh the costs.

Integrated Communications

All of the above can be pulled together into a coherent strategy. Understand your brand so well that its message can be communicated consistently and coherently. Set strategic targets that match the planning and implementation. Don't do anything in isolation; have open dialogue between sales and marketing teams.

Retail Detail

"Buy-one-get-one-free," "three-for-two" and price reductions of all sizes seem to be the only topics of conversation in regard to retail these days. It appears to be getting to the point that some brands are on continual sale.

Obviously, the promotion of product plays an important part in encouraging traffic through a store and generating sales. I have always been sure of the importance of retail in supplying entertainment, and I have become far more aware of—and impressed by—stores' efforts to attract and retain their customers.

Let's consider the process.

Mum and child go about their daily lives receiving advertising, sponsorship and promotional messages by the million. They wake up to radio, they watch breakfast TV and they listen to radio on the way to school, passing posters on walls and bus stops. After school they read magazines, watch TV and use the Internet. All of this time, they are absorbing messages about brands. Every message is a touch point and is carefully transmitted to catch them at a time when they might be most receptive—when they can be "brainwashed" into wanting something they probably don't need.

There comes a point when all the information is in place: They have seen the TV shows, they have seen the ads, they have checked out the brand via the Internet, they have further discovered details about the sort of product they want and are happy to set off to the store (or the online site) with a happy heart that they are going to get just what they want. Upon arriving at the retailer, there is a sense of excitement; the product is almost in their hands, there is an air of expectancy. In-store, they plan to head for what they want . . . but often they never get there!

Why? All the plans were laid; it was just a question of picking up the product and paying for it. What happened?

It was all in the retail detail.

The consumer was let down at the most important part of the branding process. At the crucial point, they pulled out of their commitment to purchase. It just didn't seem like such a good idea any more. Maybe they decided to get something else instead.

I can't tell you how often this happens; all I can tell you is that it does. In focus groups, I heard mums and children talk about how the retail experience can actually hinder their purchase of the brands they planned to buy. I have also heard them blame the retailer for the way they found (or didn't find at all, in some cases) the product when they arrived. I say that it is not only the retailer who should shoulder the blame; marketers should look closely at our role in the process and what we do to help create purchase-point inertia.

For many years, experts have been talking about retail experiences, and how retailers cleverly entice (some say trick) consumers into unplanned purchases. The toy industry is no exception, in that stores are carefully planned and laid out. It is easy to be drawn to promotions and sale items, though I don't believe this is enough to distract buyers from their planned purchase. I believe sales items are potential add-ons.

What is happening is that consumers are being let down at the final touch point. Upon finding the sought-for product, seeing it in the store environment and maybe even picking it up, consumers often are not as enamoured as they were before. The gloss has gone.

This comes down to many factors, including ambience. This needs to be factored into marketing plans.

It all starts at the development stage; will packaging stand out from other items on the shelf? Also to be considered is a product's position on the shelf—is it being highlighted with signs? In what environment does the product sit? A single product requires something that shouts; a range of products calls for something that appeals—not only getting attention but helping to define brand ethos. We should all think more carefully about the quality of this communication.

The store and catalogue environments offer much to those who wish to take advantage. I firmly believe that this is the point where competitive advantage holds its greatest sway, yet I am often disappointed with in-store displays. It's not that they aren't heavily branded, but that they show no real creativity; the "wow" factor isn't there. There seems to be a lack of ingenuity, maybe even a lack of knowledge of what is possible. Remember not only do children love "wow" but so do their mums!

This is a shame because we are in the entertainment industry; our products entertain, but their in-store displays do not. If you have spent money securing a coveted in-store position, you should invest time and effort in getting the display just right. There is an adage in the sponsorship industry that says you should spend at least the same amount telling people that you are the sponsor of an event as you did buying the sponsorship in the first place. In other words, just having a presence isn't enough; you need to exploit it. This is where marketing efforts fall short. For example, upon making deals to "sponsor" a part of the store, we then don't invest in exploiting this sponsorship by telling consumers that we are doing so—and why.

The same is true with catalogues. Much money is invested in these pages from which your product is being sold directly. Yet how much time and effort are spent on the final delivery of the artwork? This is the final moment before purchase; surely it deserves plenty of attention.

Who's Looking at In-Store Displays?

Having established the need for in-store entertainment, it is now important to find out whether consumers are watching what you've done.

There is, of course, a wealth of data collected on consumer spending trends during the Christmas holiday shopping period. One recent holiday season, a colleague and I stood in major retail stores for an extended period of time watching people shopping in individual toy stores and larger retailers' toy sections. We wanted to ascertain how they were shopping, which aisles they visited and whether they noticed, paid attention to or walked straight past promotions, on-shelf displays and end caps or pallets. What we learned was surprising.

The average consumer traffic, we found, was above 190 adults per hour. Of these, 16% stopped at displays by the entrance, and a similar number glanced briefly. This means a whopping 68% walked straight past. And to our surprise, these figures were repeated throughout the store: 68% ignored the pallets and 66% ignored end caps, no matter where the displays were situated. There was one huge display inside a major retailer that was accompanied by music, yet, once again, only 15% stopped. Upon entering a store, the majority (61%) of consumers would take the quickest entry, and would therefore miss out on a few aisles immediately. Only 27% stopped to look at the bargains on offer.

We found these figures quite startling, and they should send a shiver down the spines of those who pay a high price for such display positions. When retailers ask high prices, you should be asking what you will get for your money!

I can only speculate as to the possible cause of these statistics, and suggest some remedies.

Consumers probably are entering stores with their minds set on exactly what they intend to purchase, and they go straight to the relevant section, pick up the product and proceed to the checkout. Many brands, through advertising and PR, have already reached their target audiences. Secondly, I suspect the Internet is playing a role, too. Its influence on shopping is gaining year on year, beyond simply purchasing online. I suggest that the Internet has influence in the purchase process for the vast majority of brands, whether as a tool for browsing brands and competitors, price-checking or selecting where to buy.

Another reason for ignoring displays is time. Many mums have lists and will be busy trying to get something quickly as they move onto the next item and then the next. They are not inclined to stop and browse.

Age plays a role, too. Displays are for specific brands targeted toward specific ages; as such, they will not be of interest to the mums of other age groups.

Finally, I wonder if consumers have become "promotion savvy," leading to apathy and even cynicism. Consumers likely don't feel a sense of wonder about discounts anymore, and therefore don't feel the need to stop at such displays. A promotion has become another "advertising" message among the many thousands received daily.

I couldn't understand why consumers preferred to stand and look at aisles of product and not take a good look at the end caps relevant to those same brands on display in the aisle. It appeared that video displays, especially, didn't attract any attention, despite brands' efforts to do just that. Indeed, consumers seem to know what they want, and while they might browse the shelves, a decision on which brand to purchase almost certainly has already been made, and no amount of nudging will sway them.

It was clear to us that the overwhelming majority of stores leave consumers uninspired, and we suggest there are two areas ripe for improvement. First, displays themselves need to be more imaginative, particularly considering the vast sums spent on marketing campaigns.

Second, stores themselves should brighten up their acts. They need to consider the "wow" factor that many children's products engender and use this to their benefit and build an environment or atmosphere that entertains. We want to see some magic and an effort to encourage children's participation.

We would go so far as to say that most stores that sell toys or children's products in general are actually unfriendly environments for children, the ultimate consumer.

What if stores were to become more child-friendly—places of entertainment, where children can touch and feel products, where the items being marketed can come alive? Why not establish a "play zone" for product demonstrations and trials, so that consumers can sample potential purchases? Children would be happy to visit such places, and mums would also be entertained. Thinking further, while parents are having fun with their offspring, why not sell them a beverage? More time in-store equals more money at the till!

Our research implies that consumers have very little in-store "relationship" with retailers beyond low prices. This is fine if you only want to sell them one product; multiple sales require a better strategy.

Xmas Is Getting L8R & L8R

For at least 10 years, I and many others have been wound up by the creeping earliness of retail Christmas displays. In the mid- to late-1990s, it seemed that as soon as children were back at school, adults were being told to think about Christmas. This carried on into the new millennium, but I began to detect a shift around 2006.

Consumers don't want Christmas in August; they are happy to wait until December before launching into holiday shopping and planning. For one thing, consumers believe that the closer the holidays, the more bargains will be available; they tend to ignore Christmas-related store displays that pop up too soon. For another, consumers can create their own virtual holiday spirit by ordering gifts online. Ultimately, the watchword for the consumer is "value" and they are very happy to wait to get it.

Retailers, meanwhile, have caught on to rolling out additional shopping "seasons," with back-to-school followed by back-to-college, then Halloween, and then fireworks and the bonfire party. Christmas only has a chance to start in earnest once these buying seasons end.

Consumers may be happy that Christmas-holiday shopping is being pushed back, but what is happening to the traditional marketing model, in which millions of pounds were spent enticing early brand purchases? What is to come of the annual negotiations whereby manufacturers promise early TV advertising followed by more advertising at the key period? When *is* this key period?

A new model is needed to reflect changing consumer behaviour patterns.

Your marketing communication plans may need to be overhauled so that they are in tune with the modern audience; this, in turn, will change the way you see media channels. You should be increasing the coverage of the audience you reach and looking at how you talk to them, with less repetition and greater interaction. It will take a shift in attitude internally and externally, but the effort will be rewarded with long-term brand benefits such as consumer recognition and trust, along with retail confidence.

Christmas always will fall on December 25, but its retail season is falling later and later, and the Internet will continue to fuel this delay. It is time to figure out how you will adapt.

Lies, Damned Lies & Statistics

I love statistics. I can spend hours looking at and cross-referencing them, but I accept that I am in a minority. Statistics can tell lies, can hide the truth, can confirm mistruths and can explain things away.

Collecting, analyzing and assimilating accurate data is vital in the modern world. From politicians to brand owners, everyone wants to know as much as possible about consumers and their habits before committing to any action, word or deed. Handling data and the resulting statistics is a multimillion-pound industry that can be enlightening or confusing to those in the marketing field.

Enlightenment via data comes with a caveat: You must be brave enough to act on the data's findings. Confusion results from the collection of incorrect data and statistics in the first place.

When seeking data, you should know what you are attempting to discover and also have a pretty good idea of how you will collect and use it.

As cynical as it sounds, data and statistics can be manipulated to support the answers sought. What you should seek is research that does not simply confirm your own thoughts but digs into brands' perceptions and qualities and determines whether these suit consumers' desires. Research should not be a "told you so" exercise, but should be seen as providing "need to know" information. If you are not prepared to change things after analyzing your research results, you should not commission such study in the first place.

In the child and family markets, all kinds of data exist and have yet to be collected. Information ranging from the most general to the smallest niche has been compiled; deciding what is relevant is key. Children are moving forward, developmentally, at an incredible rate. They are a researcher's biggest nightmare: No sooner is the ink dry on the latest set of research than it becomes out of date; a child has moved on, grown up, become bored, found a new set of friends, or, to use their own parlance, "whatever!"

Children cannot be trusted when it comes to research that generalises or is dependent on the whims of a collaborative group of under-10-year-olds. So why do we seek it? Partly because we need to know what kids think at a particular moment in time and we need to let them loose with a brand—have them try it out and come back with the truth. It is easy to digest the truth and much easier to change a marketing strategy when based on real perceptions.

The difference between good, relevant research and average research is most stark in the youth market. Too many researchers haven't taken time out to understand children and their reactions to questioning, including the tendency toward "group-think."

This group, so to speak, could consist of any number of sets: the extended family, the immediate family, a brother, the school playground, mates in school, mates outside of school; I could go on and on. If you are considering hiring someone to embark on research, you must make sure your practitioners understand the context into which you are placing your enquiries.

A good start is making sure your researcher has experience working with children, and asking whether their facilitators have experience in teaching, child care or, better still, child psychology. People in these fields tend to know how to handle children, how to provide the feeling of confidence needed to say what they think and not what their friends tell them to think.

While all children are different, most share a feeling of not wanting to stand out in a crowd. They want to appear "normal" and feel safe. Being different doesn't cut it with most children. So how do you go about teasing information out of these youngsters when they are in a group situation?

As mentioned, you should begin with someone who knows how children operate and who can adapt to the context, making children feel comfortable in their surroundings and confident to voice their opinions. Once a product has been demonstrated, children should be given some product to take home. Mum should be engaged, given a diary to fill in regarding a child's interaction with a product.

What does all this mean to your market, brand positioning and communication strategy?

A researcher's role is to get information, which they do for many markets. It's up to marketers to apply the strategic implications. A specialist who can combine research capabilities with an in-depth knowledge of young people and their marketplace can help. Data results will be analysed in a way that will make sense and give proper context and prospective.

I have been asked many times if I can recommend a research company to my clients. Every time, I struggled to come up with a company that I could be certain could perform the task. The solution, I found, was to do it myself.

Maybe this is something you should consider. Doing so will get you closer to your audience and provide you with direct contact and new understanding.

Licensing

The license has become an integral part of the children's industries; the use of characters to enhance brands has become the norm. Just as the entertainment industry was changed by the film *Toy Story* in the mid-1990's, so was the licensing industry—and it has been booming ever since.

The preschool market has seen licensing "greats" such as Thomas the Tank Engine, Bob the Builder and Teletubbies lead the way, followed by the likes of Dora the Explorer. The explosion of TV channels has fuelled the desire for content, which has further allowed for the expansion of properties available to license.

Picking the Correct License and Licensor

The job starts with the licensee, who is going to be taking the biggest risk. It is paramount that every consideration is given to whether licensing is required and, if so, which type of license. So the first task is to look at one's own strategy in terms of brands. Ask such questions as:

- Is it a new range?
- What are the short- and long-term goals?
- Who is the consumer?
- What age and gender are being targeted?
- How much influence will the parent have?
- What are the distribution targets?
- What are the sales targets?
- Is the range seasonal?
- Will the range extend into many territories?

These are a few components of a strong strategic plan. Once such a plan has been constructed, marketers can decide whether a license will help achieve goals for a product.

While gut feelings and experience can help in such decisions, a bit of science is useful as well.

On the following pages I have compiled a table called "market mapping—licensing" that can serve as a guide to a buyer's feelings about a licensed product at the time of purchase. It describes six scenarios pertinent to the licensing market:

1. Love the license; don't know the product
2. License to sell product
3. License to enhance the brand
4. Brand requires license "add-on"
5. Harmony of brand and license
6. Product/brand doesn't need a license

We will try to place these headings into scenarios in regard to the mindset of the purchaser/consumer, figuring in context, emotion, propensity to purchase and barriers to purchase. In the last section, we summarise all of the above and assess the potential.

The chart should be used to cross-examine your own brands and understand into which scenario they may fit. You then should be able to see more clearly whether licensing is the proper route to pursue, and, if so, what needs to be done to clear the path.

Occasions Mapping -

Purchase occasion	1. Love the license; don't know the product		2. License to sell the product		3. License to enhance the brand			
Context	Will buy anything with license	Will trust anything with license	Product needs lift	New launch requires exposure	Brand confident but not absolutely sure of itself		License is a nice "fit"	
Emotion	Give me everything with this license, please!		Like license therefore trust product / brand	License cool; product ok!	Good product; nice license		Love license; product looks ok!	
					Don't like license		Want product; license helps	
Mind Position	Wow, thanks; yes please!		The license has made me want it.	This product is better than I thought!	I may want it	Want brand but not with the license	License is the clincher	
Risks	Quality of product may diminish the value of the license		Product lets license down	Imperfect harmony of license and brand	Product lets license down	Imperfect harmony	License lets product down	
"Sense" of occasion	The license clearly is king. Good license to take if launching a product or wishing for simple introduction to licensing		Here a product that needs reviving would look for strong license or a brand has little identity of its own and requires the push from a license.		There are a few danger signals here as nothing is decisive. Without positive action the programme has good chance of failing. Strategy must be spot on.			

Licensing

4. Brand requires license "add-on"			5. Harmony of brand and license		6. Product / brand doesn't need a license
Good product but needs a kick start	Great license; perfect fit with brand		Like both; don't notice the license	Brand enhances the license!	Confident brand; selling well; trusted by consumer
Love brand; license makes it cooler	Love brand; license ruins it!		Love it; would like it; hope can afford it	Hate the brand or hate the license; either way, no thanks	Want this brand; will want this brand with or without license.
Product interesting	License interesting				
May go for it; license doesn't help	License makes it better; could be ok	Not sure; the mix of brand and license doesn't make sense	This is good; I'm comfortable; the license doesn't ruin my brand	This is good; I'm comfortable; the brand doesn't ruin the licence	Don't understand why there is a license on this; but I like it anyway!
			Love the marriage of the two!		
Imperfect harmony	License lets product down		Wrong license!		Wrong license!
Again positive affirmation of requirements is needed. Many things can go wrong. Time should be spent getting the right strategy.			The perfect scenario for a licensing programme.		A license here will really be for brand vanity and, of course, extra profit!

Each scenario clearly has different routes leading to a potential purchase. The scenarios at the edges (1, 2 and 5, 6) have much clearer paths; there is a confidence that either party knows what they are into licensing for and the purchaser will understand this proposition. There is either harmony or the brand/property knows what it stands for, building confidence. Where the scenarios are a little blurred (3, 4), the path to success is more tricky, creating potential negative consumer perceptions and misunderstandings.

What I hope is clear from the mapping table is that the decision to use a license boils down to being positive about brands and their positions. If licensing is deemed a "nice idea" and "something we should try out," you should think twice before embarking on a road that may be unfulfilling to the consumer and very expensive to the manufacturer.

Getting the Right License

Children can fall in and out of love with characters at the drop of a hat; sometimes the relationship can last a year; sometimes a decade; others a lifetime.

Marketers all are searching for the next big thing. With youths, though, I find that no data analysis can help accurately predict success, no matter what some say.

One of the reasons this market is so engrossing is that kids are not predictable and are gloriously fickle about everything, especially products and brands that could fall into a "fad" category, which, like it or not, toys and games usually fall into.

As for predicting where the next trend is coming from, no one can confidently say they can do so. Do you have a good sense—or any sense at all—of what the most popular toy will be next holiday season?

In the world of children (and their mums), licensing is a familiar concept. Everyone, consumers included, is aware of what it is, how it works and, ultimately, how much extra needs to be paid for it. In my world, licensing makes money for clients, and is seen as a safe option and a solid base on the bottom line.

I can't help but think of licensing as a necessary. But, ultimately, being safe and secure, warm and cuddly makes things boring. Licensing has taken away the need for creativity, for sparking new product development. Where are the risk-takers? Nobody wants to try something new.

You might not see it this way. You might believe that you always are on the lookout for something new. But how many people really choose the risky, exciting option ahead of the safe but dull?

Licensing is the safe and dull. It will never be a craze, but it most certainly is a trend—one that comes as close to a science as we can get in this market, and therefore appeals to boardrooms and shareholders.

Yet as comfortable as many are with licensing, I am astounded by the paucity of the output licensees generate from their licensing relationships. I am a fan of licensing, but only if the relationship is developed to the full. I am always disappointed by the loss of opportunity between licensee, licensor, media owner and retailer.

Licensors point out that it is generally down to the licensee to exploit the relationship's advantages. But often these potential partnerships are not fully explained before—or after—license agreements are signed.

It is also true that many licensees are not geared up to understand the opportunities afforded them and therefore nothing is exploited.

Much money is spent on licensing, and one should expect to gain sufficient return on this investment. The key is to create synergy—the pooling of communications resources to provide a cohesive brand plan.

Licensors spend a lot of time and effort supporting retailers. Joint promotions and advertising are important, as is licensee cooperation.

The children's film and entertainment world is fairly formulaic, but in recent years I have noticed a change in the way the licensing industry conducts business.

Over the last few years, it has struck me while visiting retail outlets that the model I was used to had changed, and that business plans and marketing strategies should be adapted. The basic character model used to be the norm, and it was relatively simple. A film was to be released and licensees signed up for an opportunity to create or be involved with the launch marketing, and to participate in the retail programme, promotions, public relations and advertising. The film launch date was key, and everyone worked with that timing in mind. Some products were put on shelves to coincide with the film's release, while others were phased in. When the video/DVD was released, another opportunity arose to take stock and make hay. In all, the window of opportunity could last many more months.

But children's lifestyles are changing, as is their appreciation of the world around them and the characters they connect with.

In July 2006, three films launched in the United Kingdom were intended to be licensing blockbusters: Pirates of the Caribbean, Superman and Cars. All set out with the goal of becoming a box office hit and a licensing sensation. In-store presence for each was massive, with spectacular displays.

But I was left perplexed.

Why were these films launched right on top of each other? Some said it was because they wanted to avoid coming up against the soccer

World Cup, especially while England was still struggling through it. I don't understand this argument. Another option to the World Cup, for many consumers, would have been most welcome. Many people, such as mums and young children, are not interested in football and would have welcomed the chance to get away from the TV. Plus, after the first two weeks of the competition, there were days when there no football was being televised at all, marking a missed opportunity for entertainment providers.

I also don't understand why each range was launched to the consumer with promotions and discounts. Some giveaways and competitions are a must when launching a new range, but I watched an entire industry collaborate in the devaluation of one of its greatest assets of the last 15 years—the licensed film character range. Most of us have seen firsthand the work that goes into developing these, and the effort it takes to get them to market. Yet we have reached a point where wholesale retail reductions are being offered on ranges to coincide with the film launch, and in some cases, prior to a launch! If consumers pondered the matter, they would think we are nuts; we've allowed them to hold off on purchases and shop for last-minute bargains during the holiday season, and now we are giving away margin on licensed ranges before many have even had the chance to see the characters in action.

Where was the long-term planning? What happened to a marketing push that coincides with the DVD launch or online availability or satellite premiere, not to mention the holiday push when the film might be shown on television? Over-promotion diminishes these opportunities, putting all of the pressure on the master toy licensee to keep the character fresh. The rules of the game have been changed forever. The long-term model will be replaced by a short-term push for cash. Consumers now have been trained to expect price reductions at every launch, and I expect retailers will panic and give their customers what they want.

Amazingly, there is a positive to be gained from this situation. Completely by accident, the industry may have modernised itself.

We are now in a new communications era, and traditional lead-ups to launches are no longer feasible. Audience fragmentation, more nimble, portable computers and faster, more mobile communications mean that the instant film download is upon us. Some have even promoted the idea of releasing films in theatres and on the Internet simultaneously, to reduce piracy. This represents the opportunity to build a business plan around the Internet and mobile telephones and computers.

For example, master toy licensees should drive licensors to create long-term strategies beyond the usual mix, to have plans for a brand online and digitally. Otherwise, it is possible that the toy range will be the first casualty.

Many children primarily watch satellite TV; listen occasionally to the radio and perhaps once a week or fortnight go to the cinema to find some new character heroes, but from an increasingly early age, they are using computers and mobile communicators. Children's marketing strategies that do not include an online/digital/mobile strategy are beginning to look like no strategy at all.

Each year I have the privilege of spending a few days at licensing shows around the world and I see licensing more than ever as king of children's marketing. It is illuminating to see the world's characters and brands "on sale." Faults still remain within consumer product companies—particularly a lack of insight and strategy—yet licensing-related business is booming.

Licensing teams are not responsible for creativity and brand development; this is the task of the entertainment arm that created the coveted characters. Entertainment companies must talk directly to consumers; to do so successfully, they must have a relationship with and understand them. Film and TV companies have direct access to their audience; the resulting dialogue has helped develop most entertainment properties during the past decade. They engage, and take care not to patronise, their audience. These companies are trusted by their audience, and this trust allows for the many brand extensions that follow.

In what other market are brands anticipated as eagerly as they are in the film industry? Where else can a brand such as Ben 10 take off as quickly as in the children's TV market? These brands are not the result of luck but of careful development through understanding of consumers and through work to remain relevant.

Not only are TV and film companies ahead of the game in regard to understanding of audiences, but they recognise the need to continuously reinvigorate and reinvent. They know they must create compelling and relevant content that engages and excites and also breeds familiarity.

In developing entertainment properties, the creative process involves much research and many conversations with potential consumers. This helps build an entity that will remain popular for some time to come. This is a valuable lesson to be learned from licensing: Licensed properties have long-term strategies that take into account a product's history and/or plans to build a franchise into the future.

TV companies in particular spend much time with and utilise many media channels, continuously interacting with their consumers, learning about them and the ways they are developing, the language they use, their habits—the ins and outs of their world. This is then developed into relevant content and long-term brands.

How many other industries can say the same? The majority of brands aiming at children or families are short-term in aim, designed to make hay whilst the property is hot. There is little recognition that the property could be around for a long time—that there are opportunities beyond the next 12 months.

The TV and film industry is based on three fundamental business functions: Understanding the audience; creating compelling, relevant content and long-term thinking. Who in other child-facing industries can honestly say these three are the core business functions of their current or future brand portfolio?

As an examination of the history of great children's brands shows, thinking and learning more about consumers will allow for greater creativity in product development. There is no reason to believe this won't be true for the future as well.

To invent and market a new, untested product is risky, to be sure. I challenge you to think "why not," and to believe in your company's creativity. New products don't have to be revolutionary, just different. Wouldn't it be a fantastic endorsement of the talent in the toy industry if every company developed one range each year based upon the three functions of audience: understanding, creative development and long-term strategy? Not all would make it, but I would bet that each year at least one product line would emerge that would excite and put the buzz back into the industry.

Agencies

I didn't always enjoy my own experience working within agencies, but I did learn an awful lot from some great minds.

The problem with many agencies is that—with a few exceptions—they are simply money-making machines that don't care enough about clients' businesses. I want to share a few observations that might be useful when searching for help from outside sources, because having the right people is especially important when dealing with children.

Children's Specialists: Who Needs Them?

As I have disclosed, I run a business that specialises in marketing to young people. Why is this type of service needed?

The truth is, not everyone does need this guidance. In many cases, child-specialist agencies grew from misguided intentions. Some arose b cause they had several child-centred clients. They declared a desire to serve clients' strategic needs, installing research techniques to better understand clients' business, but in truth simply wanted increased revenue.

Clients began to see that they were being asked to pay extra for a new service, which amounted to an admission that they weren't getting the needed strategic input in the first place, and that agencies themselves had much to learn regarding marketing to children.

What's more, when some agencies set up long-term monitoring, the groups they were studying were, in fact, the children of the agency staff. And the staff themselves did not truly desire to become leaders in youth marketing; they aspired to bigger, more prestigious clients.

These weaknesses lead to the demise of most child-centred agencies. The surviving firms, such as my own Jammy Rascals, used clients' time to gain insight into their marketplace and genuinely took the time to understand the marketplace, rather than simply seeing the trend as another way to make money.

Still, the truth is, most media agencies are "buying shops"—they are heavy on administration and they need volume to make a profit. They are not geared to client service. A sobering thought is that if you spend between £2 and 4 million per annum, you are unlikely to be in the top 50 of the large agency's clients. What does that tell you about the service you likely will receive?

If you are a "big" spender and want to purchase volume TV spots, then these "buying shops" are the agencies for you. If you have smaller budgets and need to eke out every penny of value, you may want to take a look around.

Search out specialists who want what is best for their clients, rather than what's best for the agency's bottom line. True specialists will seek an active dialogue between your brands and the target audience, and will recommend strategies that do not waste money and do not require funding for superfluous research.

Good client service, innovative thinking, challenging advice and multi-dimensional communications understanding should be available at a price that certainly is no worse, and often is better, than the buying shops. Your specialists should be equipped to deal with small budgets and put in the time and effort needed to gain precious standout.

From my experience, I can cite several examples of strong media opportunities that were not been fulfilled due to lack of budget commitment from clients. The main reason in almost every case was that the clients never were made aware of the opportunity in the first place. In many cases, the agency was the barrier; often because it hadn't taken the time to create a strategy beyond buying TV space.

It's time to start searching out new opportunities. For example, search out grassroots sports, where children are being encouraged to participate and where your money will be welcomed. Budgets of all sizes can be accommodated that would provide exposure at point of contact with this audience and create that all-important active relationship.

Other examples abound in the arts and entertainment, which can open up a new dimension in communicating with children. These are the opportunities that agencies specializing in children's marketing should know about and be talking about to clients. Agencies should be able to advise on how to maximise such opportunities.

Back in 2004, I asked the following question, and it's still relevant today: Who is providing creative media thinking? I was at a toy fair that year, and I found brilliant stands, brilliant people, and brilliant products. The main topic of conversation was the state of the market regarding retail promotional giveaways, but this was closely followed by exasperation as to the predictable way in which TV ratings were being used.

People in the toy trade and many others condemn the pressure they feel from retailers to pay for promotions. The retailers, who don't even know what a GRP truly is, nonetheless expect lots of them. Marketers then turn to media agencies and instruct them to buy as many GRPs as possible for as little as possible. So on one hand, marketers condemn retailers for a narrow-minded "pile it high, sell it cheap" attitude, but on the other you instruct your agencies to adopt the same strategy.

The market, on both sides, has stagnated.

Improved communication is about quality: quality of the creative message, quality of the media strategy, quality of the media plan and quality of the media buying.

It is not about quantity. When will this market come to grips with the fact that a quality communications plan is about reaching as many members of your precise target audience as often as you can in a way that engages them and attracts them to your product?

The currency is *coverage, frequency* and *message*—not GRPs. I repeat, the currency is *not* GRPs.

There are many ways to build a strategy that delivers a plan based on the above criteria. All of the usual factors that come into play when planning TV campaigns are present: budget, time scale, market forces, retail relationships, target audience, ready-made TV ads, TV programming.

Back in Chapter 4, I discussed the impact of coverage and the need for innovative thinking in the use of GRPs. I demonstrated that you can achieve high coverage levels with fewer GRPs and then use the money saved to improve communication with your audience, improving its quality and tangibility.

Does this conversation sound familiar?

BRAND OWNER: "Hello, agency. Here is a brief for my product. It targets boys ages 5 and 6 and we have £x to spend. We already have a TV commercial. We need to advertise during key holiday time slots and go early if possible to lend some support to the retailer."

AGENCY: "OK. We'll send you a TV plan. Could you make sure you book it by the end of July? What is the time length of the ad?"

BRAND OWNER: "20 seconds"

AGENCY: "Cool. See you next year."

That's it, simplified. Just enough time for the agency to negotiate a rate, come to a few monthly meetings, buy the TV campaign and collect the commission.

Where's the strategy? Where's the creativity? Most of all, where's the thinking? Media owners should be tearing their hair out. They spend millions of pounds developing their medium, brand and/or product, and trying to understand child consumers. Most crucially, they deliver these consumers to advertisers.

Why do they bother trying to sell this knowledge to advertisers, though, when all advertisers seem to want are GRPs? They're not interested in other things that may be available and the relationships this entails. Most of all, they don't want to compromise the retailer relationship by thinking outside the GRP box.

But thinking outside the box is what is needed to engage the children and get them talking about your brands.

Unfortunately, most media agencies see simple TV buying as a guaranteed income in November, with very little work on their part. It's good business; who can blame them for not wanting to rock the boat?

Agencies aren't the only ones who spur this course of action.

Marketing budgets drop because of the squeeze put on them by major retailers, leaving brand owners under pressure to cut costs. Where better to start than with media? The brand owner then puts the squeeze on the media agency. They already expect the best buying in town; now they want their agency to do so at a much reduced commission rate. The agency has no choice but to accede to the request and the brand owner is delighted with their negotiation.

Herein lies the rub. The agencies are now working on tight margins themselves, and any creativity and strategic insight comes at a cost (a staff member, a planning consultant). This is a cost that can be lessened by reducing time spent on the account. Volume buying requires less work than thinking. Block-booked TV campaigns require very little administration.

So it may appear on the surface that in the current market, nobody needs to think anymore. The truth of the matter is that we do. The critical question: Who's going to pay?

The communications plan requires cohesion between all parties—retailers, research companies, PR or advertising and media agencies. The GRP is not the currency that provides the glue. Coverage and frequency do. And a cohesive plan requires thinking and analysis.

Which brings us back to the crucial question: Who is doing your thinking for you?

Digital

Nothing ever stands still. This is why I love with the children's market; it challenges and cajoles and keeps people on their toes, encouraging creativity of thought and deed. Children are at the forefront of change; they are the embracers and developers of new technology.

For children, the future, perhaps alarmingly, is now!

One piece of research that I find particularly astounding, which has ramifications in sales and marketing—especially those who ply their trade to children—is this: In a recent survey, 65% of 15- to 24-year-olds said that if given a choice, they would choose their computer over the TV. This startling statistic not only endorses the computer as the trusted tool of the masses but also one that stands as an indictment of the television as we know it. (By the time you read this, the computer-favouring percentage likely has increased—possibly exponentially.)

Let's not be naive in thinking that this statistic hasn't filtered down to children—and, ultimately, the whole family. Society is hooked on computers. We can't live without them, and with the advent of Voice Over Internet Protocol (VOIP), which ultimately will reduce telephony costs to nil, our reliance will become almost complete. Children in many places are already there. They use computers in schools, where 60 percent of children in the United Kingdom have access to broadband connections. They use them at home, where 70 percent of nine- to 11-year-olds claim to have their own computer. Ninety-five percent use their computers to play games, but they also use them to download information and, most importantly, for constant communication.

Consider these findings:

- 96 percent of children between ages five and 10 have a computer in the home; 88 percent have access to the Internet at home.
- 78 percent of children in this age group use the computer in school.
- 40 percent of children eight to 10 years old and 31% of those five to seven years old use the Internet three to six days weekly.
- The average session lasts more than 15 minutes, and this is increasing on average by 10 seconds *weekly*.
- 48 percent send and receive email, 32 percent use instant messaging, 20 percent use text messaging and 22 percent collect mobile phone accessories.

We already have a nation of computer-savvy children who are using technology for a multitude of applications. The TV has not been replaced as an entertainment tool—*yet*—but it is one-dimensional in comparison. The computer is becoming vital to children in the multimedia environment, so much so that I suspect TV's efforts to go interactive will be perceived before long as a poor relation, too restrictive when compared to the computer and its capabilities.

The computer has become the new TV, with GRPs relegated to a supporting role within the overall communications mix. The TV simply can't compete with what can be achieved on the computer; it's just a matter of time before all programming will be streamed online.

I must put in a quick caveat here. I am not saying that children's TV channels will disappear; far from it. They have been leading the multimedia generation for years and are in prime position to be the ultimate benefactors from the change. They have seen the light and are waiting for us to take the cudgel up with them.

So what should you be doing? I urgently suggest taking a look at your online strategy, including your own web sites, your own multimedia communication plan and their roles in your integrated mix. How are you communicating with the computer generation? You can use the Internet (and other applications reached from the computer) for advertising, promotions, public relations, sponsorship, direct mail, Customer Relationship Management (CRM) and even point-of-sale through online retail. Children will pass along your brands to friends instantly—immediate word-of-mouth! The perfect synergy to it all is that you control the output *and* you have access to the consumer input. You have the chance to develop an active relationship with the consumer, which is vital in today's cluttered market.

And what about the social networking phenomenon? Facebook, You Tube and My Space have become a huge stage on which to place your brand. You are going to need to be confident of your brands' attributes and also be prepared for comments that you may not want to hear, but honesty from the audience is what you want and most certainly will get! If you put a brand up for scrutiny on social network sites, children will feel bound to say exactly what they think. But this is what we want to encourage. As I said in the early chapters, we need to give children more respect and this is why, for them, social network sites are important. There, nobody is patronising them or telling what they can or cannot say. If you are happy to engage on this level, you will get some great feedback for your brand.

How much time and effort have you put into addressing these opportunities? Can you afford to keep ignoring them?

And what about the future? Where is the Internet going?

Internet users are moving from a reliance on providers to becoming instigators of content. They are taking ownership and controlling their own data, through the likes of blogging and twittering, in-page ranking, E-bay reputations and Amazon reviews. The web is booming not as a technological tool but as a platform and a socially interactive community. Control will continue to be in the hands of users, who will choose how they interact with the Web just as they have traditionally chosen their own social interactions at home, in schools or in the playground.

The world has moved into an era of cross-collaboration and social application, and people will search out sites with which they have a degree of self-identity, where we think we belong. The basic tenet of all children's relationships with others is that they want to belong. This opportunity, if harnessed, represents a powerful worldwide brand extension (similar to self-chosen sponsorship) and will ultimately represent opportunities for retail, e-tail and multimedia companies.

Streamed TV and video, instant messaging, SMS, mobile marketing, in-game sponsorship and advertising, music downloads, voice recognition and web-cam technology are developing at an alarming quick rate and represent untapped niche marketing opportunities. The virtual world is the perfect medium in that it will allow us to develop marketing strategies designed specifically for its audience and cut out the waste. In most cases, online media is accountable, giving your business a gauge of return on investment.

Wow—I hope you're as excited as I am.

It's time to stop thinking of the computer and its media opportunities as an add-on to your communications and marketing strategies. The time is now for the computer to take a lead role in brand positioning and communication.

Don't wait until your products are overtaken by new brands you've not yet heard of—the next Annoying Thing and Arctic Monkeys (for those reading this in the future these were, respectively, a phone ringtone and a rock band, both of which became fashionable as a result of digital media). Get your online strategy ready now!

Web Sites—What Does Yours Do?

With online retail sales growing exponentially, the Web is not just important but paramount to marketing efforts. As more and more people come online looking for information and entertainment, they will find your site. Are you ready for this?

We know how important retail is to your marketing strategy, and significant effort has been made to attract in-store buyers. Now the store has moved; what are you doing to support it?

Everything you do on-line has to be part of the marketing strategy, which includes protecting your brands' ethos and delivering the same message online that is being communicated via advertising or packaging. We all know the stories of consumers going into a retailer to buy one product and finding themselves coming out with a competitor's because, in-store, the purchased product had a greater presence. Well, this is where the Web is going—only the Web isn't only the place of purchase; it is the first point of contact, too.

Your own Web site is the initial point of contact. Is it up to scratch? Is it doing the job? It is probably doing the job it was intended to do when it was designed, which was to give a point of reference and enough product information to allow visitors to understand the range. At the time this was fine; now it's not.

Your site needs to showcase your product and brand, but also appeal to children, their mums and retailers. When you take a good look at your site, you will probably find that it offers good information about products, tells where they can be purchased, suggests a point of contact for retailers and offers a customer services section. But this type of site provides information for trade relationships and for consumers *post*-sale.

What happens when the consumer is looking for more than post-sale customer services? What happens when a child, pre-sale, decides to find out as much as they can about their favourite character and happens upon your site? This hypothetical searcher has been finding entertainment related to the brand wherever they've digitally travelled (a TV channel site, YouTube, MSN messenger and even on their mobile phones) and here they are at your "post sales" site. Is this going to feel like a let-down?

I suggest a few ideas that can help you revamp your web site without spending a fortune.

First, I suggest developing a consumer Web site, with a front page offering one section relevant to children and one relevant to adults. Upon entering the site, children will follow the fun route, which will provide plenty of brand interaction, games, general mayhem and enough rope for the children to become engaged in and even lead the content. The mums will follow the "fun but a little bit more serious" section, which will have lots of ideas and plenty of product information, FAQ and customer service information—most of what you likely already have. And the trade visitors? I think the above would suffice: Their positive interaction with the brand at this stage will be a boon, and one section for "trade sales" in the adult portion is enough.

Second, if you feel your site is fine as it is and acknowledge that it is solely a trade site, you might consider building "micro sites." Rather than pushing consumers to your original site, you go in search of consumers, buying space for your micro site on other companies' Web sites. This is no different than buying advertising space on TV, except that your media are Web sites, where you can measure your exposure immediately in "hits," and add this coverage to your overall marketing plan. A micro site is considerably cheaper to create than a TV ad; if you buy your media innovatively, you will still be able to gain on-air exposure to back up your micro campaigns.

Both of these ideas make good use of the investment you have made already and add a much-needed consumer-specific element to your digital strategy.

Do not take your site's content and ability to speak to its audience lightly. The presentation of brands online is very important and can be a let-down for visitors if, for example, the wording isn't given the same consideration as it would be should for packaging. Wording can make or kill a campaign, and if you are devising an online strategy, you should give careful consideration to the way you use words within content. Therefore, if you are looking for a Web design company to develop your site, consider having a separate writer come up with the words—someone experienced in developing copy for the toy market, and in talking to kids and mums, who can match the correct words to a web designer's creative skills.

On final thing you may want to consider is whether you want to start a dialogue with your Web visitors. This is dependent on whether you are confident about your relationship with the consumer; you shouldn't just be looking for compliments! This may be a way of testing your brand's engagement with children and whether you are ready to build a larger CRM model and, ultimately, whether you are in a position to enter the world of blogs, Twitters and social networking.

6

And One More Thing!

We have covered a great deal in these pages, and I am sure that you will feel confident viewing the children's market as unique and in need of special attention. I want to sign off by sharing with you an article I wrote for the U.K.-based magazine *Toys N Playthings (TnP)*. This was my last column after three years of writing for the publication, and it asked a simple question:

What happened to the children?

This may seem like an odd question on the surface, perhaps, but it is extremely relevant in today's license-dominated environment. I want to talk about children, and I ask: How high are they on your list of importance?

When developing a range or products, are we all looking for the easiest route to market, the tried and trusted model, or are we thinking about the end user? I suspect that most of us can answer yes only to the first part and I can understand why. We are in a multimillion-dollar business that traditionally demands the safe option, one that can be easily positioned to retailer buyers who can then satisfy their bosses by guaranteeing profits. We have put the capital "C" in Conservative!

What a shame. In three years of writing articles for *TnP*, I like to think that I have challenged everyone, including myself, to be more creative in their actions, whether that be in developing ranges, distributing them, or most especially, in communicating these brands to the consumer.

I know I have been consistent in trying to persuade you to put children first—to allow them a voice, to take heed of what they are saying and to take this into consideration when producing a product.

Yet we are now so dominated by licensing that I fear we are beginning to lose sight of the goal, which must be to provide products that children will love and that parents will trust.

I have no problem with licensing or with licensors, which are an integral part of the relationship between product and consumer. But I do feel the pendulum has swung too far the wrong way. Surely licensing is about getting the closest synergistic relationship between quality product and quality brand and using this as the basis of a successful business plan. My concern is that while this is the ideal, and every licensor will strive for it, in reality it has become more difficult to achieve, especially in the era of huge movie releases and expensive TV series.

I do question whether we haven't lost sight of our main reason for being, the reason there is a toy industry in the first place. Is the tail now wagging the dog so hard that we cannot stop it? Children are the reason we market toys, but licensing has such a powerful pull on the business model that I wonder whether we are looking at the license too much as the lead and then adapting our ranges to fit them.

The clamour to get in on the next "hot" license property is staggering. Is it because we just don't feel able to take a gamble any more and are searching for the "sure thing" more than ever? All businesses, at some stage, are about taking risks. With hot property licensing, the risk to the manufacturer, the risk of failure, is being mitigated, because if the range fails it can be blamed on the performance of the film or TV series. No-one loses face!

Of course, there are many exceptions to the scenario I am describing, most significantly in the realm of girl's collectibles. Barbie and Bratz are multi-million dollar brands and have never relied on third-party licensing except as brand enhancements, which is absolutely the way it should be.

However, if the model continues as it is now, the gains made on the balance sheet will not take long to fall, as we continually change the characters on the toys but make little effort to change the entertainment value on offer. I believe we are already into the realm of "hot license fatigue" and that mums will soon become extremely cynical every time a new film is released. It is my opinion that most products are much safer seeing licensing as a great brand extension as opposed to a must-have accessory!

Perhaps I'm being naïve, but surely it is less of a risk to develop products, first and foremost, for children. By being aware of your consumer and supplying what they want and how they want it, you can market products that fit their lifestyle and development and which they will appreciate and trust.

I admit that this route is more long-term and doesn't create the short-term gains of film licensing, but the benefits can be far greater if a brand can last for many years as opposed to 12 months. When you have a long-term product you then have the range extensions and the probability of applying the best synergistic licensing partnership.

Children are the key; we should spend more time getting to know them and watching how they grow. The reason I love this market so much is that it is always changing; it is getting harder to accurately predict not only how children behave from generation to generation, but actually from year to year. However, scrutinising their behaviour and understanding how the media is dictating their rate of growth will give a distinct advantage in developing the most suitable and exciting entertainment ranges, which will stimulate and excite.

Keep an eye on the media; the rate of change is set to continue for many years to come. The key point of distribution for media communications is shifting. Children are leading the shift and the TV guys are the quickest to follow. TV is king, but not in GRPs; TV is king on a multi-layered platform, destined to be transferred to the computer, which will be the TV. (get your head 'round that!).

And finally:

Children are getting bolder younger, but they are still immature and naïve and in need of safety and security. Their world is changing at a rate that we can't appreciate without their help; we should take note of what they are telling us and strive to market great products that they will love.

I for one intend to spend the coming years doing exactly that. I hope that you will, too!

Lightning Source UK Ltd.
Milton Keynes UK
UKOW04f2115050315

247373UK00001B/96/P

To Cate
Thank you for
your support

Michael C...

BARRELED OVER

BARRELED OVER

MICHAEL CAVOLINA

TATE PUBLISHING
AND ENTERPRISES, LLC

Published by Tate Publishing & Enterprises, LLC
127 E. Trade Center Terrace | Mustang, Oklahoma 73064 USA
1.888.361.9473 | www.tatepublishing.com

Tate Publishing is committed to excellence in the publishing industry. The company reflects the philosophy established by the founders, based on Psalm 68:11,
"The Lord gave the word and great was the company of those who published it."

Book design copyright © 2013 by Tate Publishing, LLC. All rights reserved.
Cover design by Allen Jomoc
Interior design by Mary Jean Archival

Published in the United States of America

ISBN: 978-1-62902-119-5
1. Fiction / Thrillers / Suspense
2. Fiction / Action & Adventure
13.10.28

CHAPTER 1

My name is not important. I'm a survivor and that is. My mind is sharp and my wits keen. Trouble is, that's all of me that works anymore. They feed me through a tube because my throat won't take food. They have this thing they call a catheter up my penis so I can urinate and there's nothing satisfying about that. Oh, I almost forgot, I have a bag, too. Yeah, I'm a survivor.

It's April someday or other in the afternoon. I'm sitting quietly in my chair because walking ain't, sorry, isn't, something I can take for long. Jack didn't like me saying ain't like I'm from the Bronx or something, which I am. I am well spoken but it's easier to make people understand how pissed off you are with a little Bronx cheer in your voice, as gravelly as it is.

Jack held on for all he was worth, which was significant, but in the end he had so much morphine on board that he spent his days so stupefied he didn't know if it was raining or sunny, and he didn't care. He was a tough guy and I know he believed that the pain was his penance. On the rare day in the last six months that he chose to bear the pain of lucidity, he had made me promise to tell his story. He had spent his last months in terrible pain, dictating to me.

I got a tape recorder and put it all down for him. My tumors were slower to grow than some of my compatriots at the sanitarium, and I was told I could last up to a year or more before the pain was too great to stay in reality or the cancer got to my brain. So I better get started.

The view from my perch in the Italian Alps is spectacular and this place I'm in is a hospice whose location cannot be found on any map. How I got here and why I'm cloistered is part of Jack's story and ultimately mine. I'm one of the few survivors that were removed from Manhattan Island. We were among the unlucky ones. We lived. We were a few miles from Ground Zero, twice removed.

One year ago, this month, our worst nightmare came true. Yeah! Some fool finally did it. Two small megaton bombs so dirty that 4 million New Yorkers and those who were there to visit would eventually die from them. And for those of us who survived the blast, it was constantly on our tongues that we must have lived evil lives or we would have died that day. Because being alive was hell.

The blasts occurred in two places. Native New Yorkers knew the sites were well picked, as they cut off Manhattan from ground transport to New Jersey. They also played to the prevailing westerly wind, known in the wintertime as the Hawk. The first explosion occurred on the George Washington Bridge off-ramp on the city side at 7:55 a.m. It took out Washington Heights and all of the bridge. The area to the north and south of the bridge for a radius of forty city blocks was vaporized. Buildings that were standing since the 1920's were melted by the extraordinary heat of the blast. Further away, the shock waves shook buildings loose from their foundations while the blast wind toppled them, one on top of the other. Secondary explosions from broken gas mains had the effect of mortar rounds hitting randomly throughout the northern end of Manhattan. The devastation was instant and immeasurable. At that hour, hundreds of thousands of people were at home preparing to leave for work or on the street heading to a bus or subway stop. What wasn't leveled in the blast area was burning. What was not killed was battered by the shock wave and received a lethal dose of radiation.

Being farther away from Ground Zero was no comfort. The buildings that withstood the heat and shock of the explosion caught fire and burned, trapping residents in smoke-filled halls and elevators. Few people north of 125th Street survived the attack.

The GW Bridge, as New Yorkers and New Jerseyites alike called it, once a grand sight from either side of the Hudson, was gone, along with several thousand commuters.

The second blast occurred at the mouth of the Holland Tunnel, where it opens to lower Manhattan, at 8:00 a.m. Both blasts appeared to be on timers and set to the apex of Friday morning traffic. This one took out a chunk of Lower Manhattan Island—buildings, shoreline, tunnel. It was like a few million tons of TNT in a very small package.

The strategic placement of the second device was diabolical. The effect of the blast and heat was as if the lower third of Manhattan had been cut with the grim reaper's scythe. Nothing stood. For the fortunate, it meant instant vaporization. For some a little less lucky, it took a little longer to die, like the poor slobs in the tunnel who looked up after hearing the noise only to see the Hudson River pouring into their morning coffee and ruining their day, forever!

CHAPTER 2

I met Jack Duncan, Sr., on the morning of the attack. Even for pre-spring April, this day was icy cold. The Hawk moved through the streets toward the East River carrying bitter cold and damp winds at breakneck speed. An eerie stillness gripped the city as everyone rushed to end the agony of their commute from the suburbs to their cells in the nondescript office buildings that made up the skyline of the city of New York. April was never this cold, Jack Duncan, Sr., thought as he crossed 34th Street.

Duncan was not the kind of man to wait outside Pennsylvania Station at 7:45 in the morning on any morning. Walking on any street in Manhattan north of Wall Street and south of 46th Street was akin to slumming. He was a denizen of Central Park East, better known as 5th Avenue. Some called it Avenida Del Oro for the vast amount of wealth controlled by its residents. Jack danced with the elite of the city and walked with the Titans of Wall Street. He was out of his element this morning.

Jack was a man of extraordinary wealth. Had it been his nature to seek attention, he would have been listed in the Forbes Top Ten. But he was not so inclined and was nearly phobic about publicity, not at all unlike his friend at the Company.

Jack Duncan, Sr., was the American success story. Orphaned when his father was killed in the Philippines at the outset of WWII, and his mother died two years later when influenza and grief, combined with overwork, did her in. He was blessed, though, and taken in by the Sisters of Mercy and raised in an orphanage where he was educated in the religious truth of Catholicism and the secular truths of the Board of Regents of the State of New York.

Jack was a good student and soon found himself at a prestigious preparatory school run by Jesuit priests, educational pragmatists who found Jack to be a nearly perfect subject. He was quick to grasp material and needed little coaching, which was the Jesuit model of the excellent student. He was selected in his sophomore year at the school to pursue a scientific curriculum. It was a perfect match. He found chemistry and it found him and took him through the Pennsylvania State University on a full scholarship.

The war in Korea was winding down in 1953 when Jack graduated with a BS in Chemistry. He was fascinated with hydrocarbons and had studied how the Germans, master engineers that they were, had attempted to develop synthetic oils to operate machinery in place of ever-scarcer supplies of processed petroleum products. Jack applied for and was awarded a scholarship to Baylor University, in Texas, to study geology and petrochemicals. He was immediately smitten. His sense of service and love of a challenge combined to drive him almost relentlessly in his pursuit of synthetic oil.

Out in the cold of midtown Manhattan in 2008, Jack wasn't thinking about synthetic oil, much as he hadn't for nearly fifty years. He was there to meet his grandson, Jack Duncan III, who had just graduated from college and was coming to New York for a much-needed time out and a chance to reintroduce himself to a grandparent with whom he had never had enough contact.

Jack had sent his driver to pick up young Jack's mother, but the Limo had run into a traffic jam of monumental proportion on its way in from her estate in Short Hills, New Jersey, just across the George Washington Bridge. The bridge was at a standstill. Four independent cabs had managed to play bumper tag and the 4 drivers, who were of middle eastern descent, were having a melee that would have made a Friday evening at O'Neill's Bar and Grill look like a quilting bee. They effectively blocked the eastbound lanes of the upper roadway of the bridge.

Jack had hired a car to bring him to Penn Station, but the driver, short on English, wouldn't sit in front of the station for fear he'd be ticketed for illegal parking. Like all cabbies and private hacks in New York, the driver had a host of parking tickets and the commensurate bench warrants for failure to pay. So it was that Jack scurried inside the womb that was Penn Station.

It was 7:55 a.m. and young Jack's train was to arrive at 8:00 a.m. from State College, Pennsylvania, where he had spent the last four years. Duncan hurriedly approached a Redcap.

"What track is the train from State College arriving on?" he quizzed the man. "Track 19," he shouted to be heard above the dull roar that was Penn Station at the height of the morning rush.

Jack looked around and found his bearings. He was close to the track end of the station and he could hear the train whooshing to a stop. It took him less than a minute to find the gate. As he started toward it, the ground under him shook violently. His ears ached from the accompanying noise. It was louder than anything he had ever heard. He screamed from the pain and fright. It seem as though he could hear the sound of wind whistling by, but it was the speed of that wind that terrified him. He had seen a moving picture of an atomic blast, with its bending trees and unbelievable blast wind, and could only hope that his memory of that film and reality were on different planets. He fell to the floor, dazed and disoriented, and lay still for some time. He couldn't tell how long, but it was only minutes. I know because that's when I entered Jack's world—just as mine, Penn Station and its caverns, was being shook all to hell.

⟨ɷɷɷ⟩

I was a denizen of Pennsylvania Station and like so many of my ilk, a veteran of the Vietnam conflict, who never came to grips with the killing and maiming of women and children, no matter what their politics or reasons for engagement. The war had left its scars and no matter how hard I tried, I couldn't shake the memories. Drinking helped. At first, it allowed me to sleep, which allowed me to work. Soon, it became my crutch. Before long, I was drinking before sun up.

My job went, I sold my home, and I took to the streets where I found brothers-in-arms who were fighting the same demons. It wasn't as if I had to stay there. I had my disability check and adequate savings to rent a place, it was just that I liked being with other tormented souls. Truly, misery loves company. Winter pushed all of us inside, and I soon found my own spot in the bowels of Penn Station. The morning I met Jack, I was returning underground from a night spent at a midtown "D"-rated hotel. It was warm and the doors locked, but most important it had a shower in the room and hot water. I was clean and in warm clothes when the commotion began.

———◈◈◈———

The second blast was like being slapped in the face to awaken you after you've been floored by a haymaker. It stripped away the cobwebs from the first blast and knocked me down, where I landed heavily on Jack's legs.

"Aah! Goddammit, you've broken my leg!" Jack attempted to scream, but his curse came out as a whimper. "Help me up," he tried to order. "I've got to meet my grandson over there."

He was pointing in the general direction of the track gates, but there was no there anymore. He was dazed and in pain, and trying to mentally arrange the pieces of a puzzle without a picture of any relevance to guide him.

When Jack and I had gathered our senses, we could smell it.

"What the hell happened and what is that smell?" Jack demanded. He looked as if he knew the answer but wasn't sure he wanted to believe it.

Burning flesh, burning glass, burning steel, burning concrete, but we couldn't tell where it was coming from in all the chaos, but

I'd smelled all those ugly odors of death before, and the memories came rushing back like a tidal wave.

"It's everything you've seen in your worst nightmare," I answered above the noise that engulfed us. "It's the end of the fucking world. Someone just nuked New York."

There was pandemonium behind us. Sirens blaring, women shrieking, men sobbing, and the wounded screaming screams we had never dreamt of hearing. It sounded like every village we had flushed the VC out of by setting it on fire and volleying shots at those who decided that getting shot at was better than burning to death. It brought me back to reality. Something wrong had happened, something horribly wrong.

"We've got to get out of here," I bellowed. "This place won't stand it much longer. This way," I yelled, pointing toward the south end of the station.

I knew that time was not in our favor. Jack started to get up but screamed and fell into a heap on the floor.

"My leg, it's really broken," he sobbed in a barely audible voice. "Help me. I've got to find my grandson. I can't leave without him."

Jack looked toward the track area. Passengers from the train Jack III was to arrive on were just stepping off the train when the first explosion occurred. They had fallen to the platform along with the other passengers who had already disembarked other trains. They were not hurt, but stunned and dazed at the noise and the violent shaking that had followed the initial explosion. Most of them rose to their feet and hurried toward the terminal. Many arrived at the gateway to the terminal just in time for the keystone of the arch to the main station area to give way and the stone arch to fall, and with it the wall it held up.

Jack lay motionless. He sensed the world had moved a notch off its axis. He was right, but he had precious little time to ruminate. Pennsylvania Station had been shaken to its very core. From the roof to the Long Island Railroad tracks below, the structure was wobbling like a punch-drunk fighter after ten rounds, and was in grave danger of caving in on itself.

My fall had fractured Jack's leg in two places and he couldn't stand if his life depended on it and it did. "Let's go!" I yelled as I picked up this old stranger who had become every soldier I had shared a foxhole with nearly forty years earlier.

I had to get Jack up and out, and quickly. I hadn't had time to assess my own damages; there would be time enough for that later. I didn't imagine at the time that that thought was prophetic. I picked Jack up and headed toward the 34th Street exit. He was limping and in terrible pain, but he knew that we had to get out of there and it had to be now.

We made it to the street and headed east. South was too chaotic and I knew some places on the east side where I could get help for Jack. His eyes asked the obvious question. "We're going east," I said. "There are some hospitals. We'll get that leg splinted."

As we moved east, we saw smoke wafting across the roofs of towering buildings, giving the impression that they were burning. Sadly, it was not an impression. Manhattan Island was ablaze. It was far worse than I imagined. In my mind's eye, I had pictured the event, trying to visualize what kind of tragedy my mind could conjure up. I had dreamt up some grotesque images, but reality lost nothing to my dream.

We turned north on Park Avenue and continued east along 42nd Street past the Park Avenue tunnel that ran through the old Pan Am building and turned south again on Lexington Avenue. It seemed that midtown was still intact, at least on the surface. There were the normal sounds of a crisis here, sirens and police cars moving up and down the avenues and east and west along the streets. We had no way of knowing that they could only move a few blocks in any direction.

CHAPTER 3

We arrived at the hospital after some hard walking with Jack hanging on to me and agonizing over every step and me numb from the knee down.

"Where to," I asked the first person I saw in hospital garb.

"Over there," the orderly replied, pointing at the door where the ER sign had been.

"What happened?" the orderly asked, looking for all the world like a man who really didn't want a truthful answer.

"It's the big one, at least two nukes," I reported mechanically.

We were hustled into a waiting area and left to sit tight. The hospital was organized chaos. The staff moved with alacrity in a zombie-like trance. No amount of preparation, or exercise, or drilling, had prepared them for what was there and what was to come.

We sat in the holding area knowing that we would be there for a while. We saw the victims come rolling in. There were no dead bodies, as the word had been passed down to leave them where they laid. They were only to care for the living. The ones we saw were living but not alive—with burns so tragic that the flesh was gone and bones were visible, with arms and legs broken and twisted like twigs in the wind, with wounds with the weapons that made them—shards of glass and pieces of twisted steel—still sticking out of them, and screams that would make the Banshee shudder. "If you can't Band-aid it, leave it," the head of the ER department ordered. "We haven't the capacity or the staff to do more." His voice trailed away in sadness.

The night shift was still on duty as only replacements who lived nearby could find their way in. The ER staff was desperately trying to find beds, cots, gurneys, or anything flat enough to lay the wounded on until they died. Triage was more often a death sentence than a chance to receive care. Doctors moved quickly away from those whose hope of survival had floated away in the smoke and terror of the morning.

"Damn, this hurts," Jack spoke through clenched teeth. "Can we get some help?" He was becoming agitated. He was in serious pain and wanting information. He was able after several tries to find a fireman. "Can you tell me what happened?" Jack asked him, holding on to the man's bulky coat so he couldn't go without giving Jack an answer.

"At least two devices detonated at the bridge and tunnel, possibly a third at midtown on the West Side. I don't know more than that," the man replied, gently removing Jack's hand from the sleeve of his coat. "I've got to go," he said, and pointed to the fire truck getting ready to make another morbid collection run, like the carts stacked with bodies during the Black Plague.

Jack knew intuitively that it was not another Oklahoma City bombing, but he wasn't prepared for what he heard. The fireman only passed on what he knew but it was more than Jack could handle. When he heard that the bridge and the tunnel were gone and that buildings all over Manhattan were on fire or collapsing or blowing up from gas pipe breaks, he began to perspire, turned ghostly white, grabbed his chest, and slumped to the floor. "Get me a gurney and find a crash cart," the fireman barked at the nearest orderly. "This man's going into defib!"

The fireman carefully lifted Jack onto a gurney and got an orderly to check his vital signs, which were exactly what they should have been for a man whose heart was breaking. "My family," was all Jack could get out before the pain became too much for him to speak.

He knew that his daughter-in-law would have been on or near the bridge when the first blast went off. He knew that the station was collapsing as we left and he hadn't seen Jack III and it was likely that he was dead or mortally wounded, crushed under the rubble of that once majestic building.

The traverse from Penn Station to this east side hospital left an indelible picture in Jack's mind. He had seen the pictures from WWII of the Dresden firebombing but this was far worse. Blackened and broken buildings that clung to life by leaning on each other.

He had no idea how his wife, Veronica, had fared, but the picture in his mind left little doubt that she had succumbed.

The medics at the hospital were as good as people walking through the aftermath of a bloody battle could be. They did their jobs with a professionalism that bordered on lack of concern. They didn't or couldn't look at the wounded. They did what they had been trained to do as if they were working their magic on cadavers. They were happy to have Jack. "Get that man over here," the head ER Doc barked. "He's a live one and I want to have at least one I can send home in something other than a body bag."

The stress of the morning was beginning to show and treating someone who, aside from his broken leg, which he let them know about the first time they moved him, was not full of holes or burned beyond recognition and didn't have bones protruding from places where bones aren't supposed to be, made Jack an oasis in the firestorm of hell that the ER had become. He was the one patient they all wanted to work on and the one they could look at without feeling the overwhelming need to vomit.

"There," the doctor said after giving Jack a large bolus of opiate. "I think that will get him comfortable for a while,"

It didn't take long for Jack to get stabilized and sedated. He was resting comfortably when the fireman came back in. "Doc," he shouted as he moved quickly toward the front of the ER, "Penn Station has collapsed. We got a shit load of wounded coming this way."

The word that there would be a second wave was hard enough on a staff that was stretched thin, but that Penn Station collapsed at rush hour with thousands of people trapped under the rubble was devastating.

The roof we had been under not long ago must have given way into the mezzanine level, which in turn fell through to the track levels below. To understand the devastation is to revisit the San Francisco earthquake of 1989, and the pictures of the elevated roadway that fell in on itself. In Penn Station the bottommost level with commuters from Long Island hurrying to the next level and the New York City subway system which would take them to the far end of Manhattan and the Bronx. The topmost track level harbors trains from all over the country. Above that is the Mezzanine with its marble floors and brass clad ticket windows.

The roof and the super structure had been shaken violently to the very foundation which had cracked and crumbled allowing the entire building to implode.

Jack didn't move but I could see a tear in the corner of his eye and heard him sigh above the noise as he laid his head back and passed out.

"Doc, is he going to be all right,".

"He'll be okay for now," he answered cryptically. I would come to understand the hidden meaning of his words all too soon.

Jack woke about an hour later. He was agitated and wanted to speak to me. I was getting my ankle taped and heard him calling. "Come here," Jack commanded. I hurried to his side as quickly as my wounded pin could move me. "I have a lot to tell you," he said quickly. He was in full confession mode and wanted to be heard. He didn't care that the confessional was the middle of an overcrowded emergency room.

"Can you get us out of the middle of this," I asked an orderly. "Roll him this way," he said pointing. "It was a supply closet," he laughed. "It's empty now and you'll be out of the way in there."

"Thanks," I said as I rolled Jack's gurney out of a tidal wave of new victims arriving at the ER like the rush hour tide at the subway stops at Grand Central Station. We ended up in what amounted to a laundry bin. At least it was quieter.

"This is on my conscience," Jack said.

"What are you talking about?" I asked him.

Jack was becoming lucid again as his meds wore off. It was obvious that his real pain was inside.

"This is my doing," he murmured. "This is my doing." His voice had taken on a frenetic tone I had heard so often in the rice paddies of Vietnam.

"What are you talking about?" I asked him again, thinking he was having post-traumatic stress. That is, until he looked at me with eyes clearer than I have ever seen and told me with the sincerity born of truth, "I am the architect of this tragedy."

I could imagine much in the fertile fields of my mind, but I couldn't plumb the depths of this self-aggrandizement. "Who the hell are you?" I shouted at him. "How the hell did you do this?"

This is the story he told me in my words.

CHAPTER 4

Navigating his way around the Baylor University Campus was as difficult as dragging his stuff behind and in front of him. After a few false starts, Jack finally found his dormitory room. As he approached he saw the door was ajar.

"Hey, pard," Jack heard a voice from inside the room call. "You my new roomie?"

The voice belonged to J. B. Johnson, perpetual student and first in line to inherit Houston Oil and Gas, his daddy's oil company.

Jack smiled at the young man sitting on the cot across the room. "I guess if this is room 103, then I'm your man."

Jack entered the university in 1953 to add Geology and Petrochemicals to his Chemical Engineering degree as the basis of the research project he was determined to make my life's work: synthetic oil.

"Take the cot over there by the desk," J. B. offered. "You'll have more need of the desk than I have or ever will," he chuckled.

Jack believed that we are all here for a purpose and his, naively, was the betterment of mankind. His roommate on the other hand, a silver spoon baby, also was here for a purpose—eating and drinking and sleeping with all the girls he could get. Life, according to J. B., was for having fun.

"What are you studying?" J. B. asked.

"Geology and petrochemicals," Jack announced proudly.

"Whew," was all J. B. could muster, "a real bookworm. You gotta meet my daddy. He's the head of Houston Oil and Gas and is always looking for guys like you. Me, I just like the atmosphere here, if you know what I mean." He laughed as he drew the curvy figure of a girl in the air with both hands.

Jack laughed loudly at J. B.'s antics, but was worried that he might become too much of a distraction. But, he decided that he could use the comic relief J. B. would provide. Some decisions, made in haste, give credence to the old saw.

"I could use someone who knows their way around the west end of this state," Jack told J. B.

"Hell, I was weaned in West Texas and the Permian Basin," he replied.

"Then it's settled," Jack said.

Geology was more fun than work. Field trips to the arid regions of West Texas provided an outlet for him to bleed off the pressure of a double Masters by day and work on his project in the lab at night.

On the weekends, J. B. rolled out his Corvette and they'd head to San Angelo or Abilene, pick up motorbikes, and go off into the boonies to collect rocks.

Jack sort of liked J. B. He had no inhibitions, which Jack chalked up to having too much money and altogether too much booze. He trusted him, too, in part because J.B. had no desire to do much more than be a drugstore cowboy: eat, drink, party, drive his 'vette, wear his cowboy hat and boots, and chase tail, but mostly because he was much Jack's opposite number. Where Jack was focused and prepared, J. B. was scattered and spontaneous.

On one weekend, when J.B. was particularly over the top, Jack got in a barb about his lackadaisical attitude. "J. B.," he said trying not to laugh as he did, "your face that tells me you aren't stupid, just too rich and lazy to be smart."

"Jack," J. B. countered, "you're gonna own the world, at least the part that I don't."

They talked openly, J. B. telling tales about the shady deals his grandfather, and later on, his father were in on, taking entire oilfields out from under bewildered wildcatters using trumped up deeds and corrupt local justices to back their spurious claims.

"My father's name," J. B. began one story, "is T. J. Johnson, after his father, but his friends call him Cully. By my reckoning, he's as crooked as the limb of a Mesquite tree and as sour as its berries. He built his oil company by being faster and smarter and more larcenous than the next guy. He knew how to play the local law in West Texas, where justice was still being dispensed by Judge Roy Bean. Dad had a nose for oil and a better nose for a fool. He knew who and how much. He hated northerners, especially those who brought eastern money with them. They were a challenge to his way of life and he would go out of his way to see that they didn't find what he knew was there. If they did, he found a Justice of the Peace who would rule in his favor on a backdated deed or lease giving him control of a newly proven field.

"Cully shot a man in Abilene," J.B. went on, "over a well the man had brought in. Cully had dummied up papers that gave him mineral rights to three sections, about 1,920 acres, of land, including the well. The man got himself a lawyer, but Cully had the J. P. When all else failed, the man filed a paper in Federal Court to have Cully's claim overturned. Cully was not going to let him have his day in court. He bushwhacked the guy a few miles out of Abilene, moved the body miles out into the desert, stripped him bare, and let the critters and West Texas sun do the rest. The FBI got on the case, but never found the body and besides, Cully had cultivated a host of powerful friends in Washington with green fertilizer."

J. B. was the opposite of Cully. He was laid back where his father was out front. He was drunk when the situation needed sobriety. He was open when he needed to be guarded. He didn't give a damn. Jack was convinced that J. B. was going to spend his inheritance by the time he was thirty, but as he said, he trusted him. So much so that one evening after they shared their dorm room for about six months, Jack invited him along on one of his trips to the "library."

"J. B.," Jack called to him as he was getting ready to go out, "come with me. I've got something to show you that you might be interested in."

"Let me get my boots," J. B. yelled, hurrying to catch up. J. B. couldn't stand not being in on everything and suspected that Jack was up to something though so far he had been unable to pry it out of him. So he ran after Jack like the last one downstairs on Christmas morning.

When they reached the small and very well hidden lab, J. B. was floored. "What the hell is this?" he asked.

"It's a lab, you ass," Jack replied sarcastically.

"I got that much, Einstein," J. B. said in mock anger. "What are you doing down here?"

"Planning to blow up the world,"

J. B. laughed.

"I'm trying to develop a formula to make synthetic oil," Jack said earnestly. "Oil won't last forever. When the last well has produced the last barrel of oil, what are we going to do for cheap energy?"

J. B. sat on that for a while. There was a ring of truthful inevitability in Jack's words. Then he asked, "How far along are you?"

"Years away," Jack replied. "There are so many pieces that need to fit together and this lab doesn't have the facilities to even make the pieces."

J. B. was shocked. Jack could tell what he was thinking, Could this guy with the big brain and big ideas put an end to his gravy train? That is, until he saw the magnificent irony of the whole thing.

"Jack," he cooed, "did you come all the way here to put the oil industry out of business? Did you think you could keep this a secret?" He laughed so hard he looked like he was in pain. "Why are you taking on this big ass task?" He would have said Herculean task, but he had lost his copy of Edith Hamilton's

Mythology on the beach at South Padre Island after puking his guts out following an all-day binge.

"A man has to do some good in his lifetime, you know, payback for what he has," Jack said defensively. He could only guess why J.B thought something so serious was so funny.

"J. B.," Jack demanded, "quit laughing. This is serious and it's secret. I trusted you enough to share this with you, so please have some feeling for its importance to me."

"Sorry," J. B. apologized, "I'll keep it quiet."

Jack knew intuitively that he had made a mistake letting J. B. see what he was working on.

———

A week later, Jack returned to the dorm and found all of J. B.'s things gone. He had left a note saying he was taking a work vacation from his educational vacation. Jack smiled at the thought of him doing an honest day's work.

He noted that J. B. was the family's black sheep. His attitudes and life were shaped by his parents' divorce when he was five. His father had turned to business and an occasional roll with a secretary or barmaid, and his mother to the bottle. She went to Phoenix to dry out and had fallen off the radar. His father just kept doing what he always did: business.

J. B. grew up on his grandfather's ranch. It wasn't a bad place, just all business. He learned to find his pleasure where he could. By the time he was twelve, he could drink like a roughneck, gamble like a wildcatter, and fight like a treed polecat. He had a charm that made women think they could change him by giving in to him. Texas was replete with a fine crop of very angry young ladies who found out they gave way too much and had come away empty.

Mostly, J. B. wanted nothing to do with the business. He had agreed to go to Baylor to see if there was anything he could find in the curriculum that might interest him. Sadly for the family, J. B. so far remained just plain J. B., a drinking, carousing, womanizing, fighting fool.

Jack learned the hard way that working in the den of the beast to discover its Achilles' heel was something to do quietly and in secret, and a secret two people share is no secret.

HOG was the second biggest oil company in Texas. There was only one thing they wanted more than money, and that was to be number one. The week after he left Baylor, J. B. had gotten drunk at a family gathering and had a set-to with his father. He was in charge of bringing in a new field, but after a week on the job, he had yet to set foot on it. In typical J. B. fashion, he laughed at his father's serious manner and told him he was wasting his time drilling for oil when it could be made in the laboratory. This time it wasn't his shoe leather he inserted in his mouth, it was Jack's.

CHAPTER 5

Saturday afternoon in the basement lab of the chemistry building was a good time to work on private projects. The campus was busy watching football. Jack could work without distraction. The project, which he compartmentalized, a definite Jesuit trait, was going well and he was making rapid progress on a difficult phase. He thought he might be able to head back to the dorm in daylight.

In less than an hour it was done. As he walked out into the daylight and shielded his eyes from the setting western sun, Jack was grabbed by a very large man intent on shoving him into the back seat of a limousine.

"Get in," the man said.

"What the hell are you doing?" Jack shouted as he tried to break away.

"Get in the car," the man said again. This time Jack's refusal was met with a hand as big as a Texas steer and a door that slammed noiselessly shut, locking him in the leather prison that was the rear seat of a Mercedes limo as big as his dorm room.

There, in his best Rexall Ranger attire, sat J. B. Jack hadn't seen him in several months and looked at him with a eye that said he was less than pleased by the cloak and dagger way he'd been hustled into the car.

"Nice wheels, huh," was the sheepish way J. B. greeted him.

"Where are we going?" Jack asked, fairly spitting the question at him.

"You'll see. Some folks want a word with you. Folks that don't take no for an answer," he replied. "I'm here to keep you company." J. B.'s tone was different than his usual who-gives-a-shit attitude. In fact, it was anything but comic and was, to Jack, downright scary.

The car moved out of the Baylor campus and headed southwest from Waco toward Austin, the state capital. The car was solid and rode smoothly over Texas roads that were hardly more than dirt paths. It rode in silence, but not as deep as the silence that passed between J. B. and Jack. The sun had set and the fading light gave Jack the feeling that he was in a tunnel, moving deep into a blackness from which he would never emerge.

Jack found an interior light and switched it on. J. B. took this as his cue to start a conversation, but Jack only wanted to look at his watch, and shut off the light quickly, along with any conversation.

As angry as he was at J. B., his presence kept Jack from feeling like he was in solitary confinement. Just as the feeling of claustrophobia began to crowd over Jack, the car came to a stop and in a few seconds the door opened. It was pitch dark.

The driver who had whisked him off the Baylor campus held a small flashlight.

"This way," he said walking in front and signaling them to follow him. In the dark of a moonless night, some requests are not debatable.

The path wound around a small pond that was visible by flashlight, but Jack could hear the rippling of a larger body of water in the night breeze. He had no idea where he was. His mind began to imagine the worst, but he didn't think anything bad would happen with J. B. there. Then it hit him. "Son of a bitch," Jack hissed at J. B., "you let it out." He had been betrayed.

Jack had learned the hard way that although Texas is a big state, its about as small as Rhode Island when it comes to rumors about oil and the things that impact it. His misplaced trust and J.B.'s big mouth had put his project front and center with some pretty influential people. While he was publicly becoming an expert on the composition of hydrocarbons and where to find them, and privately trying to solve the puzzle that was the formula for synthetic oil, J. B.'s father was watching Jack as closely as Eliot Ness watched Al Capone.

The house appeared out of nowhere. Jack described it as a house because there were no other words for it. It was colossal. From the front, wings stretched out on either side for what seemed the length of football fields. The gabled roof covered three stories. It was completely lit.

Jack was about to come face to face with power, power that he could only imagine from stories he had read about the robber barons of fifty years earlier. He felt a shiver down his back.

CHAPTER 6

Sister Philomena, Jack's eighth grade teacher and a fine example of a Sister of Mercy, was a woman of stature. She was five feet ten inches tall and weighed in around 200 pounds. She looked mean and was just as terrifying. It was her M.O. to take the biggest and burliest male students in her class, wale the tar out of them on the first day of class, and then ask the class if she was going to have any trouble with them for the rest of the year. She never did.

Jack remembered the first day in class with her and what she did to Big Billie. It scared the hell out of him, which in a very Catholic sense was the job of the nuns.

Jack felt just as scared that night. He was still somewhere in Texas, that's all he was sure of.

The driver escorted them into an anteroom where Jack was left in the company of J. B. He hated him right now. A man who sells himself for a dollar is not to be trusted, ever. He would revisit that thought over and over as the years went by.

"Hi, Veronica" J.B. said as young woman entered the room. She was strikingly beautiful, with Grecian features and auburn hair pulled back from her temples, accentuating her cheekbones and baring her supple neck. She possessed a grace borne of the best Eastern and European finishing schools.

"Hello, J.B.," she said as she approached him and gave him a perfunctory hug. Her manner told Jack that she was bored with J.B.

"How are you, Veronica," J. B. answered as she turned and moved toward Jack, and, holding out her hand in a European fashion, introduced herself.

"I'm Veronica Shiver," she offered. The name meant little to Jack. To be exact, he didn't care if the vision in front of him had a name, as long as she didn't leave his sight.

After what could have been an eternity, Jack tried to introduce myself.

"I'm Jack, eh, Jack Duncan," He fairly stammered, still holding her hand.

"I'm pleased to meet you," Veronica said, smiling a smile of delightful surprise. "I had no idea a scientist could be so attractive," she flirted, drawing a less than friendly look from J. B.

"I've heard that you're interested in synthetic oil," she said. "Is that true?" Veronica's voice left Jack defenseless.

"Yes, miss," He replied like a schoolboy. "I am."

"Could I enquire why?" Veronica posed politely.

The question of science helped him get his footing.

"There is a finite amount of oil underground," Jack began. "When it begins to run out or becomes too costly to extract, and supplies dwindle, there will be conflict. If I can substitute an inexpensive synthetic, it will guarantee our energy supply and possibly help to avoid future wars."

Veronica smiled at Jack in a way that was both frightening and delighting. She seemed pleased by something she saw in him that he didn't know was there and was to learn later: an irrepressible desire to succeed at whatever he attempted, whatever the cost.

J. B. saw the look and knew that she had sized Jack up and liked what she saw and would be the end of any designs he had on Veronica. He had been around her since childhood and knew her well enough to know that she had chosen Jack and would get what she wanted. He smiled to himself wryly. Jack had no idea what a ride he was about to go on.

"I find that an interesting perspective," Veronica said. "How long do you think it will take to develop the first samples?"

"I'm not sure," Jack replied. "My small lab makes experimentation slow and difficult. There are equipment issues and, of course, time."

"Have you thought of the ramifications of a discovery of this magnitude?" J. B. heard her ask as she led Jack out of earshot.

J. B. knew that Veronica wasn't as ruthless as Cully Johnson, but she was capable of emasculating an adversary with a glance or a well-placed barb. She was bright, but more important she had business savvy. She kept complete control of her emotions when things got dicey and could analyze a situation on the run. She understood that oil was not a provincial enterprise like so many of her Texas oil friends thought, but a global issue worth trillions of dollars and she wanted her share.

Veronica was the daughter of the governor of the State of Texas, and crude oil was her passion. She knew what wealth could buy and coveted it as much as any man could, but power was her aphrodisiac and she was willing to go through hell to get it, even if that included marrying J. B. She would control J. B., and through him she would control what would become the largest oil company in Texas. She was everything J. B.'s father wished J. B. to be, and he saw the future of his family and their wealth in her. He knew his son, and knew how little he cared about the enterprise. But he knew that Veronica would do what was necessary to maintain it. He planned for them to marry, even if he had to empty every liquor bottle in the State of Texas.

Veronica had been happy to go along with this plan until today. She had read the dossier on Jack Duncan. She knew about his early years in an orphanage and his education. She also knew he was a man of conscience with a populist bent. His research into synthetic oil was threatening to Cully Johnson, but not to Veronica. She saw the oil business for what it was: a zero sum game. The winners would reap vast sums of money and the accompanying power until it was gone. Jack, she thought, might be the future.

"Hi, Dad," J. B. said, half as a hello and half as a signal to Veronica that someone else had entered the room.

Veronica looked at Jack, smiled and took his hand again.

Cully Johnson, all six feet of him without his signature boots, strode into the room with his characteristic bull-in-a-china shop way of going and took notice.

He walked directly over to Jack and extended his hand. "I'm T. J. Johnson," he said, "but my friends call me Cully."

Cully shook Jack's hand like he was pumping a well.

"I know you're Jack. Pleased to meet you. Come on, y'all, we have a bunch to do."

Cully put a lot of stock in proper public behavior, but little in what he did in private. Having properly introduced himself, he took them through the main hall of the house into a lavishly furnished living room.

The room's motif was decidedly twenties in character. It was filled with furniture that had certainly heard the Charleston, including a settee that could only be described as the chastity belt of love seats, an S-shaped sofa that kept a couple on opposite sides. Jack also noticed the Tiffany lamps that lit the surroundings and the man in a leather chair the size of Texas, whose face was not familiar to him.

Veronica walked demurely across the room to the man in the overstuffed leather chair, leaned over and whispered, "Daddy, I'm going to marry this man". This brought a quizzical look from the man in the chair, then a broad smile. He wasn't sure what had caused Veronica to say this, but he was glad of it, for as much as he liked Cully Johnson, that's how much he disliked J. B.

"Daddy, I want you to meet Jack Duncan," Veronica said aloud as she introduced him to her father.

"Pleased to meet you, son. I'm Governor Shivers," he said, extending his hand.

The governor greeted Jack like a long-lost son. Cully got the message.

"Get you a drink, son?" the governor offered.

"Yes, sir," Jack managed, somewhat overwhelmed. Normally, he was not a drinker, but the events of this evening needed a strong belt to get them down and keep them there.

Soon after, a bell rang. "Dinner," the governor announced, inviting them into the adjoining room.

A fine French provincial table, long enough it seemed to Jack, to seat thirty people in regal comfort. This evening's group was easy.

"This way," Veronica whispered as she took Jack's arm and escorted him to a chair at the corner of the table. She sat next to him. The governor sat at the head and Cully and J. B sat across from Veronica and Jack.

"Here's to the future of the oil business and the State of Texas," the governor said, raising his glass. Three waiters entered the room with silver trays of Gulf shrimp and cocktail sauce, horseradish, and Tabasco. Jack had eaten shrimp cocktail in New York, but never saw it served on silver. The governor was a no-nonsense guy and dove into the shrimp hands first. Texas politicians socialized with Texans who didn't much stand on ceremony.

"Like this," Veronica instructed as she took Jack's left hand and placed a shrimp fork in it. The governor smiled.

Dinner was more than Jack had eaten at one meal in a lifetime—spinach salad with a warm vinaigrette dressing, a perfectly seasoned standing rib roast with au gratin potatoes, and the governor's favorite freshly baked German chocolate cake. As coffee was being served Cully spoke up.

"I, we, the governor and me," Cully began, "that is," he continued. He had apparently rehearsed his speech, but without a barrel of bourbon on board, he sounded like an eighth grader performing on parents' night.

"You need a little more bourbon," the governor offered chuckling. "Miss Veronica," he asked, "would you mind?"

"Jack," Veronica said, "we've brought you here without asking if you would care to come. Please forgive us."

If she had asked him to swim the English Channel doing the backstroke and holding his breath, he damned well would have.

"We've been told a lot about you by J. B., who also asks to be forgiven for inadvertently allowing a breach of the confidence you shared with him," she continued. "We also know that there is wisdom in your quest. The oil will run out and if there is not a viable alternative there could be serious political and military consequences. Because of this, Cully and my father want you to join Houston Oil and Gas. They believe that you would make an excellent vice president of exploration and development. All Cully asks is that you allow Houston Oil and Gas to fund your research. Arrangements would be made for you to finish your masters and a doctorate if you so desired, and HOG would build a state-of-the-art laboratory for your use while at Baylor, which they would donate to the university when you've completed your degrees."

Veronica's smile seemed to promise more than a research facility.

Jack could barely think. What had started as a frightening misadventure became a dream. He nodded in assent and tried to answer. A stuttering "yes," was all he could manage, while looking at Veronica. "Yes!"

The thoughts in Jack's head made the blood rush to his face. Veronica got the message, and taking his arm, announced that they were going for a walk. Governor Shivers protested, but his protest was smiled down by a very radiant young lady. As they left the room, Jack heard Cully offer J. B. a tall glass of Kentucky bourbon. J. B. was easy to distract.

Veronica took them through French doors to a veranda overlooking a lake. It was dark on the lake and the only light available was from the Tiki torches Veronica lit.

Jack was in a state of confusion, having just met a vision who took away both his breath and good sense. He committed himself and his project to HOG.

"Jack," Veronica asked, "do you believe in love at first sight?"

He tried to answer yes, but the words never made it past his lips as Veronica kissed him. Jack knew he was falling, but where he would land was like the ending of a Saturday matinee serial: wait 'til next week. In his case, it would be decades.

CHAPTER 7

"Jack?" Veronica called as she entered his laboratory, unsure of where he was in the maze of glass beakers and tubing.

"Hi, Veronica," Jack waved from behind a row of beakers at the far side of the lab. "I'm almost done."

The lab was completed, stocked, and staffed. Veronica was a regular visitor at Baylor and Jack was in, pardon the pun, hog heaven. he was paid handsomely for the research work and for summertime forays into the Texas backcountry to find potential oil drilling sites. He had an uncanny knack for finding viable oil fields. It was as if he possessed a built-in divining rod, a Y-shaped stick that points down to an underground water supply, only his gift was for black gold.

Jack's studies moved ahead rapidly and in less than three years, he completed both of his masters' degrees and started a doctorate in chemical engineering. He was fulfilling all his dreams except one—the one he had every evening about Veronica. He had taken the bait and she had set the hook.

Veronica came to Baylor for Easter weekend, 1956. The school was closed and most students and faculty had gone home for the spring holiday. She had come with a purpose—to reel in her catch.

As they closed up the lab for the evening, she asked, "Are we ready?"

At first Jack played at being clueless about what she was talking about. "Ready for what," he teased.

"Oh, you are just impossible," she shot back.

"This impossible," Jack queried as he kissed her passionately on the lips. "Yes, I think we're ready," He whispered as he held her close.

"When do you think we can?" she asked. "You have so much to do."

"June would be fine," He offered.

Veronica had wanted a May wedding, but time was too short for that; the logistics of getting the governor's daughter married made her agree to wait a month longer.

———

Veronica and Jack married in June, 1956, at the Governor's Mansion in Austin. It was a wedding befitting Texas royalty. Veronica planned everything down to the smallest detail. A wedding gown of fine silk imported from Japan. Jewels from Tiffany and Bridesmaid dresses from Saks Fifth Avenue. The meal would be catered by the Plaza Hotel in New York with the best Texas beef, Maine Lobsters, Italian Veal, along with Champagne and Truffles from France.

The ceremony was held outdoors under a tent big enough to house a circus and the five hundred people who would attend. Everyone who was anyone was there, including President Eisenhower. It was the first time Jack met Ike, but it wouldn't be the last.

Cully was in his element. This was a crowd he could work. He was the only son of a two-fisted, hard-driving skunk of a wildcatter. He didn't remember much about his mother. She left when he was two, tired of his father's drinking, gambling, and womanizing. She had nowhere to go so she left him with his father.

It was a hard life early on, but he stayed in school long enough to read and write, and then took off for the oil fields. Roughneck, Cully would call them, the men who worked the oil rigs. The work was hard. The hours were long. The risks were uninsurable. He cut his teeth there, learning the oil business the hard way.

They were good lessons in a business where the good guys were the thieves and robbers. His father taught him how to skin a guy without him knowing he'd lost all his money. He could work a crowd and a bottle of bourbon as well as anyone.

Cully cornered Eisenhower, who wasn't an easy man to get alone, but Ike also wanted a word with Cully in private. Ike was a pragmatic man who was always alert to security issues that threatened the country. He was not a friend of military suppliers but he knew that they played a role and that they would support any military action that increased their bottom line. So it was that he sought out Cully to discuss such a situation.

"May I get a favor from you?" Ike whispered.

"What can I do for you, Mr. President," Cully asked cooperatively, but with the unspoken reservation of someone who didn't trust a politician even if he was standing in front of him.

"I am planning an excursion next year and might need the services of that young man, Duncan," Ike said. "Can you arrange it without asking where or with whom?"

"Sure," Cully said. He rarely had the opportunity to have a chit in with such a big player and offering Jack was the least he could do to earn the favors that would go along with helping the president.

"I'll contact you when it's time," Ike said as he moved off to the reception line.

Cully licked his lips as he sipped his bourbon. He wasn't the brightest bulb on the tree, but what he lacked in intelligence he made up for in cunning and guile. He would continue to cultivate Ike as a friend, as if Cully had any friends. To him, friends were people he could manipulate for his own gain. He thought Ike could provide some opportunities to be there first, wherever there was.

How big a score Cully had just made might not become apparent for years or ever, but Ike was in his debt. That was tall enough cotton.

The summer passed and Jack moved through his doctoral program with the ease of a man passionate about his work. Soon he would be finished and Veronica and he could move to Houston and set up a home there. Life had changed dramatically.

CHAPTER 8

Jack was sitting up and showing signs of real physical distress. The best I could do was to give him more painkillers and cold water. As they took effect, he started in again, smiling a bit as he talked about the early days in texas as if they had passed in an instant.

Veronica, though, as Jack later related, would have described the four years after Jack arrived at Baylor in an entirely different manner. She had fallen for him the first evening at the lake house, and waited patiently until he completed his doctorate. She supervised everything in his life to be sure that he didn't waste a moment that they could spend together. As dedicated to his studies as Jack was, so too was Veronica to the proposition that she would spend the rest of her life with him.

She had accompanied him on a few of his geological field trips that doubled as oil surveys and was amazed at his ability to sniff out an opportune place to drill. In return, she made sure that Cully was true to his word and kept Jack's research laboratory staffed with highly qualified scientists.

Veronica had a head for business. She spent a great deal of time helping Jack develop his knowledge of the financial side of the oil business. With her help, he had brought to fruition some highly profitable ventures for HOG. This earned him a seat on the company's planning counsel, a fact she relished.

She noted that their relationship with J.B. soured during this period. He had, on Jack's arrival at HOG, taken a greater interest in his own future in the family business. It had become obvious to J.B. that Jack was far more qualified to move up in HOG than he ever could. He knew in his gut that Jack would end up in charge. No one at HOG took J.B. seriously, a fact he knew was his own doing. Jack, on the other hand, was treated like the second coming. Veronica knew this would piss J.B. off. She watched as he moved further and further away from his friends and came to work less and less often. It didn't seem to bother anyone that he wasn't there, Except for him.

Worse than that, he still believed he would have married Veronica, if he ever stopped chasing skirts. It would never have occurred to him that his drinking, carousing, and showing up for work when it suited him might have made Veronica gravitate toward anyone but him.

When Jack and Veronica married, she knew that J.B. would try to take some form of revenge on Jack. She spoke to him of her concerns, but he thought wrongly, as he would learn later, that J.B. was too busy with his boozing and skirt chasing to have anything like that on his mind.

The birth of Jack Duncan, Jr., on April 24, 1957, was the capper to the last four wonderful years for Veronica. He was quick to grasp things, like his father, and had his mother's good looks. Jack and Veronica were elated.

Cully was to be Jack, Jr.'s godfather. The irony of God and Cully in the same sentence was not lost on most of the population of Houston, Texas.

CHAPTER 9

"Have you been to the lab lately?" Veronica asked.

"Just this week," Jack answered. "The experiments we're conducting on rearranging carbon atoms are on schedule, but the equipment development is slower than I'd like it to be. I'm going to hire two chemists when we get back from vacation."

Though Jack had continued researching synthetic oil at Veronica's insistence and hadn't lost his desire to complete the project, Cully kept him so busy that there was precious little time to spend in the lab or at home for that matter. Veronica never complained. he made an astounding amount of money for a twenty-seven-year-old in 1957.

Jack had spent the last six months bringing in a field in the Permian Basin near Odessa in West Texas. It was time for a rest and he planned to take Veronica and Jack, Jr., to Hawaii.

Cully enthusiastically encouraged them to go there, so much so that he sprang for the tickets and hotels. Jack was delighted. He had long ago accepted Cully as a friend and mentor, but Veronica was more skeptical. She trusted him only when she could see both of his hands. She knew he was up to something, she just wasn't sure what.

On the day Veronica and Jack were leaving, Cully stopped by as she knew he would and asked if he could borrow Jack for a few days while they were in Hawaii.

Veronica looked at Cully in a way that sent a shiver up his spine.

"And if I refuse," Veronica asked piquantly, "will you take back our tickets?

Where are you sending him?" she demanded.

Cully had arranged for Jack to visit a new area west of Hawaii that had enormous potential and was as yet uncharted, but he didn't answer her question.

"It's in this package," he answered as he handed her a manila envelope. "Don't open it until you're in Hawaii." Cully said, as he beat a hasty retreat. She had read him right and Jack would have to go.

—◦/◦/◦—

Hawaii was as beautiful as the brochures, and the hotel was first class. Jack had taken Veronica to paradise, but after two weeks the job called. The notes Cully left in the envelope instructed him to pack enough clothes for about four days and meet a man named Strange at the entrance to Pearl Harbor.

"Be careful," Veronica cautioned as she kissed him.

"I will," he promised her, wondering what he was getting into.

Jack thought the meeting place was unusual, but no more so than the name of the man he was to meet, which made him chuckle. It would be his last laugh for a while.

"Jack Duncan," the Petty Officer at the gate to the Naval Facility at Pearl Harbor said.

"Yes," answered Jack.

"That way, sir," the young sailor directed him toward a large, blacked-out building across the quad from the gate. "He's waiting for you, sir."

Jack crossed the quad and worked his way past some smaller workshops on the way to the blacked-out building. His contact was standing at the entrance.

"I'm Jack Duncan," he said as he offered his hand.

"They call me Strange," the man said ignoring any attempt at civility.

He was of average build, average looks, and average mannerisms. He'd blend in anywhere. Whether Strange was his first or last name mattered little, but it fit him like a glove. His eyes were steel blue and devoid of emotion. He was curt and discourteous.

"In here," Strange ordered as he turned back into the building.

Jack was getting that same uncomfortable feeling that he'd experienced the night that J.B. had waylaid him years ago.

"Where are we going?" Jack demanded, his irritation obvious. Strange didn't answer. An orderly took his bag and they were taken into a room with several lockers and a bench.

"Change into these," Strange instructed as he opened the locker in front of Jack. It held the uniform of a naval officer. He looked at Strange, who was changing into a tan lieutenant commander's uniform. He quickly followed his lead.

An orderly entered the room and gave them standard issue duffel bags packed with additional clothes.

"Please follow me and stay on the gang plank," he said as he escorted them through a maze of scaffolds and half-lit passages down to a staging area that seemed ten stories below the water level. As they emerged from the last passage, Jack froze. He had seen pictures of large vessels and had even toured a Triton Class WWII submarine, but he had never seen anything like the leviathan in front of him.

"What the hell is that?" His voice trailed off as he spoke. He didn't expect an answer and didn't get one. Whatever it was, it was in a dry dock so he could see from the conning tower to where the keel should have been. Jack looked at this five-story boat, which could best be described as a cigar with a dorsal fin, and thought, this is a submarine, but what kind of submarine he couldn't imagine.

"Let's go," Strange said. Noises that spoke of water entering a chamber woke Jack from a state of shock and moved him along with such speed that Strange had to hold him back even though he had no idea where he was going. He just didn't want to stay where he was.

"Follow me," Strange said as he maneuvered them onto the last gangplank. At the other end stood a man Jack recognized as the Captain by the eagles on his collar.

"Good morning, gentlemen. I'm Captain Nelson. Please follow me," he said.

Without further introductions, he escorted them onto the vessel and down a hatchway to a deck that held the galley and conference rooms. This was no WWII submarine. This was a floating hotel. The captain excused himself as the boat was getting underway. He was needed in the control room.

"I'll rejoin you shortly," he said.

Strange, who seemed familiar with the layout, navigated them to a small room. Two officers were already there, sitting at a table. They both stood up as Jack and Strange entered the room.

"Good morning. I'm Commander Jansen, the Executive Officer, and this is Lieutenant Commander Davis, the Science Officer," the first man said.

"I'm Jack Duncan," Jack offered, extending his hand.

"Can we get some coffee?" Strange interjected cutting off the pleasantries.

Coffee was poured as they waited for the captain to return.

Captain Nelson soon arrived, and the meeting, which Jack hoped would clarify the jumble of questions that were piling up in his head, began.

Nelson got the big one out of the way quickly.

"Mr. Duncan," he began, "this is a nuclear submarine. It is the prototype and has passed all its pre-commissioning tests. It can cruise at over twenty knots underwater and remain there for a month or more. It has its own air re-circulating system and the most advanced navigation system available. Mr. Davis," he said, turning to the science officer, "if you will."

"Thank you, captain," Davis said, as he began to explain the mission. "This vessel is fitted with a ground penetrating radar system that can map deep into the ocean floor. We are able to dive deeper than any other vessel and make a radar record of the area we survey."

Jack was beginning to get an inkling of what this was all about.

"Thank you, Mr. Davis," the XO said as he began to fill in the details. "We're going to the South China Sea. The President believes that America has finite reserves of domestic oil. Alaska has oil but logistics and god awful weather make it somewhat undesirable at present. The French have studied the region we're going to and have indicated that there might be oil there. The president is relying on your expertise, Mr. Duncan, to determine if there is."

Jansen went on. "For years the French had been asked by the Vietnamese to leave Indochina. After a final battle at Dien Bien Phu, they accepted the invitation. As you know, President Eisenhower and the UN negotiated a divided Vietnam with the Communists in the North and the Democratic Republic in the South. It's an unholy peace. Nevertheless," he summed up, "the president sees the region as a strategic locale, especially if there is oil there."

Jack began to sense that there was more to this than a clandestine look under the water at a potential oil field.

Captain Nelson took over. "This mission is top secret and is unknown to anyone other than the five men in this room and the president. You gentlemen are in uniform because it was necessary for the crew to believe that you are navy officers observing a series of routine tests."

A shiver went up Jack's spine. Something was not right. They were deliberately leaving things out of the briefing. He was an engineer and used to dealing in facts. The classified nature of this mission told him there was danger attached to it, and he was being led into it blind. He wanted out, but they were already underway.

After settling into a two-bunk "stateroom" just large enough for two men to stand in, Jack confronted Strange. He wanted answers, but Strange was not quick to deliver. Everything he had been taught at the Company school, yes, that Company, pointed to secrecy as the means to a longer life than the usual covert agent's tenure. Too much knowledge and too much talk made a man a prime target for the other side.

Jack's doctorate taught him to analyze situations and this one didn't pass the smell test.

"There's more to this than I'm being told," Jack challenged Strange.

He ignored him.

"Maybe you don't have the answer to my question," Jack baited him. "Maybe you aren't in on the game." He had pushed Strange's button. "I asked you a question and I want an answer," he persisted, "or this mission goes on without me." Strange pulled a pistol out of his locker and pressed it to Jack's throat.

"I'll blow your fucking head off if you don't quit asking questions you have no business knowing the answers to," Strange shouted.

"Shoot," Jack yelled back at him, looking him straight in the eye. "I'm done here and so is the mission if I don't find out what this is all about."

Jack's reaction was not in his playbook. He knew Strange had received his orders from the White House, and he was there to see that the mission was accomplished.

"We are on our way," Strange said grudgingly relenting, "to Vietnam."

Jack got that much, as it was explained in the briefing that they were going to the South China Sea.

"There's more," Jack challenged him. "What else are we committed to do?"

"We're also to scout an area in the central highlands for oil and gas," Strange said. "This will be risky and will require us to travel in uniforms without insignia with a squad of army raiders trained in infiltration tactics. We have to be invisible," Strange said. "If the mission were known, it might induce the Russians or the Chinese to enter the conflict before the South Vietnamese government could solidify their position politically and militarily. We'll move in quickly, survey the geology, make a determination, and move out in the same fashion."

"How much time do we have to accomplish this?" Jack asked, peeved that he was being dragged into what could be a war zone.

"You'll have two days," Strange replied.

"Why is this part of the world strategic?" Jack asked.

"We are at war with the communists." Strange began, "although we don't shoot at them and they don't shoot at us, we look for an advantage wherever we can find it, on the theory that what's good for us is bad for them. The president believes it is in the national interest to develop whatever resources there may be in Vietnam. It would not be in our best interest, yours and mine and the country's, for anyone to know what we're doing."

"Why are you here?" Jack asked in a less hostile manner. His conciliatory tone breaking the ice.

"What I am about to tell you is classified at the highest levels," he replied with deadly seriousness, "if you ever speak of it to anyone, I would have to kill you and them."

Jack nodded at Strange to indicate he understood the gravity of what was about to be told to him.

"I'm part of an unnamed super secret intelligence agency, My job is covert operations in the Middle East and Asian area. Vietnam is in my sphere of influence and it's on the front burner since it became apparent that the French were going to be thrown out. It was rumored for some time that there were oil and gas reserves in the central highlands and in the South China Sea. You and I have been tapped for the mission because your boss, Cully, is a powerful friend of some powerful people in Washington.

"The deal is," Strange went on, "that if you have reason to believe there is oil and gas in the region, Ike will commit to putting troops here in greater numbers, with an eye to helping the south take the entire country. For your trouble, Cully would get first crack at the oil."

Jack couldn't believe his ears. The government of the U.S. would go to war if he thought there was oil and gas in Vietnam? He tried to get his mind around this.

Seeing his distress, Strange interrupted his internal struggle. "Jack, if there is oil and gas in Vietnam and we don't get in and aid the south, the Russians and the Chinese will back the north. The whole of Vietnam could fall to the communists, and they would get the oil. Are you satisfied?" he asked finally.

"Yes," Jack replied. He was a patriotic American and couldn't let an enemy of the U.S. get hold of such valuable resources. At least that's what he told himself. It made his misgivings more palatable.

CHAPTER 10

The trip went quickly. The submarine was powerful and slid silently and effortlessly through the water while Strange and Jack busied themselves with preparations for the land mission. The sub was met off the coast of Vietnam by a Navy destroyer, and the two men deployed to the surface ship.

A helicopter from the destroyer was to take them to a staging area inland, where they would be deposited at an undisclosed location. The thought of the flight had Jack in a state of panic. He'd seen them in newsreels, but helicopters looked like nothing that could stay airborne.

An hour after their departure from the destroyer, they landed in a secure area where they were to meet up with the group of soldiers who carried on the Ranger tradition of skillful clandestine infiltration and assault.

The rangers arrived soon after Strange and Jack. They were led by an army major, a tall man in his thirties in excellent physical condition. He was a West Point graduate who spoke in short crisp bursts that invited no rebuttal. He and his men wore olive drab fatigues without insignia and dark green berets. His men looked like they would follow him into hell because they knew he would get them out the other side.

The second in command, a sergeant major, was an older man, the most grizzled but clearly the strongest of the cadre. He was a veteran of WWII and Korea, where he had distinguished himself as a capable recon squad leader. His mission had been, and still was, infiltration behind enemy lines to remove enemy observation posts and spotters. He was still alive, which meant he was very good at his job.

The sergeant major was an old acquaintance of Strange from the Korean War, Jack learned later, where he was assigned to accompany Strange on a mission deep into North Korea to eliminate a double agent who worked for the "company" but had been flipped by the Chinese communists. They had to kill him in North Korea or the communists would know their agent was made. They moved by night and hid by day. After several days of traveling this way, they made camp in a thicket about two miles from the Yalu River. From their vantage point, they had a clear view of the main path from the river crossing.

They waited there for the agent, who was returning that night from China. The sun went down and night set in, cold and cloudless. The moon rose to fullness about midnight and its light reflected on the river. A boat finally appeared. The men on it were talking loudly as the front line was far to the south and they didn't expect to be overheard. It was the perfect opportunity to move into their kill position. One kilometer later and it was over and it looked like the North Koreans did it. The sergeant was as good as his reputation. Even with a Korean sniper rifle.

The rest of the group was made up of highly trained and dedicated soldiers who had volunteered for this special force.

<hr>

They boarded the helicopter again to move to a landing zone within a few hours of their destination. Jack sat nervously with his back to the rear wall as far from either door as he could get. It amused the soldiers but none of them did more than grin. His fear of this creature he was flying in was written all over his face.

These were real men with real guns—AK-47s so there would be no evidence of an American presence—and they had given Jack one too, a loaded Russian pistol.

They were flown to a drop zone in the highlands at dusk. If the mission was to remain a secret they would have to move in relative darkness and landing where and when they did was the least chancy. The helo hit the ground with a thud. Jack fell forward and rolled over the door edge and onto the ground with a thud of his own. Strange was on him instantly, keeping him from standing up in the confusion of the moment and risking losing his head.

"This way and stay low," Strange signaled as he pulled Jack beyond the perimeter of the chopper's blades. They were quickly joined by the rest of the party. The chopper made a quick departure and they were soon alone in the dark of what appeared to be jungle.

"Thanks," Jack said.

"We're silent," Strange whispered.

That is with the exception, Jack thought, of the incessant hum of the jungle which made his skin crawl and made him promise himself that he would sleep standing up. He didn't keep that promise, though. He never slept.

Strange and Jack walked at the rear of the group, with one soldier behind them. They marched for about two hours when the absolute silence was broken by the sound of several men coming up the trail behind them. The leader of the group signaled that there would be no gunfire. Knives were drawn and the order given to take out the intruders.

"There," Strange said in a voice barely audible above the jungle hum and pointed. There was where Jack went as quietly as he was able. Strange came, too, and crouched next to him with knife drawn.

With little more than a grunt, three pajama-clad Vietnamese rebels, called Cong or VC for short, were dead, their throats neatly slit. Right now it was too dark and dangerous to wander far enough off the trail to dispose of the bodies safely. The major signaled to make camp. His men would get rid of them in the morning. They had to be well hidden or the mission could be compromised.

Jack was appalled. He had lost his father in the war in the Philippines, but never gave the possible manner of his death any thought. Now it hit him, and hard, and he had trouble maintaining his equilibrium. He sat down lest he fall. The danger inherent in this mission came home. The stakes, he thought, were very high.

Morning arrived with a cacophony of sound and three dead bodies. The major signaled for the soldiers to find a suitable place to stash them and to cover the bodies with leaves and debris. After they had disposed of the bodies, they marched north for another hour. The trek was uphill most of the way. Eventually they came to the edge of an open plain and made camp in the trees that surrounded it. No fires were permitted. What food they had were c-rations left over from the Korean conflict, little green vacuum cans of ham and beans and other inedible mixtures, along with cigarettes, waterproof matches, and a few sheets of toilet paper. It was hardly a luau.

Strange and Jack studied a map American intelligence smuggled out of Vietnam before the French left in a huff. It was made by a French geologist, who marked sites that he thought held promise for oil or gas. They used it now to plan how they would proceed.

The major called Jack to the front. He reiterated that they had two days and then they would move out. "The area is known to be a crossing point for VC moving about the countryside, and we may not be as lucky as we were last night. Get started."

Jack moved the equipment into position and began work at the sites marked on the map. The results were positive. Over the next forty-eight hours, he and Strange moved about the plain checking the terrain and the geology of the area. Jack's ventures into oil-producing areas in the hill country of Texas had been lessons well learned. The geology of the sites examined on this plain in Vietnam was similar to those he had examined at home.

He knew that there was a very strong likelihood that the ground held significant natural gas reserves. Oil was more of a maybe, but HOG had drilled in less promising fields and hit pay dirt. By the end of the second day, he was certain of his results and very ready to go home.

As Strange and Jack were collecting gear from the plain, Jack heard them. In the noises of the jungle it sounded like a cavalry charge.

Strange came quickly and moved them down the trail, past the spot where the Rangers assembled, while signaling the major of the impending visit of some unfriendlies. He indicated that he thought there was about seven of them, though how he could tell that Jack didn't know. Without an order given, the soldiers set up a deadly ambush and took positions on either side of the trail.

Jack took his pistol out of the holster and took off the safety. It was operational, but he wasn't so sure about himself. He had fired pistols at Cully's range on the ranch, but this was a situation he hadn't faced before.

Strange said quietly, "If any VC gets through, we will have to kill them or risk being discovered, cut off from our pickup, surrounded, and killed or captured."

Jack started to protest but a short jab in the ribs from Strange's gun butt brought him back to reality.

They waited. They could hear the VC talking animatedly and paying little attention to the trail ahead, unaware that an enemy was in the area. When the Rangers could see the last man in the group of VC, they opened up. Six of the seven VC were dead instantly. The seventh, wounded in the arm, moved forward on his hands and knees to a point beyond the soldiers' crossfire. He raised himself up and stared into the muzzle of Strange's pistol. He raised his rifle in reply and Strange pulled the trigger of his gun. Nothing happened. It was jammed. The VC had Strange in his sights.

The recoil of the gun nearly knocked Jack over. Regaining himself, he fired again and again, emptying the clip into the dead VC.

Strange looked at him with a surprised smile.

"Let's go," the major barked. "Get the VC off the trail, grab the equipment, and get the hell out of here." The gunfire would, no doubt, bring more VC. They had to move immediately if they were to get out of there at all.

The trip back to the pickup site was made at a quickstep. Jack struggled to keep ahead of the rear guard, and after almost two hours of forced double time they reached their destination. The major had radioed to his base while they were on the run and in a few minutes a helicopter, which had been on standby, came in. It was just in time, as they could hear a large group of VC moving at considerable speed behind them.

"Get in," the major shouted to Strange and Jack as the chopper landed. They ran and quickly boarded. As the helo climbed away, they heard gunfire below. The side gunner opened up with a machine gun mounted to the chopper and sent the VC scurrying for cover. It was enough for them to make good their escape.

After what seemed an eternity to Jack, the chopper later set down in the clearing where it had first picked them up. They covered it up with camouflage netting making it less visible from the surrounding jungle.

"Over here," the sergeant called from the hooch just inside the jungle. Strange and Jack entered the hut, where they were given food and drink. They were told they would have to wait until sunset to make the helicopter flight out because of heavy enemy activity in the area. Jack sat on the floor and closed his eyes. He wasn't tired. He just needed to sort things out.

"That was a brave thing you did out there, Duncan. You all right?" the sergeant asked.

"I'm okay," Jack offered unconvincingly.

He had gone on a secret mission for the president with a man who was obviously a secret agent, found oil and gas in a strange part of the world called Vietnam, and killed a man, shooting him until his gun was empty. His mind flashed to third grade catechism: Thou shalt not kill. He pushed the words out of his mind. Thinking about right and wrong was too painful, but his mind had other ideas. He saw an image of death and destruction and knew that any decision to come to this place would be the cause of much of it. Again he pushed the image out of his mind. There were national interests at stake, and besides, the U.S. military could handle some backwater rebels without breaking a sweat. They were not the French.

CHAPTER 11

J ack and Strange retraced their steps back to the sub and moved to the area of the South China Sea that they were to survey. It took just a few hours on the outward journey from Hawaii to master the technology of the new ground penetrating radar. The actual tests were completed in a few days.

Jack learned a little more about Strange on the way back to Hawaii. As they were sitting in the galley of the submarine nursing a cup of the worst coffee the military could provide. They had come through this adventure unscathed and. Strange's face creased into what had to be a smile.

"How did you get into this?" Jack asked him, genuinely curious.

Strange explained that he joined OSS during the big war and parachuted into France to help organize the French resistance in an effort to slow down German reinforcements by destroying rail lines and booby trapping roads to the coast during the Normandy invasion. He killed his first man in France, a Nazi sympathizer who had overheard a meeting between him and his French counterpart. The man followed Strange and hid in a wooded area. If he made it back to the Germans, it would have made the invasion even more difficult than it would come to be.

Sensing that they were not alone, Strange broke off the meeting in a hurry. He sent the Frenchman back to the village hoping that the intruder would follow. He did. Strange set off toward the shore, but doubled back and took the Nazi sympathizer by surprise. It was over in a moment, but the disturbance had aroused a Nazi soldier returning from an evening with a local woman. The soldier had him at gunpoint, but Strange was trained in hand-to-hand combat and easily overcame the man, killed him, and got away.

He spent the remainder of the war in France and Italy neutralizing Nazi spies and sympathizers. After the war, he stayed in the OSS. The cold war made his experience as a covert operative and assassin very valuable. He was billeted in Europe and moved with stealth in and out of the Middle East where oil in that region had the attention of the superpowers. In 1949, he was sent to Iran. The young shah, who was more of a despot than a leader, was not keeping the Russian (in 1949 the Chinese communists were still engaged with Chiang Kai Shek for control) communists in his country under control. They roamed the country setting up political networks in an attempt to gain control over the oil. This was problematic to President Truman, who knew that keeping the communists away from Middle East oil was critical. Truman's counterparts in Britain had told him so, repeatedly.

He was given a dangerous mission worthy of a chess grandmaster; he was to make an attempt on the life of the Shah, fail, and make it look like the communists had done it. The logistics were the sticky point. Pinning it on the communists would be simple; they were ubiquitous. They tried to be surreptitious, but only managed to be obvious. Wherever the Shah went several communist party members took cover in vantage points along the route. It must have had something to do with their national tendency to spy on everyone. But it played into Strange's hands.

On the day of the attack the shah was on parade. Strange placed two of his operatives in the crowd below and across from his own position, which was just above the Russians. When the Shah passed, Strange fired two shots, dropped the rifle and spent shells onto the Russian position, and made his way down to the parade route. His operatives let out cries and pointed at the

Russians. It took only moments for the Shah's secret police to surround the Russians and leave them with no way out and in a packet of trouble. Dour though he was, Strange always laughed at the memory of the chaos that ensued.

"After my experiences in the Middle East," Strange said, "I spent the next few years moving in and out of Korea, Japan, China, and Southeast Asia. I was used by my handlers for a variety of operations, mostly involving taking out an enemy spy or an inconvenient opponent. I had been to Vietnam many times while the French controlled the colony. I had built up a cadre of operatives in advance of the imminent fall of the French. I knew the resources that had kept the French in the region: rubber, copra, rice. I had an idea that there might be more, but it was never confirmed until this mission. I've been in many tight spots," Strange told Jack, "but I never stared down the barrel of a gun at close range with a weapon in hand that didn't work. I'm not a man of sentiment, but I have to thank you for saving my life. I'm indebted to you."

Jack listened to the story with awe. He knew Strange was the real thing, but his story was unlike anything Jack had experienced. He was a man who killed for a living and lived for the adventure. It was surreal. To Jack killing enemies and narrow escapes were the stuff of Saturday matinees, and best left that way.

In a few days they were back in Hawaii. Strange and Jack parted company where they had met. As he said goodbye, Strange handed Jack a card with a Washington, D.C., number on it. "If you ever need an assist," he instructed him, "ask for Wolf." He turned away and drifted away into the streets of Honolulu.

—⁘—

Veronica had been beside herself with worry. She just knew that Cully had sent Jack into some vermin-infested jungle and that he would come back with malaria or some other dreaded disease. She was relieved to see him in one piece and insisted that he take a few days to rest up before they went back to Houston.

On the beach the next day, she asked about the mission.

"I'm sworn to secrecy," Jack explained. "I can tell you that I got to ride in a submarine and on a helicopter and survey some unique territory with an interesting crew."

Jack told her a little about it, but left out most of the details, and Strange. It was a plain vanilla story about a field trip to someplace in Southeast Asia that Veronica didn't buy for a minute.

"Okay, Jack Duncan," Veronica chided. "You will tell me this story."

He resolved to, but not on a public beach. Strange had warned him that talking about the mission could be dangerous, and talking about it in Hawaii, Strange had pointed out, within shouting distance of Pearl Harbor, was tantamount to putting up a Barbasol sign on a highway. Jack promised Veronica he would fill her in when they got home.

CHAPTER 12

C ully was waiting at the airport chomping at the bit for a rundown on the trip. He arranged for Veronica to be driven home in the limo, while he drove Jack to the office. He was very agitated; he had been waiting for him to return home for several days and the pressure to know what was going on was getting to him.

"Give out with it," Cully said as he poured them each a glass of bourbon back in the office. That settled him down a bit.

"What I can tell you," Jack began, "is that there is an abundance of oil and gas in Vietnam and off the coast in the South China Sea. How we are going to get to it is another matter. It will be expensive, because of the distances to be traveled, and the political uncertainties of the region will make it even more difficult and dangerous to develop."

"How long before the region is settled and we can get the oil?" Cully queried Jack.

"That's a question you'll have to ask Ike"

"Speaking of Ike" Cully laughed as he handed Jack an envelope. "This came for you today. It was left for you by an unidentified man who said that you were to open it as soon as you got here and call the number inside immediately. Someone of importance is waiting for you."

Jack opened the envelope and saw that the note was written on White House stationery. It read:

Dear Jack,

I am pleased that you have returned home safely. I know that this is short notice, but I am anxious to meet with you, my schedule allows for a brief meeting tomorrow. Please join me for lunch. I will have a plane waiting for you at Hobby Airport. Please call this number: 202-555-2222.

Sincerely,
Ike

"Holy smoke," Cully said when Jack read it to him.

He called the number as instructed and was put through to the president's secretary. "This is Jack Duncan," he said.

The voice at the other end instructed him to be at the Houston airport that afternoon. There was no right of refusal.

Jack hung up the phone and called Veronica.

"Pack a suitcase for me," he said excitedly, "and bring it to the office. I'm going to the White House."

"Today?" she asked.

"Yes," he exclaimed. "I'm having lunch with the president tomorrow."

After Veronica arrived, Cully offered to have Jack driven to the airport, but Veronica wouldn't hear of it.

"I'm going with you," she told him in a tone that brooked no discussion. "I'm still looking for the story of your trip and we'll be alone on the plane so you can tell me there. Besides," she continued, "I'll not have you wandering around D.C. by yourself."

They drove in silence as Jack wondered how he would explain the circumstances of the mission, the killing, and the inevitable war that would ensue as a result of his soon to be delivered report to the president. The Vietnamese had thrown off the yoke of the French. The Communists from the North, under the leadership of Ho Chi Minh, were determined to unify the country, by infiltrating and overthrowing the democratic regime in the South. An American presence there would add fuel to an already burning fire and very likely bring the Communist Chinese and perhaps the Russians into the fray. He thought about lying about what was found in that Asian backwater, but he understood the strategic importance of keeping the communists out of that region.

On a very large Boeing 707 not unlike Air Force One, Jack and Veronica sat in comfortable swivel chairs of dark leather. The flight attendant poured them each a bourbon and soda, which he swallowed in one gulp. He was tired and stressed and did not want to have to make any decisions, especially ones that could cause people to die. He had killed one man already. That was enough.

Jack kept his word and spent the next hour reliving the nightmarish excitement of the days in the bush to Veronica. He made no mention of Strange, though. He had made a promise to not expose him.

Veronica was horrified. "Jack," she made him swear to it, "don't ever put yourself at such risk again. I would be lost without you. I love you," Veronica's voice faded as he fell asleep.

Jack slept for the rest of the flight to Washington, and awoke as the plane began its decent into National Airport.

The rest had recharged his batteries and he was looking forward to a shower, and then a good meal in one of the Capitol's better restaurants. He was not disappointed.

After dinner, they strolled lazily back to the hotel. Veronica was in an amorous mood and Jack was glad to be alive and even happier to be with the woman he adored.

CHAPTER 13

The White House was always busy with tourists who stood for hours to see the symbol of the presidency of the United States of America. Jack had never been to Washington, D.C., before, and was awed by the monuments and by this building that housed the executive functions of the government. Everything was starched and ceremonial, from the Marine who stood guard at the door to the guides who conducted tour groups it had a very formal atmosphere.

"Mr. Duncan," a member of the president's staff called to Jack, "this way." She ushered him into a private room where a table was set with the finest linens, glassware, and china, all with the presidential seal.

"Please sit here," she said and showed him to a couch where he was to wait for the president. "When the president arrives, you are to stand and wait for him to initiate introduction. Remain standing until he instructs you to sit down."

The staffer then gave Jack a short briefing on the proper way to greet and address President Eisenhower. He smiled at the thought of J. B. being subjected this protocol and the image made him laugh out loud.

In a few minutes the door opened and the president walked in, followed by the Secret Service agent assigned to guard him. Ike looked tired. The cold war was raging and the reports that the Russians had launched a space satellite were wearing on him. The nuclear threat was becoming more than just words as the

Russians demonstrated that their German scientists could design rockets that could pinpoint a target across the world. It was a difficult time to be a leader.

"The last time I saw you," the president greeted Jack, "you were getting tied up to that beautiful woman. How is Veronica?"

"She's fine, sir," he replied nervously.

"Come with me." Ike walked over to the lavish table that had been set for them. "You must tell me all about her. I've heard that she is a graduate of Shipley School in Bryn Mawr and the Sorbonne."

Jack was mystified by the knowledge Ike had of his family. That is, until he remembered that his father-in-law was the governor of Texas and, like all politicians, lived in a glass house that offered only a modest amount of privacy.

"Yes, sir," he responded, "Veronica has a classical education."

"Her presence dresses up a room," Ike added wistfully. "I remember her as her father's companion at many social functions after the death of her mother. You're a lucky man, Jack."

"Thank you, Mr. President."

Ike continued, "The Secretary has briefed me on the military aspects of the mission. I'm told that you conducted yourself in a very heroic way."

"Actually," Jack said with sincere humility, "I was scared to death."

Ike looked at him with admiration. He knew what it was to be afraid, to overcome that fear, and to do what was necessary without hesitation. He smiled. "I fully understand," he said.

Though flushed with embarrassment, Jack smiled back at this man who was the principal reasons the allies were able to maintain their cohesion during WWII. His demeanor and leadership during the D-Day invasion took nerves of steel. Jack believed that he would not lead the country into something that was not in the national interest.

"Let's eat first then you can tell me about your findings," Ike said.

Lunch was an array of summer salads and cold cuts served boardinghouse style. After a desert of cheesecake, especially flown in from Lindy's in New York, Ike was ready to get down to business.

"There is evidence that the highlands have significant gas and oil reserves," Jack began, giving Ike clinical descriptions of rock formations and soil type that compared to what he had seen in producing fields. "As for the area off the coast," he went on, "there are potentially serious oil reserves there."

"You have some second thoughts?" Ike asked. Something in Jack's demeanor touched that old soldier's instinct that another shoe was out there and could drop; he wanted no surprises. The general didn't run a successful campaign in Europe without being about to root out nagging reservations in his field generals, even unspoken ones. Ike told him to speak his mind, so Jack addressed his reservations bluntly.

"Everything I saw in Vietnam tells me there will be terrible loss of life if we entertain taking sides in this civil war. The soldiers on the ground there said the South is corrupt and the North is bent on unifying the country. I'm not a military man, but I am a student of history and can see the strong parallel between this conflict and our Revolution. We can send thousands of soldiers just as the British did and, just like we did to the British, they'll pick us off from behind trees, around rocks, and out of caves. The jungle I spent several days in is their home. They know it and can use that to their advantage, just as we did against the British. They can hit and run to places we can't maneuver through. In short, sir, we would be fighting ghosts who never have to quit, and could melt back into the trees and come out fighting at any time and place they chose. We are not the French when it comes to engaging an enemy, but the French had decades there and knew their strengths and weaknesses, and were still sent packing by people who don't know the meaning of the word quit."

"I would have given much in the middle of the war," Ike remarked, "to have people around me with your ability to assess a situation. I have been told by my advisors that there are inherent risks in any involvement in that area."

The president rose and took Jack's arm. They walked outside to a quiet spot in the Rose Garden. "Jack," Ike said pointedly, "this is not something for you to carry on your shoulders. I'm only asking you for a scientific opinion. Whatever happens, you should know that your report is only one aspect of my decision." Ike didn't want him to feel the responsibility he was clearly feeling. "There are other considerations. We are monitoring the association of the North Vietnamese with the Russians and Chinese."

But Ike knew there was no escaping the inevitable and thus asked the question that would seal the fate of many young American soldiers.

"I need to know if the reserves of oil and gas may be significant enough to warrant supporting the South Vietnamese against the North."

This was what Jack had feared. Even though Ike gave him a pass, he was about to give an answer that could very well put us in a shooting war. He sensed that many hundreds of men, perhaps thousands, might be killed. But the national interest and those of his family and employees overtook the negative images and he answered the president with a resounding yes. He had convinced himself that it was for the greater good.

"I believe that reserves in the region approach the volume of reserves in the U.S."

"That gives credence to the reports we received from our French contacts as they were leaving Vietnam" Ike said. "They too believed that there were vast reserves in that area. It was a factor in keeping them there so long."

As they left the garden, Ike said, "Please take this. It's the least a grateful president can give for your service." He handed Jack a small box and instructed him not open it until he was on the plane. He put it in his jacket pocket and said goodbye. They exchanged a warm handshake and in an instant Ike disappeared.

"This way, Mr. Duncan," a voice broke into his thoughts. It was the young lady who had brought him into the room earlier. "A car is waiting to take you back to your hotel."

"Thank you," Jack said as he was escorted out of the White House.

———◦◦◦———

"What was he like?" Veronica asked. "He seems like such a nice man."

"He was very warm," Jack answered. "He wanted to know about you."

"Really," Veronica said, trying not to show her pleasure at being mentioned in a private meeting with Ike.

"He gave this to me," he said pointing to the box he placed on the table in the hotel room.

"Open it," Veronica said excitedly.

"He asked me to wait until we were on the plane."

The car that took Jack from the White House was waiting to take them to the airport. The mystery of the box made the trip from the hotel to the plane all the more exciting.

When they were finally airborne, Jack opened the box and found a Silver Star Medal.

There was a note along with the medal. He read it aloud.

> Jack, I have had the honor of commanding many men in battle. Your heroism under fire as reported to me by the leader of your group was exemplary. Please accept this Silver Star as a token of your President's appreciation of your actions. For reasons of national security, please keep this between us until the situation in Southeast Asia has stabilized and is under American control.
>
> Sincerely, Ike

I listened to this part of Jack's story with a lump in my throat and some very terrible memories trying to come to the surface. He looked at me in a way that told me he knew that I was one of those about whom he worried.

He told me, as we sat in the ER, that during the years between his foray into the highlands of Vietnam and the broader presence of American "advisors" in the country significant changes occurred in his attitude. He had been a young man of great integrity, but he was also, by education, a pragmatist. Over time, he evolved from a man who first weighed the morality of an issue to a man who put his family, and HOG, first, regardless of the effect it had on it had on anyone outside the family.

Oil reserves in the U.S. would someday be a memory and we would still need oil for our security. The oil under the South China Sea could keep the spigot open indefinitely and give HOG the opportunity to be the principal player in the oil game.

CHAPTER 14

The pain in Jack's leg flared up again and I gave him more painkillers from the stash I had squirreled away. He was getting into the meat of the story and it was helping him forget events of the morning and mitigate the pain in his leg and his heart. After a few minutes he was able to continue.

Jack chuckled a bit as he described Richard Nixon and the Presidential election of 1960.

"I asked him what was so funny?

"I remember it" he laughed, "as closely contested between Nixon, Ike's Vice-president, and Senator Jack Kennedy, a WWII hero. But the Texas oil apparatus was well represented on both tickets. Nixon was a business friendly scoundrel who could dance as well as the next guy for an oilman's dollar, and while Kennedy was the more progressive candidate, but he brought a Texas hound dog of a politician named Johnson along with him.

Any Texan," Jack noted, "knew Lyndon Johnson as a legendary politician who was accused of everything from dumping ballot boxes of unfriendly districts into the Brazos River to arranging for the untimely demise of a rival. Johnson was oil and he was oil's man."

There was a fondness for Kennedy in Jack's voice. He won the election by the narrowest of margins, with many a republican moaning about the number of votes that came out of an unlikely precinct that was home to many of Chicago's past, translated as dead, inhabitants. But, Jack saw that Kennedy was a good president whose soaring rhetoric elevated the mood and the outlook of the country. He had grand ideas as well. He was determined to send a man to the moon and on a more planetary level, pass major civil rights legislation.

Six years passed since Jack's trip to Vietnam and they had been good ones for Houston Oil and Gas. Jack was pleased with the progress of the company; he continued to develop new fields and Cully managed refinery capacity and sales. There was plenty of oil to go around and prices made it affordable for the consumer, while the oil depletion allowance made it profitable for HOG. They bought their way into the refinery business and had plans to continue to integrate the business vertically.

Jack's visage darkened as he talked about 1963. The war in Vietnam was not yet in the collective minds of the people. Those who knew were political junkies or friends of soldiers who had been there as advisors. President Kennedy was having a difficult time dealing with the corruption of the South Vietnamese government. The leadership was waist deep in the drug trade and less interested in the conduct of the war than in lining their pockets.

Jack's tone made clear his interest in Vietnam was personal. He'd been there, he'd killed there. He was an oilman, and he knew there was oil there. His early fears of death and destruction in Vietnam were replaced by his fears that HOG wouldn't be able to get to the oil. He was not thrilled when rumors spread that Kennedy was considering pulling out and letting South Vietnam fend for itself. There had to be something that could change the president's mind.

"Something changed" I posited.

As Jack sat back against the wall of the small room we in habited, his look and tone confirmed that something important had happened at this point in his story.

"I brought the news of the potential pullout of Vietnam to Veronica," he began almost solemnly, "she was a good listener and my most trusted counselor, and equally concerned about the potential loss of the reserves in that region. But," he continued, "she was even more distressed about another development that was buzzing around the oil patch.

Veronica, as the former governor's daughter, had developed a pipeline to Washington. There was little that affected the oil patch that she didn't know of almost before it happened. She had been leaked some information from an insider in the Kennedy Administration that the President was considering dropping or reducing the oil depletion allowance to cover the cost of his two biggest programs; the New Frontier and putting a man on the moon. She spoke with her father, who had a conversation with the vice president, and confirmed it with a few well-placed expletives."

"Veronica," Jack related, "felt it would destroy everything we'd built and HOG might have to close. Her anger was apparent. She was dead set against it happening."

I asked Jack about the oil depletion allowance since I had no idea what it was. He said the allowance was simple and gave the short course. He said that if a man invested $100,000 into an oil field that field tested out to have $10,000,000 dollars of oil in the ground, and assuming it produced $1,000,000 per year, he could deduct from his taxes 27.5% or $275,000 each year. That meant over the ten years he could deduct $2,750,000 for a $100,000 investment.

"You said she was dead set against letting the depletion allowance go away," I said, "what did she plan on doing to stop it?"

"It was brilliantly simple," Jack began with a hint of a smile, "She put her mind to it and came up with a solution that was larcenous, risky, and immensely doable. She developed a plan that would not only save HOG, but also raise its status and net worth.

If the oil depletion allowance evaporates, she told me, then abundant oil will evaporate, too."

"How would this plan accomplish that?" I asked Jack.

"Fields would stop producing," he explained. "Refineries would break down for months at a time. There would be shortages.

This would bolster the price of oil and mitigate the loss of the depletion allowance, but it would by necessity have to involve all the major oil companies following our lead."

"How would you get them to cooperate?" I asked.

"By playing to their greed," Jack said smiling. "That was the easy part. Accomplishing it without getting put in jail would be a bit trickier.

Manipulating production was definitely illegal," he continued, "as was colluding with other oil companies to set prices.

It also went against my Catholic nature," Jack confessed, "but my family would suffer financially and the possibility existed that without the depletion allowance HOG would fold. Hog relied on the extra income the allowance provided to keep up its aggressive exploration of new fields."

"Then you were in bed with Veronica on this? I asked, laughing at my own joke.

Jack looked at me with a 'that's enough of that' look but went on with his story.

As he arrived at the office Cully was just getting off the phone with Veronica, who had explained as much of it as she dared over an open line. But told Cully to go over the details with Jack.

Jack described the scene as he sat down at Cully's conference table and told him to get a bottle of his best Bourbon and lock the door to his office.

"There's a lot I don't have answers for yet," Jack told Cully, "but the basics are simple. We exaggerate normal occurrences. We slow everything down and create artificial shortages."

"You need to call the vice president and confirm what my Father-in-Law told Veronica. We need to know how likely it is that this will happen and if there is any way to head this off."

Cully picked up the phone and got an operator to connect him with Johnson's office.

The VP gave him the bad news. Not only was the oil depletion allowance going away but the president was going to remove his support from Vietnam, too! Kennedy's New Frontier and trip to the moon would cost a good deal more than he anticipated. He needed to raise the funds by canceling corporate tax breaks, including the depletion allowance. Johnson told Cully that this was causing great distress in high places. Cully wanted to know if there was anything that could be done to dissuade the president. The VP said that there was, but he couldn't discuss it on an open line. He would sit with Cully and a few of the 'boys' and give them the down and dirty. Cully felt the vice-president's tone was strained.

Cully hung up and confirmed the worst. Kennedy is going ahead with this bull, and he intends to walk away from all that oil in Southeast Asia.

"Can you get me a list of all the scheduled repairs in all our processing plants? Jack asked Cully. "Then call your friends at each of the other major producers and get the same information. Try not to give up too much until I've talked to the heads of the other companies."

Jack took it upon himself to set up appointments with each of them individually. He knew that what they were proposing was very close to price fixing, but the risk of losing the business made the gamble worth it. He also knew that Johnson would try to look after his friends in the oil patch if he had any hope of running for president someday. He was as loyal to his Texas friends as a politician could be.

Jack noted that successful Texas oilmen are all cut from the same cloth. Like Cully, they'd skin you alive if there was a dollar to gain. So his meetings with the other oil company executives were as simple as a wink and a handshake. They were not overjoyed at having to face angry stockholders and explain that some Yankee had stolen away their dividends and would do most anything to avoid that issue. One by one Jack convinced them that using HOG to set the market price would leave them in the clear with their Board of Directors and would keep them away from any charges of collusion. Each agreed that if and when Jack signaled, they would, over a two to six month period, back down production. They would arrange to have their refineries close for repairs at peak demand periods, and would see to it that these repairs took much longer than anticipated. Taken together, this would squeeze the market dry. There was no question of this plan getting out, any hint of it would land them all in very hot water.

Jack also noted that Veronica introduced another element. A few years earlier, the offshore oil-producing states had banded together to form the Organization of Oil Producing and Exporting Countries; OPEC. This cartel had yet to have its influence felt, but Veronica had an idea that given the right impetus it would fall in line with HOG and the major players.

I could hear the pride in Jack's voice as he described how Veronica had formulated her plan based on her observations of the direction the nation was taking. Her assessment that post-war population increases, the G.I. Bill educating the soldiers who had come home from the war, the robust economy, increased suburbanization of cities, the new interstate highway system, and cars—would need fuel to keep it going. Controlling the flow of fuel would mean controlling the U.S. economy. Squeezing the populace at the pump would cause everything else in the economy to ratchet up, too. If there was resistance, they'd squeeze harder. Veronica knew they could buy the politicians to stay out of the way or destroy those who interfered. In this, Jack knew she was ruthless. They were prepared to move forward with the plan if the administration went forward with theirs.

Jack sensed from the beginning that the plan would make OPEC, the oil companies, and HOG billions of dollars over the next thirty or forty years. And it was so simple. Just close the oil spigot here at home and open it for a time in the Middle East and at the right moment shut all the spigots simultaneously. The price of oil would go sky high.

Jack acknowledged that he was mired in this intrigue and tried not to think about the morality of what he was doing, and when these thoughts arose, he put them out of mind.

CHAPTER 15

Jack joked that Texas was a place unlike any other in the world and on the whole didn't care much for anyone who spoke without a Texas twang or drawl, including the President. Kennedy was in Dallas to raise campaign funds for the upcoming presidential election. He and Johnson had barely carried Texas and there were fences to mend.

Jack was in Dallas on business that morning and had by chance ended up at a spot along the parade route not far from a grassy knoll, where the president's motorcade was to pass. As he waited, he saw Strange standing behind a bench at the back end of the knoll and wearing a long trench coat on a warm fall day. He wondered what Strange was doing in Dallas?

As for Strange being there, he got the answer in a puff of smoke from the barrel of a rifle. For a brief instant, he thought he was back in Vietnam. He was standing close enough to hear the impact of the bullets that killed the president on the 22nd of November. It was all over in a few seconds—the shots, the screaming, the motorcade rushing away. In the confusion, he glanced back at the grassy knoll and watched as Strange disappeared down a storm drain. Jack knew. The immediate arrest and subsequent murder of Lee Harvey Oswald, the accused assailant, covered up a plot that Jack could only conclude was the responsibility of the CIA and other powerful interests. Cully had said that Johnson thought it would take drastic measures to change the president's mind. None of them had ever dreamed that this was what he meant.

Jack felt the repercussions would be immediate and he was right on. President Johnson set everyone's mind at ease about the oil depletion allowance. It would not be up for discussion in his administration. Jack had been told by Veronica that Johnson had read the minutes of his lunch with Ike, and knowing that there was significant oil in Southeast Asia and believing that American firepower and sheer force of will would clear out the rebels and let American Oil interests have it, he was determined to escalate. Johnson also had friends in the armaments business who had poured millions into new weapons systems. They needed coverage, too. Johnson felt the war in Vietnam would serve as a live-fire testing ground for those systems. Jack wasn't surprised at the dramatic mobilization of American forces in 1964 and 1965. The numbers of soldiers under arms was raised to levels not seen since WWII. The draft mechanism was at all systems go. The demand for oil by the military kept the oil companies, HOG included, working around the clock. It was a good time to be in the oil business.

CHAPTER 16

The noise in the ER grew exponentially as the meat wagons, as the Docs called them, came in with a yet another load of the maimed and mangled. This group was the most seriously wounded as they were from an area on the Westside just past Penn Station.

As we sat there in stunned silence, I began to believe that this was indeed a Greek Tragedy where the hero has a serious flaw and upon exposing it, takes down all around him and in most plays, himself. Paris had his Helen of Troy, Achilles had his heel, and Odysseus managed to piss off Poseidon. Jack had surely pissed off the gods for this one.

In a short while, the ER Docs were still shipping out those they couldn't help, things quieted down. Jack started to tell his story but I interrupted him. I thought I had found his tragic flaw.

"If Johnson was now President and the loss of the oil depletion allowance was not in the immediate future, why did you go ahead with your larcenous plan?"

"Why not?", he answered gruffly. "There were millions, perhaps billions of dollars to be made while hedging against the next time some politician gets a silly notion."

"Okay," I said weakly backing away from this line of questioning.

He began again, without interruption, to tell his story.

While Jack was lining up the domestic oil companies as co-conspirators, Veronica had already used her position as the governor's daughter to entice OPEC representatives into the web of conspiracy. OPEC countries were at best despotic and constantly trying to bolster their military and police apparatus to prevent their people from getting out from under their often draconian rule. Veronica found the OPEC ministers were easy to convince; they were needier and greedier than the Texas oilmen.

Jack's arrangement with the U.S. oil suppliers would already slow down domestic oil production. With Veronica having OPEC close the spigot, the resulting shortages would create an economic catastrophe. When the prices had ratcheted up, she would signal them to flood the market at whatever the market would bear. The domestic oil producers would piggyback refinery costs on imported prices. Consumers, having been bitten once, would pay whatever was asked, without question, to avoid another shortage.

Jack convinced Cully that HOG needed to be a player in the Middle East, to hedge a bet that U.S. reserves were limited. Veronica's contacts inside the OPEC structure, which was still a loose confederacy, arranged a tour of the oilfields of the Saudi Kingdom, Iran, and Iraq for Cully and Jack. The flight was long and they had to change planes several times. They laid over in Rome and left the next morning for Cairo and then on the Riyadh, Saudi Arabia. Neither of the last legs of the journey served alcohol. Cully was sick from the heat and lack of Bourbon.

Jack was on a fishing expedition. HOG needed assurances that OPEC had the goods. Agreeing to a plot to raise the cost of oil was one thing; having enough oil to make the necessary impact was another. Veronica's vision for OPEC was based on estimates of bigger oil reserves than anywhere in the world. He would see for himself.

There was enough oil in the Middle East, British reports kept saying. If this were true, Hog could effectively carry out the plan and put control of the price of oil beyond the reach of the U.S. government.

Cully was not a numbers man. He saw the oil business as very simple. I pump a barrel of oil and sell it for the going price and let the depletion allowance take care of the rest. It was a good thing for HOG, before veronica and Jack showed up, that Cully's accountants knew that if they ever cheated him, they would become the next meal for some wild critter in the farthest part of west Texas.

Jack took some time during the trip to lay out how the plan and the money would flow. Cully, as Jack pointed out, was not a numbers man, but given time could get the basics.

Jack broke it down as simply as he could telling Cully to think of it in terms of a finished barrel of oil. Cully knew the cost of a barrel, the time it took to refine, and what came out of it. What he didn't pay much attention to was the numbers. He had his accountants. Jack explained that a barrel of HOG's crude oil was multiplied 700% at the refinery. With Texas sweet currently bringing $6.00 at the wellhead, HOG would make a gross profit of $42 on a refined barrel of oil. If the price of a barrel was raised by someone outside the U.S., and thus outside U.S. government regulation, HOG's gross profit would still be seven times whatever price was paid for that barrel. If the price went to $30, the gross profit on a refined barrel of oil would be $210. The price-setting agreement between HOG and the majors, made when the oil depletion allowance was on the chopping block, was still in place and the majors would follow HOG and rake in huge profits. Cully wished he had a bottle of Bourbon to toast this grand scheme.

Jack and Cully inspected the Saudi fields, saw the Shah's operation, and got a look at the fields near Basra in Iraq. His sixth sense was in overdrive and he tingled with excitement. There was oil everywhere.

Larger amounts of Middle East crude, which was priced below domestic crude, would have to be shipped to the US without much fanfare. This could be accomplished by keeping prices low at first. Then, in conjunction with the slowdown in tapping domestic crude, as agreed by the domestic oil companies and which included the capping of many new wells and delaying drilling in proven fields, HOG and the other players would make it appear too expensive and not economically feasible to continue investing in domestic oil. OPEC would slow the flow and raise the price. The effect would be sudden and dramatic. In a very few weeks the cost of gasoline and home heating oil would skyrocket and oil company profits would rise in direct proportion.

Cully was surprised and delighted. While his own quantum of larceny was greater than most, this was as clever a license to steal as he had heard in many years. He had always known about Veronica, but he hadn't been sure of Jack until then. Cully never had to ask how they would get to the right people in Saudi Arabia, Iraq, and Iran. Veronica was involved and Cully knew that she could talk a drunk sober.

"J. B. can't know about this," Jack warned.

Cully nodded his assent.

They were now a conspiracy.

———◦/◦/◦———

Jack watched and waited for the right time to present itself. The war in Vietnam was now a raging battle that, as had been predicted, was being borne by the American military. And it seemed that the longer the war went on, the more people chose sides. The young men and women who would bear the brunt of the expanding presence in Vietnam began to oppose the war. Some even burned their draft cards and marched in the streets. It was the beginning of a national protest by young people who did not want to become cannon fodder for a war they saw no purpose in fighting. Children dressed in clothing like nothing their parents had ever seen, demonstrated at the Pentagon. The country was divided. Those in favor of the war claimed patriotism. Those opposed pointed out that blind patriotism was not a reason to spend human lives, international goodwill, and real capital. It was becoming apparent that the war was being fought for something other than who governed the Vietnamese.

Jack still believed that the oil in Vietnam was a justification for being there. It was also the diversion they had been waiting for. It took the public's attention away from economics and oil. Although the plan might take five or six years to unfold, the time for rolling it out was approaching.

He saw the world chaos as the perfect foil for escalating oil prices and knew he needed only to be patient and wait for the right moment. His patience was rewarded. While the war was raging in Vietnam, there were corresponding chaotic events going on in other parts of the world. Gamaal Abdul Nasser, the despotic ruler of Egypt who had envisioned a unified Arab middle east, ordered an embargo on the Straits of Tiran in the spring of 1967. He had moved a large force into Gaza and the Sinai. All indications were that Egypt was about to start something with Israel. As that pot was simmering, Syria was sitting in the Golan Heights and shelling northern Israel.

Jack knew this was not going to last long and with memories of the Holocaust still fresh in its collective mind, Israel took the initiative. In June, 1967, Israel attacked. The Israeli Air Force took out most of the Egyptian Air Force and air defenses in a pre-emptive strike. The Syrians and the Jordanians jumped in, but it was over nearly as quickly as it started—in six days, to be precise. This war was the flash point: The enmity of the Arab world toward Israel was the excuse HOG needed to put their conspiracy in motion.

America's support for Israel was not winning us friends in the Arab street, and Jack saw that it would provide the cover the whole conspiracy needed. The OPEC countries could raise prices and appear to be putting it to the hated Americans, making them heroes in their own countries, while they were in bed with American oil companies. They were friendly enemies with a financial interest in each other.

The fall of 1967 had come. Jack needed an insider in the Middle East, someone who could move about and not be seen, someone who knew who did it to whom behind the sand dunes, someone who could open doors. He knew when to cry Wolf.

CHAPTER 17

Jack spoke with disdain of the election of 1968. By the end of 1967, he felt that Nixon had the inside track as the democrats owned the Vietnam war and Nixon promised peace. The voting age had been lowered to 18 and that was all the young people in this country could hear. It was, however, a promise that would take over five years to make good on.

Jack was delighted that Nixon would win. He was pro business and would likely turn his back on a little larceny if he could take a sip of the nectar. It wasn't that he was crooked he just couldn't turn away from an opportunity to make money. He had entered politics a poor man; he would not leave that way.

Jack placed the call to Strange two week ago and was fretting that Strange hadn't gotten the message or had forgotten his promise. Shortly before midnight, when Veronica and the young Jack were asleep and Jack was examining a field report, the French doors to his office opened and he sat up in alarm. A familiar face with a finger on his lips asking for silence, approached.

"You got my message," Jack whispered. He was surprised at the ease with which Strange broke into the house.

"I mustn't be seen in Houston," Strange said, placating Jack's obvious misgivings. "I was in Central America when I got your call. I left as soon as I could and need to get back."

Strange filled Jack in that Castro was still furious over the Bay of Pigs, and was spreading his brand of communism throughout Central and South America and had to be stopped.

Jack poured him a drink and then they moved to a room in the rear of the house where they would not be disturbed. He thought it better not to mention seeing Strange in Dallas in 1963, and got right down to the reason for the call.

Jack took the next hour to lay out the plan as it was developed.

"I'm in," Strange said before Jack could ask him. Strange knew immediately he could count on never working another day when it was implemented. He didn't care where he had to go or who he needed to take out.

"I need you to go the Middle East, and, through your channels, arrange accidental meetings between highly placed members of the courts of the Saudi Prince, the Iraqis, and the Shah of Iran," Jack told him, "and with members of the ruling families of rest of the OPEC members. They can take place in various cities throughout Europe. Can you make this happen?"

"Yes," Strange answered and they spent the next several hours going over his role in detail.

If the Saudis, the Iraqis, and the Iranians went along, the rest of OPEC would have to follow. Neither of them anticipated any problems. Money had a way of smoothing over any rough spots along the way. They would be proven right.

"What we need down the road is a war, a flare-up that gives OPEC a plausible reason to cap the spigot. At the right time, you have to move your assets in a way that makes conflict inevitable," Jack said.

When do you want to do this" Strange asked?

"Everything is okay now, but Nixon promised to end the war in Vietnam." he answered. "I don't think he can do it in less than 3 or 4 years. We're too embedded. Late in 1972 or 1973 would look to be the target."

"Good, that'll give me time to get a proper the fire lit," Strange said. "As for the other, I'm leaving tonight. I'll finish my business and head to Venezuela to layout their role going forward. The Venezuelans are like most Central and South American countries—fed up with being pushed around by the Yanqui. They would be the first to step up. From there," he continued, "I'll start with Kuwait. I'll signal you when all the arrangements for the meets are in place.

Jack would find out later that Strange was in Central America setting up a network of assets whose mission was to suppress the populist movements being fostered by Castro. This Central American involvement would come in handy later on.

CHAPTER 18

Jack stopped talking. It was nearly 11:00 a.m. Around the crowded ER, people in hospital scrubs were making life and death decisions in a makeshift triage. There was blood everywhere and cries of pain and despair floated heavily on the air.

"My leg is throbbing," he said. It was hot and swollen. "Can you find me something for the pain?"

An orderly heard Jack moan and ducked into our space. "Up there," he said pointing at a cabinet in the corner that once had a lock on it. I found enough hydrocodone, a generic form of the powerful painkiller Lortab, to take care of Jack for a week. I got some water and gave Jack two tablets.

In a little while, when he was less uncomfortable, he began to speak again. "I want to point you to the signal moment in the chain of events that led to the tragedy I've brought on myself, and on thousands, perhaps millions, of innocent people," Jack said, his eyes speaking to the level of his sorrow.

"I knew that Veronica's brainchild would change the landscape of the U.S. forever. The immediate and perhaps permanent economic effects would be felt across the middle and lower classes. In time, the comfortable economic life they'd enjoyed throughout the post WWII era would begin to decline. The upper class would become wealthier." Jack said as his breathing evened out.

"I also knew that as wealth moved upward, so would political power. It was reasonable to believe that if people were too busy trying to survive they would be easy prey to any politician or party that promised them relief from their plight or played to their fears. The movement of the middle class wealth to the privileged class was a heady aphrodisiac. I moved toward its light." He went on.

"I saw that the war, keeping the strategic oil reserve up to secure levels, and providing petroleum products for an expanding economy, was sucking up huge amounts of domestic crude. Supplementing domestic oil with cheap imported oil, which could be sold in the U.S. for the same price as more expensive domestic crude, would be necessary to keep it up.

It wasn't hard to slow down or shut down production on domestic wells and follow that with increased imports to a point where there was no going back.

The Arabs," he continued "didn't like the U.S., but they were despots who had a pervasive feeling of insecurity and saw the money to be made as the key to remaining in control. It was child's play to convince them to raise prices gradually, and at the opportune moment to stop exporting completely. As for the home front," Jack went on, "the oil companies had friends in government who wouldn't allow interference. Campaign "contributions" would see to that."

The memories and his guilt were painful. Jack's conscience had reemerged as he wiped a tear from his eye.

"Why are you crying?" I asked. "The painkillers should have kicked in by now."

His tears overwhelmed his reluctance to tell me.

"I was remembering Bobby Kennedy," he said tearfully. "I didn't directly ask for it but I know I had a role in his assassination."

I looked at Jack aghast. I had been listening to him confess to serious criminal activity, but I was having trouble getting my mind around this piece of business. I believed him when he described the events in Dallas in 1963, and that he was not involved in any way, but I was having trouble believing him when he said he was involved in this tragedy.

"I've pieced together a picture of how it could have happened. If you withhold judgment, I'll tell you what I discovered.

In April 1968," Jack told me, "when Bobby was making gains toward being the Democratic Party's presidential candidate and would give Nixon a run for his money, Cully, Veronica and I agreed that throwing a lot of money at Nixon's campaign might help keep the tide turned in his favor.

Unbeknownst to either of them, I met Strange in Manhattan. I told him that it was critical that they find something on Kennedy to derail his candidacy or our conspiracy could be set back years. I told him that Kennedy would not let the oil companies ride roughshod over the economy. In his own manner, he assured me that he would see to it that Nixon won. I didn't give it a second thought until the June evening when all hell broke loose and Kennedy lay on the floor in front of the TV cameras dying. I had a panic attack. This was Strange's response?

It took me nearly twenty years to get enough information out of Strange. He had uncharacteristically let slip that he had a friend who had a friend who knew Sirhan Sirhan, and for me to make an educated guess about what happened. Strange had taken my message to heart. Having Kennedy in the White House, with his bulldog way of finding out where the bodies were buried, was not in Strange's best interest. Discrediting Kennedy was not enough. He would have to be moved aside—permanently."

"Strange left the meeting," Jack continued, "and went directly to the Middle East to appraise the situation from the outside. He was interested in finding out who in the area was not thrilled at the prospect of having another Kennedy in the White House. It didn't take him long to find a patsy. He settled on a young Turk," Jack said, "a man whose character was questionable. I don't know whether he was a criminal or had a skeleton in his closet. It didn't matter. In Strange's world there was always a way to get people to do the damnedest things. One of his operatives made contact with the assassin and let him know that his family was in peril if he failed, then delivered him to the right place at the right time with the right weapon. Then Strange," Jack told me, "erased his own operative to close off any link to himself. It is as likely the truth as anything."

Jack added one further aside. He talked about J.B., who had been working the oil fields in West Texas managing production at the wells when he wasn't drowning his sorrows in booze and easy women. Jack reached out to him as often as he could, but J.B. was smarting at the loss of what he believed was his birthright and wanted to get even with Jack. His alcoholism was beginning to play with his mind and he was consumed by his own rage. As a boy, he had played in his father's office and knew every place to hide and observe deals that no one was supposed to see. Now that he was too big to fit in any of the cubby holes he hid in as a child and listen, technology could do it for him. He waited for the weekly sweep of listening devices. When the room was ostensibly clean, he planted a bug in the conference table in Cully's office.

He overheard Jack and Cully discussing how to roll out the conspiracy to the other oil company executives. He would let the game play out and at the right moment attempt to remove Jack and move in for his share.

Jack's tone of voice led me to believe that this piece of the story would also have an unhappy ending.

CHAPTER 19

On the first Wednesday in November, 1968. People all over the country were celebrating the Republican presidential victory. The promise of peace and prosperity rang loudly throughout the populace. Jack knew better. Mr. Nixon, though not at the lunch he shared with President Eisenhower, was there when Ike dictated the minutes of his meeting with Jack. As noted, Nixon was a poor man when he entered politics. He was gaining in wealth daily. He had no plans to run up against the oil companies and change the status quo.

Jack was sitting in Cully's office watching the morning news and smiling.

"What are you so doggone lit up about?" Cully drawled.

"The plan is in motion."

For the rest of the morning and into late afternoon, they were sequestered in what they thought was a secure conference room. While they had tacit agreement that the major oil companies were on board, they were at work on the specific role each of the major oil companies would play, when to alert them, and where would be the best place to do that. Both agreed that barbeques at the lake house would the safest place.

The Thanksgiving and Christmas holidays passed and the short Texas winter turned into spring, which came early in 1969. Jack left it up to Cully to pass the schedule of events to his cronies at the major oil companies. Over the next few months, Jack and Veronica would have informal gatherings at the lake house and invite oil company heads. Texas oilmen never needed an excuse to eat a side of beef, drink a barrel of Bourbon, or smoke a cigar the size of a small tree.

The Lake House, which was now Veronica's, was also a secure location that was constantly swept for listening devices. Cully would be free to give the oil company bigwigs an unwritten chronology of when to begin production cuts at the wells and how far to scale back refinery operations.

The barbeques were a great success. There was good food, good booze, and a good poker game for the men, while Veronica held court with the women and games and surprises kept the children occupied. These weekend soirees became a staple of the Texas summer for oil company executives in the Houston area.

It was to one of these parties that Cully's favorite actor showed up uninvited. At first Cully feigned being miffed, but Veronica, the ever-gracious hostess, took the governor of California by the arm and introduced him to the other guests. Jack told Cully that Governor Reagan was looking forward to a run for the White House in 1976. Courting and supporting him would be more than good for them.

Cully turned on his Texas charm. The two men found they had complementary interests—Cully wanted political favor and the Reagan wanted campaign money. They discussed rumors that new wells were being capped and that less emphasis was being placed on domestic drilling. The governor said he had no idea what the oil companies were up to, and thought this visit would give him some insight.

After dinner Governor Reagan was given a short briefing on production and exploration costs, the volume of oil being used by the military and the civilian population, and the cheapness of imported oil. The information—and a sizeable campaign contribution—were received with a wink and a nod. The two men understood each other perfectly. It was to be a match that would set off a quantum shift in American economics.

Later, Reagan, the ever gracious guest, signed autographs for anyone who asked. He would be a frequent visitor to the lake house over the next few years.

CHAPTER 20

Summer was over and everyone involved in the domestic side of the plan was in place. The fall and winter flew by and Jack was ready to focus on the Middle Eastern partners. Jack and Strange agreed to communicate only if it was absolutely necessary. It was! Jack sent the requisite signal to Strange through the maze of mail drops they had set up and was anxiously awaiting his reply. One evening in late March of 1970, Strange arrived unannounced.

"How did it go?" Jack asked.

"I met no resistance to the meetings I proposed. They're anxious to move forward. The Iranian Minister of Finance will meet you in Rome on Monday, April 6. Two days later, the Saudi minister will see you in Florence, then, two days later you'll meet the Iraqi minister at the Louvre."

"Is there any other way to get this information into their hands?" Jack asked, feeling some anxiety.

"No," Strange answered. "The risks of exposing the whole thing are too high if we use normal channels for these players."

"Okay, then, lay out how this will happen."

"I've delivered the code to read the information you'll hand them," Strange began, "along with pictures of you and maps of the meeting points. These were smuggled in to the ministers in postcard packets without much trouble."

Jack listened as Strange instructed him in the methods spies use to make meetings look like chance encounters.

Then, like a puff of smoke, Strange was gone. They were ready.

In the meantime, Jack made arrangements for the coming trip with Veronica to the capitals of Europe: Rome, Florence, Paris, and London. Young Jack would stay in Houston in case anything went wrong.

At lunch that day, he looked at Veronica in a way that told her he had something up my sleeve.

"You're hiding something," she said coyly.

"Do you want to go shopping?"

"Of course," Veronica answered with a smile. "Neiman's?"

"No," Jack replied.

"Saks or Lord and Taylor in New York?" Veronica kept up the game.

"No," Jack said playfully.

"Well, where *are* we going?" Veronica asked like a child tired of being teased.

"Rome, Florence, Paris, and London," Jack announced triumphantly.

Veronica hadn't been to Europe since they were married.

"Is this pleasure or business?" she asked excitedly.

"Both" he answered smiling. "We're moving forward."

So it was done, but he had no idea that destiny would be a stowaway on this excursion.

—⦿—

Two weeks later, Jack received the wire from Strange.

It read: All in order. Stop. Arrangements firm. Stop. S.

Jack was as excited as Veronica. He had not been abroad since he and Cully had gone to the Middle East. They had spent no time in Europe and he was looking forward to sandwiching a little sightseeing around the business part of the trip.

Jack called Cully.

"We're all set," he told him.

"How long will you be gone?"

"Ten days, we're leaving April 2nd."

CHAPTER 21

Jack and Veronica had a one-day layover in New York. It had been many years since he'd been to the City. He could see it had changed and in many ways not for the better, but it was still the busiest and most exciting place on the planet.

Veronica was wide-eyed at the top of the Empire State Building and while the trip to the Statue of Liberty was windy it was worth the trouble. Jack took Veronica to diner at the Colony, a restaurant that hosted President Kennedy, window shopping Fifth Avenue, and after dinner drinks at the Top of the Sixes. It was a day of full of excitement.

"What a fabulous place," Veronica said with a sigh as they walked back to the Plaza Hotel. "It's too bad we can't live here."

"You like it that much?"

"Oh, yes," she answered.

"When we get back from Europe, we'll get a place here," Jack said. "I'll change our itinerary so we can stay here a few days. I'll have to call Cully and tell him to meet us here, I wouldn't want to tell him this over the phone and I think it would be good if he saw up close that a strong presence in New York would be good for HOG."

Veronica didn't need to answer. The look she gave Jack was all the assurance he needed.

⸻

Jack booked a Saturday flight from JFK airport in New York arriving in Rome the next morning. It was a long flight, but first class accommodations made it comfortable. They were greeted by the morning sun as the plane taxied to the terminal. It took only a short time for the first class passengers to clear customs. Soon they were headed for the heart of the city.

The cab driver was a quiet man who spoke only if he had to. He had remained in his cab as the porter loaded the trunk of the older model Alfa sedan. He had cut off another driver to get to Jack at the terminal. Jack saw through Strange's mustache and cap, but didn't acknowledge him in front of Veronica. When they arrived at the Gladiatori-Pallazzo Manfredi hotel, Jack took an envelope from Strange as he paid the cab fare. It contained pictures of his contacts. There was also a note that said that he was to meet Strange in the hotel bar at one o'clock that afternoon. That was no problem. After a short nap and a bath, Veronica would be off shopping. She would not want to sightsee without him, but shopping was something else.

Jack was excited. He was in Rome and meeting Strange in an atmosphere of great secrecy. They were about to start the biggest financial shell game in modern history.

At one o'clock Jack was sitting in a darkened corner of the bar. Strange was never late, so it caused him some concern when he didn't show up.

"Qualcosa di bierre, Signore? Something to drink, sir?" the waiter whose face he could barely see asked in heavily accented English as he placed a napkin on the table.

"Bourbon."

It took him a few seconds to see the writing on the napkin: instructions from Strange. He was to ask for a telephone and call the number written on the napkin. He was to turn his head away from the two men sitting across the room.

Jack followed the instructions, and, as the phone rang, wondered why this was so 'cloak and dagger'.

Strange answered. "The two men are Soviet agents," he said. "They check passenger manifests to see if there are any businessmen of note on the incoming planes. When they saw your name, they decided to follow you and see if the trip had any significance for them. It's just routine but we'll have to lose them."

"Where are you and how do we do that?" Jack asked.

"I'm right behind the bar," Strange said chuckling. "Leave the bar and go to the Coliseum. You'll find an entrance to the Roman subway there. Take the train north two stops. Don't get off immediately, just stand by the doors, look relaxed, and as the doors start closing get out quickly. Your tail will have no time to react."

In less than 30 minutes Jack had shaken the men loose. As he walked out of the station, Strange took his arm and led the way to a small espresso bar.

"Don't look so pleased with yourself," he said, "shaking a couple of Russian spies doesn't make you a spook."

That brought him back to reality.

"The Russians are everywhere," Strange told Jack. "They'll be a nuisance, but I'll take care of them."

How Strange would handle them was a question he didn't need to ask. He had long since stopped asking questions he didn't want the answers to. He just put it out of his mind.

"Do you have the faces in your head?" Strange quizzed.

Jack nodded yes. He studied the photos while Veronica slept.

"You'll have only a short time to conduct business. The information with the timetables is encrypted as is their role in the plan." Then Strange handed him a small profile Beretta. "It's untraceable."

Jack took it, knowing that there would be no arguing with him about this.

"Take this, too," Strange said, and handed him a key with an address tag attached to it. "It's for a villa in the countryside north and east of Rome. The best way to get there is by cab. If anything looks out of sync," Strange continued with emphasis, "give Veronica the key. Don't hesitate. Don't analyze the situation.

Just be safe. If it feels bad, it probably is. Get your wife into a cab and away, then walk off into the nearest crowd of tourists."

Jack could only nod in response. The gravity in Strange's voice said it all.

"Each of the men you'll meet has received a photo of you. There should be no hitches. When you've established contact, pass the information as quickly, calmly, and as surreptitiously as you can. After you've made the pass, leave the area," Strange instructed.

CHAPTER 22

Veronica and Jack spent the morning of the first meeting in the Coliseum. She was fascinated by the size of the structure and marveled that it could have been built by people so long ago. She spent time in Europe as a young girl, and went to college in Paris, but being here again was a joy all its own.

Walking to the Forum, Jack had the feeling that they were being followed. He was right. Stopping to look at the Latin inscription on one of the buildings, he was able to see that the two Russians he'd given the slip to yesterday were back on his tail. They were unaware of anything but him. Too bad, because Strange was following them, and he knew they would soon disappear.

It was a beautiful day for sightseeing and it passed quickly. Lunch was alfresco and delicious. After they ate, Jack planned to go back toward the Forum and then walk to the Piazza della Rotunda and take the tour of the Pantheon, where the first exchange was to take place precisely at three o'clock. Strange booked the 2:45 tour.

As they strolled along the Via dei Fori Imperiali, Jack was feeling apprehensive. He wrote it off to nerves and the excitement of executing the first phase of the plan. He should have been more cautious. What he didn't know was that J. B. had chosen this time and place to make his move. He had somehow managed to alert the Iranian opposition party that something big was going down in Rome. The Iranian finance minister would be meeting with an American oil man. It would be in their best interest, J. B. told them, not to let the Shah succeed in his plan to make millions of dollars, which he would use to keep them at bay. They agreed, and sent two of their men to make sure that the minister and whoever he was meeting with didn't return from that meeting.

It was the beginning of the tourist season and there were people from all over the world in Rome—Americans, Europeans, Asians, and Middle Easterners. Two of these Middle Easterners seemed to be pacing Jack and Veronica as they walked toward the Pantheon.

Jack hailed a cab. The hour of the tour was approaching and he wanted to be early to check out the location Strange picked for the pass.

They arrived at the Pantheon with time to spare and a sense of awe at the grandeur of the structure; marble everywhere and architecture of a kind not seen in this modern era. They walked inside and were swallowed in the beauty of the workmanship.

Jack recognized his contact and moved to the tour starting point. As they walked along with the rest of the members of the tour, the Jack and the Minister positioned themselves so that they could move into an alcove, talk for a moment, pass the papers, and move back into the group without arousing any suspicions.

The handoff went without a hitch and Jack rejoined Veronica. When the tour ended Jack and the Minister walked separately through the main entrance. Jack lingered a second to make sure there was no trouble. He was beginning to feel that finding trouble was for him like finding gum on the bottom of your shoe in a schoolyard: it was inevitable.

He saw one of the middle eastern men he'd seen on the Via dei Fori Imperiali grab the minister and hustle him up a side street. J.B.'s trap was baited.

"Veronica," Jack said excitedly, as he handed her Strange's key and hailed a cab, "go to the address on the key tag. I'll meet you there later. Don't leave until I come for you," he said with chilling emphasis.

Veronica recognized the look on his face and the intensity in his voice. She hustled into the cab and was gone in an instant.

Jack waited until he was sure she wasn't being followed and then moved as quickly as possible up the side street. He could hear voices in heated conversation coming from an alley just ahead. The men he heard spoke in a language decidedly Middle Eastern. Moving into the alley quietly Jack drew his pistol.

One of the men was holding the minister's right arm and had a gun pointed at his temple. He told Jack to put down the gun or he would shoot the minister. The minister, not a stranger to danger and intrigue, moved his right forearm to his chest and held two fingers in the V for victory position. Jack understood. There were two of them. He couldn't see well in the shadows of the alley, but knew that the second man was behind the minister. Almost without moving, Jack pointed the weapon at the first man and shot. At the same instant, the minister dove to his right exposing the second man and, seizing the moment, Jack fired at him.

Jack fired only twice but the two abductors lay dead. He grabbed the minister and moved him out of the alley and back up the side street.

"Walk back to the Pantheon," he told the minister, "and don't look back. Don't stop until you are safely inside your embassy. Leave Italy as quickly and quietly as you can."

Though still somewhat shaken, the man thanked him, turned back where they'd come from, found a cab and, as Jack later learned, was winging homeward that evening.

Jack hailed a cab and headed back to the hotel bar where he and Strange met on the day they arrived in Rome. He hoped that he would have heard about the shooting and made his way there to meet him. He sat in the darkened bar and ordered a drink. A familiar voice spoke to him from the next booth.

"Mr. Duncan," Strange said, "you never cease to amaze me. This place is too open. There is an espresso bar three stops north on the train from the Coliseum. Leave now and I'll meet you there as quickly as I can."

Jack went immediately to the train stop Strange indicated, and this time no one followed. He rode three stops, detrained, found the espresso bar, went to a quiet corner, and ordered a double espresso.

After what seemed like an eternity, Strange came through the rear door and sat down across from him.

"I killed them both," Jack said in an ambivalent voice.

"I saw you," Strange said. "I had your back if either of them flinched."

All Jack could manage was a very relieved thank you. It was reassuring to know that Strange was on his wing.

"I'm impressed," Strange said in a tone that spoke of his growing admiration for Jack's coolness under fire. "You didn't hesitate."

Jack was flattered. Now that he was safe, he was feeling a sense of exhilaration from the chase and the subsequent rescue of the finance minister.

"We'll likely have to do some P.R. to assure the OPEC guys that we aren't compromised."

"I'll take care of it," Strange assured him.

"Who were those guys?" Jack asked. At the time he had no idea that he was, in fact, their prime target.

"Iranian extremists," Strange said. "There is an undercurrent of unrest in Iran. The religious extremists are trying to overthrow the Shah and install a theocratic form of government. The men behind this," Strange continued, "are bad guys. They're clerics, but they have a political agenda that includes absolute power for them."

"Can they cause much trouble for us?"

"No" Strange replied. "They are too scattered abroad to present a problem for us, and besides, their focus is Iran. This incident was just a chance for them to interfere with Iranian affairs and embarrass the Shah. But, we've got to keep moving," Strange went on. "Stay the night at the place I had you send Veronica, you'll be safe there. Your meeting in Florence is at the Uffizi Gallery with the Saudi minister of interior. You'll make contact at the entrance to the gallery and just bump into him. You have to be subtle because our CIA is always watching the Saudis and who they meet with. Especially if it's the Russians. I'll see you there," he said as he melted out of the back of the bar.

Strange had arranged a car for Jack and Veronica to drive to Florence. Their baggage had already been sent ahead to their hotel, the Degli Orafi. After Strange departed, Jack picked up the car and, following Strange's directions, drove quickly to the house outside of Rome where Veronica was waiting.

"Thank goodness you're here," Veronica said, finally able to exhale. "What happened at the Pantheon?"

"Just a bit of a misunderstanding, it was over before it started."

"I was worried it's nearly dark," Veronica said. "Come with me," she continued, pointing toward a well-lit room, "the housekeeper was good enough to prepare a meal for us."

The housekeeper left them a delicious dinner of pasta Bolognese, Scaloppini alla Marsala, and pistachio gelato, which they devoured. It was already seven, and they hadn't eaten since lunch.

The house was lavish and all that a rich tourist could desire. It was actually a safe house for covert ops personnel. Amazing what a blank CIA check could buy.

"I left a little out of what I told you about this afternoon's activities. Two men who tried to kidnap the Iranian minister are not with us anymore," Jack said quietly.

"You killed them?" Veronica asked incredulously.

"They were going to shoot the minister, so I shot them first," he said nonchalantly, feeling ever more like the spook Strange assured him he wasn't.

Veronica was silent. She looked at him with worry and admiration. Her warrior was home safely, to hell with the losers.

They would be gloating now if the roles were reversed. Business was war and she and Jack were winning. That was all that mattered.

As Jack finished a snifter of Cognac and took Veronica's hand the housekeeper approached.

"May I have the pistol, please," she said in a tone that Jack recognized as Strange's orders.

He was reluctant to hand over the only thing that could keep them safe.

"Please, sir," she repeated, "I must have the pistol. It is his order. There is another just like it in the nightstand in your quarters."

Jack gave it to her.

She had been ordered to dissemble the pistol and scatter the pieces in the Tiber. She followed her orders to the letter.

As they were preparing for bed, Veronica made sure that there was another one where it was supposed to be. She was trusting, but not too trusting. As promised, it was there, and identical in every way to the one Jack used that afternoon. It too, had no serial number. He placed it under his pillow. He was ready for a night's sleep.

Strange was concerned that someone had penetrated their circle. Too many people knew they were here. While Veronica and Jack slept, four CIA types from Strange's cadre were hidden in vantage points that covered all approaches to the house.

CHAPTER 23

The housekeeper gave Jack the map and instructions that Strange had left for the trip to Florence. He and Veronica left the villa at first light with only a picnic basket, headed north and east, and kept a weather eye out for anyone following. Strange's instructions included what to do if they were tailed. They were to stop in Siena and turn back to Rome. There was a turnoff marked on the map just south of Siena that went east. About two miles in, a dirt track looped back to the north and on to Florence. They only needed a short lead on anyone tailing them to get on the dirt track unseen.

The drive to Siena took them through the beautiful Tuscan countryside. Jack drove as Veronica pointed out interesting landmarks. He had a landmark of a different sort on his mind and in the rear view mirror.

"There's a black Mercedes-Benz following us," Jack said in a matter-of-fact manner. "It's been there for about an hour, but I wanted to be sure it was following us so I changed speeds few times. Each time I changed they changed too."

"He doesn't seem interested in hiding his presence he's just there, the same distance away all the time."

Jack made several side trips off the main road, feigning sightseeing, and the sedan followed. He couldn't always see the car itself, just the plume of dust it raised on the dirt side roads. After the last of these experiments, he pulled back onto to main road and set a course directly for Siena.

At noon, they found the park that was marked on the map by Strange.

"This is where we stop," Veronica said as she checked the map a second time.

"We'll eat here and spend an hour resting."

There was something about the Italian countryside that was very relaxing.

After lunch, they climbed back into the car. As Jack pulled back onto the highway, he looked at the side view mirror.

"They're behind us again," he said, his voice elevating with excitement. The race was on and he had the rail.

"How far is it to the gas station where we turn around?" he asked Veronica.

"Fifteen miles," she answered.

"Look for the turn-off, it comes up about two miles before the filling station," he directed her. "It's marked it on the map."

"At the bend in the road, yes, there it is," she said as they sailed past it ten minutes later.

Strange had picked the perfect spot to lose a tail. The road bent hard to the right and the turn off was at the southernmost end of the curve on the east side of the road. Coming from the north the turnoff was not visible from the road until you were almost on it.

Jack chuckled as this whole scene reminded him of a film noir potboiler where the bad guys try inconspicuously to follow the good guys.

In just minutes they were approaching Siena. Jack found the filling station noted on the map. It was right outside of town.

"That's it," Veronica said, pointing across the road to the southbound side.

Jack didn't need fuel, but it was a perfect place to turn around and head back toward Rome. Pulling off the highway slowly and making it look like they were stopping to fill up he waited a moment for some southbound traffic, shot out in front of the line of cars and in no time was back on the road speeding southward. As he passed the black sedan, which had to wait for traffic to clear before it could turn around, Jack could see the consternation on the faces of the two swarthy men in the car. He knew they would turn around immediately, so he sped up even more. The sedan was again on their tail, but this time several hundred feet further back and behind traffic. It was all they needed.

"There!" Veronica shouted. "There's the turn!"

Jack sped quickly down the side road and turned again at what looked to be little more than a cow path. He didn't see the trail of dust from the black sedan and a gentle breeze had muted his. He pulled to a stop about a hundred yards up this trail in a small stand of trees. There they sat and waited.

"Who are these people?" Veronica asked.

"I don't know but I'm sure going to find out. I think we've had a security breach."

Jack fingered the pistol nervously. This was exciting business, but serious. Suddenly he heard the sedan come up the side road. Their car could not be seen from the road and soon the Mercedes was well past them.

"They're gone," he said after a few minutes, satisfied that the car and its passengers were a safe distance down the side road now. He followed the cow path until it grew into a road that led back to the main highway through Siena and on to Florence. He turned north, and that was the last they saw of the black sedan.

He kept close watch in the mirror as they drove on, but Strange's ruse had worked, as always.

It was late afternoon when they arrived at the hotel. They had the evening to themselves. It was spring in Tuscany and they were still young.

The following morning, Veronica, a bit gun-shy from the experience in Rome, decided to see the Dome while Jack took care of business at the Uffizi Gallery.

The meeting and handoff went smoothly and he was able to join Veronica for an early lunch.

They had time on our hands, which in Italy means sightseeing, and Florence was certainly the place to do that. They toured the galleries and art shops on both sides of the Arno River and shopped the gold merchants on the Ponte Vecchio. Tired tourists, they headed back to the hotel with their treasures. Over dinner, Jack spoke again of his nagging suspicion.

"I believe we've have a leak," Jack told Veronica for the second time.

"Who," Veronica began to say, but caught herself in mid-word. "J.B.," she said with conviction. "It has to be him. The plan and all the players would have been exposed by now if it were anyone else."

"I've come to the same conclusion," Jack echoed. "J.B. won't know what happened here so we can wait to deal with him until we return to the States."

"Jack," Veronica asked in a whisper, "how do you feel about killing those two men?"

"Truth be told, I put it out of my mind. They were trying to kill one of us, and for that, they had to die. I have no remorse."

Veronica smiled and took his hand and led him to the bedroom. She quietly closed and locked the door.

Morning came early. The telephone was ringing and Jack was closest to it, he got up quickly to silence the persistent clang of the 1950's vintage Italian telephone. It was Strange.

"Get down to the lobby as quick as you can," Strange ordered his voice as tight as a piano wire. "There are things in the wind."

Jack hurriedly dressed and headed down. He saw Strange walk into the espresso bar, and followed. It was empty save the attendant, who was dressed in a white tunic.

"Due Cappuccini, per piachere," Strange told her as he led Jack to a table in the back of the shop.

"You have to leave Italy immediately," he said. "The Italian police are investigating the shooting in Rome. Someone saw you, and though their description of you is sketchy, there's no sense taking any chances. You and Veronica must leave now or risk being picked up. The resulting publicity might scare the OPEC members away. I've booked you on a private flight to Paris this morning."

"Thanks," Jack said. "I'll make the final drop and fly to London the following day."

"I've taken care of the South American meeting. The plan will be executed, but you must move quickly. The flight is in one hour," Strange said as he moved toward the door of the espresso bar.

Jack called Veronica on the courtesy phone in the hotel lobby.

"We've got to leave, and now."

"I suspected as much," Veronica replied. "I've already begun to pack."

Jack made it back to the room in time to clean up, put on fresh clothes, and gulp down a second cup of cappuccino. The bellman was waiting outside the hotel with their bags. He hailed a cab and was loading it as they came out of the hotel. Jack noted with a smile that the driver bore a strong resemblance to Strange.

At the airport, Strange took them to a small hangar on the far side of the field. There was a small customs detachment in the hangar as this was the adit and exit for the very rich, the very powerful, or the very corrupt. They passed through customs quickly and were escorted out of the hangar to the hard stand where a private jet was waiting. Jack put Veronica on board.

He and Strange huddled at the door for a few moments before Jack followed her.

"I'll see you in New York," Strange promised. "I've got a few loose ends to tie up here."

They were off the ground shortly and winging toward Paris, where a car would take them to the Louvre and the meeting, which was moved up a day. They would spend the evening in a hotel near the Cathedral of Notre Dame, then fly to London. After a layover in London for a day, they would make the Atlantic crossing to New York. Jack would have time to call Cully from there.

Paris is beautiful anytime of year, but in the springtime and in bloom it is enchanting. Both Veronica and Jack wished they could spend more time there, but Strange nixed that.

At the Louvre, Veronica went off for a short tour of Renaissance paintings while Jack met the Iraqi minister of interior. The pass was made and he went back to the private car. He was surprised to see Veronica leaving the museum accompanied by the driver, who was, he discovered, one of Strange's operatives.

The driver had been alerted that the French Surete was looking for an American resembling Jack and that he had to get them out immediately. French police had gotten the same sketchy description as the Roman police.

They drove away from the Louvre as several police cars moved in looking for someone who might fit the description. When they arrived and found no such person, thinking provincially, they put out a local dragnet.

"This is too dangerous," Jack whispered to Veronica, as their plane climbed to cruising altitude for the short flight to London, his voice reflecting the angry countenance of his face.

"Why do you think J. B. would deliberately try to sabotage this?" Veronica half asked, half said.

"I'm not sure, but I'm guessing that he's harboring some animosity toward me for my displacing him at HOG."

Jack was tired, and very concerned that the plan was compromised. Everything was moving forward, but the risks were escalating.

Maybe Cully told J. B. about it?" Jack mused aloud.

"No" he concluded answering his own question.

"J. B. is hardly around. He's always at the refining operations office. Last time I saw him, he looked like the overly wealthy drunken Texas wannabe oilman that he's become."

"He's been sulking ever since Cully brought you into HOG," Veronica said.

Jack had no idea how close to the truth Veronica had come. J. B. wasn't playing softball, and Jack was his target.

They arrived in London and settled into a suite at Claridge's Hotel. Jack called Cully. He wanted a piece of his hide.

It was very late at night or very early in the morning when Cully woke to the rattle of the telephone. He looked at the clock and, shaking the cobwebs from his head, picked up the receiver.

"What the hell did you tell J. B.?" Jack fairly screamed into the phone. He held the receiver away from his ear for minutes as Jack unloaded all the tension that had built up in him from the unacknowledged fear of the past few days on the continent.

When he finished his rant and had cooled down some, Cully got a word in.

"Hello, Jack, how are you?" he drawled in a sleepy Texas tone.

Jack laughed out loud at his droll way of taking a verbal pounding without losing his sense of humor. They were more than just two men in business together. Cully had a genuine fondness for Jack.

"It almost all came apart. Someone found out about the meetings and there was some gunplay."

"Whoa," Cully laughed. "I thought we only did that at high noon in West Texas."

"Be serious," Jack chided him, laughing. "Have you told J. B. anything?"

"No," Cully answered. "But he could have overheard any number of conversations. I'll see to it that I'm more careful in the future," Cully promised.

"Sorry for teeing off on you," Jack said, genuinely apologetic.

"I think we need to confine any more talk to secure locations, away from the office. Sit tight in London," Cully told him, "see the sights. I'll have J. B. for lunch, find out what he knows and who he told. The problem will be dealt with."

Fortunately, Jack settled down enough for he and Veronica to take in a little of London. A few hours later, they came back to the hotel after a relaxing day of shopping. Not long after, Cully called back.

"I found the leak," he announced. "J.B. listened in to a conversation between you and me and took the bits and pieces he heard to an Arab oilman he met in Houston. I ran down the guy's pedigree. He's an operative for the Iranian ayatollahs. It has to be the connection to the incident in Rome."

It was J. B.'s swan song. Cully had all he could stand of J.B.'s drunken and irresponsible behavior.

"I've given J. B. a choice," Cully went on. "He has to be on a plane to Indonesia, today, to work a small joint venture there, and he has to shut up about any and all of HOG's business dealings, or he's out at HOG."

The tone in Cully's voice told Jack that out at HOG meant OUT, period.

He was startled by Cully's words. He had just heard him say that he would have his son killed if he was not out of the country and silent.

"Are there any other loose ends?"

"I'm not sure," Cully answered, "but it doesn't seem so."

"Why would J. B. do that?" Jack thought out loud. "What would cause him to do something so extreme?"

Cully answered pensively. "He's an alcoholic, even though he keeps the effects of his hangovers to a minimum. He's still angry at his mother for leaving and angry at me for staying. When you pile on living with his grandfather, a workaholic, you have a boy who is all screwed up.

"He uses humor and practical jokes to cover his insecurities. They help him get through the rough spots. He has no real friends. No one gets close. There are lots of women who think he's cute and clever and rich, the kind of women who don't care what kind of man he is, just what kind of bank balance he has. He uses them as much as they try to use him."

Cully paused. "Veronica scared him to death. He could hardly speak around her when they were teens. She was so refined and he was so coarse. But he really was in love with her. I'm sorry to say this, Jack, but when Veronica turned her attention to you, it was the breaking point. He lost his place in the company and he lost the woman he loved. I think he's trying to eliminate his rival. I'm disappointed, but not surprised."

"Thanks Cully," Jack said acknowledging how difficult it had to be for a father to be so critically honest about his son.

"Meet us in New York in two days and we can discuss our next move."

CHAPTER 24

New York in April is second only to New York in September. The air is fresh and the trees, awakening from their winter slumber, sport fresh canopies in beautiful shades of green. So it was that morning, three days later, as Cully and Jack walked along Central Park.

As they strolled toward the Plaza Hotel, Cully explained, "I found out that the Arab J.B. enlisted was on an FBI watch list and I had some friends in the governor's office drop a dime on him. He'll be shut up tight for the next however many years trying to show that he's only a poor Arab merchant with a large family to support. His chances of seeing daylight in the next few years are slim and none."

"We have to be sure that J. B. didn't tell anyone else."

"I've used every source from the governor's office to the Texas Public Safety Department," Cully said reassuringly. "I couldn't find anyplace that boy was in the last six months where he could tell anyone of any importance. He was mostly a loner and not smart enough to carry on something sneaky." The words stung Cully as he said them, but he was sure that they had plugged up the leak.

It was Jack's turn to be newsy.

"Remember that gunplay in Rome I told you about?" He asked with feigned nonchalantly.

"Yeah," Cully said.

"I had to kill two men."

"Stop making fun of me," Cully laughed.

"Seriously, it got tense in Rome, we were chased all the way to Siena, and the Italian and French police were too close so we had to leave Europe to make sure there was not a hint of scandal."

"I've got some news of a different kind," Jack said, catching Cully in mid-question. "Veronica and I are moving to New York. It's as much for HOG as it is for personal reasons. HOG is growing. The plan is almost in place. When we pull the trigger, the best place to manage it is right here. There's access to the OPEC ministers and the leading players of the major oil companies. It's the perfect setting."

"I'm disappointed for me, Jack," Cully said sadly. "I'll be losing two of my closest friends, but I agree with you.

"How will you set the plan in motion?" Cully asked.

Jack hesitated. He wasn't sure that Cully needed to know what the trip wire was, so he gave him some half-baked answer about consumption volumes and consumer demand. It satisfied him. Cully was an oil driller, but not so much when it came to economic discourse. Jack filled his response with references he knew would make Cully tune him out. It was also something he'd been working on with Veronica as the answer to the criticism they would certainly encounter when the cost of oil went through the roof, as they knew it would.

"That's all bull to me," Cully said. He was not really satisfied, but knew he would have to take another tack to get any more information out of Jack. They reached the Plaza, where he had booked a breakfast reservation.

After they ate, Cully turned the conversation to timing.

"If you don't want to tell me how you're going to pull the trigger, how about telling when?"

Jack continued to obfuscate. "Domestic drilling and refinery production have to be minimized. This has to be done without raising any eyebrows in the private sector or at the federal level. Nixon is on board through a series of campaign donations that have been funneled into his pocket. He will stay busy dealing with Vietnam, which is full-fledged conflict with a half million American Soldiers in country, and is consuming most of the public's awareness.".

"I can only guess at the actual date, but it will be within the next five years.

"I'm going to see my broker," Cully said giving up on trying to pin Jack down. "I talk to this guy nearly every day but I've never seen his face."

"I'm meeting Veronica for some R&R," He smiled as they parted with a promise to meet again the next morning for breakfast.

Veronica and Jack had planned to take in the U.N. complex and the Museum of Natural History.

He set up a meeting for Veronica with a real estate agent, and she had spent the morning looking at luxurious Fifth Avenue apartments. He was to meet Veronica at the U.N. He grabbed a cab and headed cross town.

CHAPTER 25

Jack sat silently for a moment. I could see he was tired and feeling the pain of his injuries and the weight of his transgressions. He sat back and closed his eyes and slept.

Finally, I was alone with my own thoughts and wondered why I ended up here in this ER next to a man who very well might be the architect of the worst man made calamity in history. It was an exercise in self-questioning that I should have avoided as some very painful memories came cascading back into my consciousness. While it is true that no one event or moment in our individual history can be solely credited with determining our destiny, but for me, 1968 was fateful. The events of that year would lead to the day that I met Jack Duncan in Pennsylvania Station.

Five years before I was a typical high school senior preparing for graduation. I was accepted at a local community college as a full-time student for the fall semester. This kept the Selective Service System at bay and me out of the draft and the army.

College and I didn't get along. I was a procrastinator and deadlines were anathema to me. Papers didn't get done on time, classes were missed, my grades fell, and my draft status rose. By the end of the summer of 1967, I had exhausted all avenues to avoid being drafted.

In October 1967, I was ordered by my local draft board to report to Fort Dix in New Jersey. The main thing I remember about the place was that it was very busy. Thousands of us, all looking like little shaved-headed G.I. Joes, marched and shot

M-14s and M-16s, walked until our feet were numb, and got screamed at by some sergeant with a third-grade education—at least it seemed so.

We lined up for everything, all of which entailed some kind of indignity. There were the shots: malaria, jungle fever, yellow fever, smallpox, cholera. There were the pecker checkers. Stand in line and look straight ahead as some guy in latex gloves, which he never changed, pulled on your private parts. There were the private eye checkers. Stand in still another line and drop your shorts and grab your socks as another guy walks behind you and looks up your ass to see if your hat's on straight.

There were forced marches with full packs, night crawls under the barbed wire with live fire overhead, and never ending parades.

As with all nightmares, you finally awake and they are over. After what seemed forever, basic training finally ended.

After two weeks leave, a brief reprieve, it was on to Advanced Infantry Training. AIT was what those designated as cannon fodder were sent to in an effort to give them a relative chance for survival. It was there I had the chance to resume my education. Classes included the care and treatment of VC prisoners, your rifle and you; an advanced course called Ambush 101; and a host of other enlightening and terrifying war games.

The Spring of 1968 came in a rush and with it my orders to ship out to Vietnam. It still scares me to this day just to think about it.

My flight to Southeast Asia, a commercial charter full of military types, was hardly memorable—lots of drinks, smokes, and nicotine stains where they didn't belong.

After several stops for refueling, the interminable journey was over and we landed at Ton Son Hut Air Force Base in Saigon.

I managed to raise myself from my seat and unstick my underwear from my butt as the plane came to a stop and opened its doors. I was hustled into a reception area from where I was picked up and driven to a staging area. I was billeted there for two days, which meant I had only 363 days to go before I rotated out. After two more days, I was ordered to load up and report to a forward base north of Saigon. There I was assigned to a unit that spent most of its time in the field hunting Charlie.

The faces of the men in that Company and the platoon I was assigned to have long since become a blur, partly because I have tried to forget them and partly because remembering triggers emotions in me I have fought hard to suppress.

My platoon leader was a good guy, a first lieutenant, which meant that he was a survivor. Most young officers where either fragged—shot from behind by their own men—or Charlie got them long before they were eligible for promotion. He never sent us out in front of him; he was always out in front of us.

My life in the boonies, if it can be called that, was filled with bugs: red ants that lit you on fire, stinging insects that raised welts the size of half dollars, and moisture that made New York's summer humidity seem like the Sahara. We spent much of our time on search and destroy missions to hamlets that housed what seemed to be the youngest and oldest people in the world; there were no people in those villages from teenage to late forties. They were all in hiding, generally in tunnels that ran for miles underground, waiting for opportunities to fight us on their terms. The tunnels served as staging areas for attacks, storage facilities for weapons and ammunition, and conduits for moving combatants around the country. When we found such a tunnel, we'd set fire to the nearest village as punishment for being VC sympathizers. Sadly we found that many of the Vietnamese looked on us as no better than the French, who they had thrown out over a dozen years before.

I had been in country for five months and was becoming hardened to the mission and to the killing when my group was assigned to fortify a fire base, a four-sided outpost in an elevated open area with dug in bunkers in the middle and trenches around the perimeter. I had been through several of these holes in the ground on previous patrols. They were not much better than large barrels with fish swimming in them, and we were the fish. I had hoped that I would never have to spend a night in one of them, as the scuttlebutt was that the VC used them as targets for mortar practice.

We arrived at the base late in the afternoon. The trek in had been eerily quiet. We hardly ever saw Charlie, as they liked to hide in no fire zones. These were locally controlled areas we were not allowed to enter because the provincial chief had paid off Saigon to keep us out so we would not interfere with his drug trafficking. Charlie frequently jumped out of these zones, fired a few rounds, and jumped back. This time we didn't even hear Charlie.

We were assigned to a bunker and fed. Then we took our place on the line. It was déjà vu from the First World War. Our position was a trench with little cover from mortar fire and nothing but barbed wire, barbaric looking wooden stakes, and Claymore mines as protection from a full frontal attack.

The lieutenant told us at chow that we were sent here because G2, the oxymoron called Military Intelligence, expected a major attack on this position as the VC and the North Vietnamese attempted to consolidate their position in this province. It didn't take long for those nicotine stains in my draws to come back. None of us were very excited about this mission. We were search and destroy, not sit and play target, but the army was as inept as it was big, and as political. It wasn't that there weren't any other groups to fill this billet; it was just the brass's way to punish some mid-level officer for speaking out about the waste of men and equipment. As the danger got more palpable, so did the smell of pot. We might be dead men by morning, but we would go out with the giggles and the munchies.

We slept at our post in shifts and fits. Every noise seemed to make us start. They were the night sounds. Then, shortly after midnight, there weren't any night sounds. It stayed quiet for what seemed to be an eternity, but it was only about fifteen minutes before all hell broke loose. The mortars started coming in like rain and thunder. The screams and shouts of "medic" pierced the night like a bayonet in the ribs. Then the noise rose. It was the sound of men running. We looked around to see if it was our guys. They were there to a man. We all knew what that meant: Charlie was running, and not away. They came in waves. We didn't even have to aim. There were so many that it was point and shoot, reload, point and shoot. We had brought extra ammo, but after nearly two hours of nonstop fighting, our perimeter defenses were on their last legs and we were beginning to run low. Then everything stopped. The quiet was deafening. The men left standing took a deep breath. They didn't have time to exhale.

The second wave came at us with AK-47's on full auto. It was like a tsunami hitting the beach. We fought with everything we had. When the ammo was gone we used our bayonets. When the bayonets were useless because Charlie was too close, we used knives. There was no way we could stop this tide. Nothing was left.

I was next to the lieutenant when an incoming mortar round landed on the other side of him. He was dead in an instant. I was covered in body parts and punctured with small shell fragments. Blood was everywhere as the darkness began to cloak my eyes and bodies piled up on top of me.

When I came to, it was daylight. I could hear voices speaking Vietnamese moving away from me. I lay motionless for the next hour, not knowing if they were nearby or had melted back into the countryside. I had to move soon. The weight on my wounds was crushing and the stench of blood and death was everywhere. At first, I could barely move, but after some struggling, I was able to finally push the bodies of my dead comrades off of me. I rolled to my side and the lieutenant's body turned over. The back of his skull was missing and his left side was gone. I moved what remained of him off my legs. I lost it. I began to cry uncontrollably. After a time my military training took over. I had to fortify my position, make contact with HQ, and collect dog tags. I suppose to anyone looking, I must have seemed crazy being the only one alive and trying to hold a position. I tried to reach battalion, but the radio was out of commission. I turned my attention to the men. There were so many dead men it took some time to collect all their dog tags. Every one of them had a bayonet wound. The VC had shown no quarter. I was lucky to have been covered by so many bodies that they missed me. I started to cry again. I was covered with blood and dried pieces of the Lieutenant and freaking out. I had no way of taking care of the bodies of the men in my Company, men who had spent months protecting me and who I had protected; my brothers.

After two days of stacking bodies in trenches as decoys—a ploy straight out of the old movie *Beau Geste*—and checking fortifications, a friendly patrol sent by Battalion when they lost radio contact with us, came on my position. From their vantage in the jungle outside of the outpost, they could see troops but no movement. It must have looked pretty strange. They tried to radio in, and suspected a trap when they got no answer. I could hear them in the quiet as the jungle had again ceased its usual commotion. I thought about yelling, but if Charlie were anywhere near it would compromise the patrol.

At this point I decided that this was no longer my war and found a bloody white sheet in the medics' supply area. I raised it on the flagpole and sat down and lit up a joint. When the patrol came in they found me leaning against the flagpole with an insane grin on my face.

Fortunately, the army thought I'd lost it and rotated me out as quickly as they could. It seemed odd to me that I didn't even return to my company headquarters. First I was sent to the hospital, where my wounds were dressed. That night I was shipped out to Hawaii on a private jet. My guess was this was an embarrassment they wanted to keep quiet.

In Hawaii, I was sent to a series of head shrinks. The army didn't want a nutcase running around talking to the newspapers about a massacre, so I was kept incommunicado. The press had begun to turn against the war and would have made it headline news. I assured the brass that I was okay and that I never wanted to think about what happened again. They gave me a medical discharge and sent me home.

For the next twenty years I battled the nightmares. Sleep was that stranger who came to visit periodically. He would have been welcome if he showed up every night, but he didn't. Soon it was a couple of drinks to help calm the memories. Then it was a half pint to sleep all night. The shaking and the sweats that used to happen only at night started coming on during the day. Breakfast was coffee laced with booze to steady my nerves, followed by a lunch of two or three drinks to get me through the rest of the afternoon. Evenings were the worst. Life became an alcoholic blur as drinking replaced eating, but it was better than the terrifying memory of men screaming for their mothers as they lay disemboweled or blown to pieces all over Vietnam.

The memories were winning. It took more and more alcohol to wash away the horror. Every waking moment seemed to flash with the explosion of bodies contorted in death's grip. I kept hoping that I would be next, but it never happened. My life spiraled down into a bottle. I lost my job, sold my home, and moved onto the streets. Life there wasn't as bad. I was surrounded by battalions of kindred spirits who had the very same dreams of the horrors that I did. In some ways, living on the street was therapeutic. It was easy to find someone who could listen to your pain, share it, and let you share his. It was a way to cope with grief.

I found myself living in the bowels of Pennsylvania Station, where I met Jack Duncan on that terrible day. Jack had said that lives would be lost if there was oil in Vietnam. He was half right. The dead found peace in the grave. The rest of us were lost in a living hell.

As I finished my reverie, Jack awoke from his short nap and began again his story.

CHAPTER 26

Jack characterized Nixon's second term in office as bad joke with a punch line beginning as badly as the war in Vietnam was ending. In either case, a disaster for the United States. Fifty-eight thousand dead, thousands wounded, and Nixon hunkered down with a scandal that had taken on a life of its own: Watergate.

Jack saw Nixon for what he was; unstable. Knowing this he stayed as far away from the administration as he possibly could. The trigger event was approaching and he wanted no unwarranted attention.

Jack was hardly surprised when in the run-up to the 1972 presidential election, there was a break-in at Democratic headquarters in the Watergate complex. The mission, led by an ex-CIA agent named Gordon Liddy, was carried out by a group called CREEP, the committee to reelect the President. This gang of thieves, all close confidants to the President, was as paranoid as Nixon was about losing. The defeat of Nixon by Kennedy in the presidential election of 1960 was a scar that wouldn't heal and in an effort to prevent a repeat, CREEP and Nixon were going to hedge their bet and find out what the Democrats were planning. At first it was hardly worth the printer's ink it garnered, but eventually it caused the demise of the Nixon administration and illustrated how easily the U.S. government could be corrupted.

Jack and Strange, in the meantime, kept the fires lit in the Middle East. Some well-placed money for munitions kept the PLO and the Israelis at each others' throats, while well placed operatives kept Syria and Egypt burning. Their 1967 defeat embarrassed Egypt and Syria in front of the entire Arab world, and they were honor-bound to get revenge. The time was drawing near.

Strange arrived in New York in late Spring of 1973, for a final meeting. HOG's offices in Manhattan were next to a café with a backdoor that opened next to the rear of a small building where Jack rented an office. The back of the office building was obscured from above by an overhanging marquee-like structure that ran the length of it and the building opposite had only 2 story truck bays. Jack could leave by the back door of the restaurant and virtually disappear.

Jack ventured out the backdoor of the café and into the adjacent office building for his meeting with Strange. The two men from such wildly different backgrounds had become friends. Jack could trust Strange, to a point, and Strange knew he could trust him likewise. It was a better than a Mexican standoff, and it worked for ten years.

Huddling together, Strange laid out the scene in Palestine.

"Are Arafat's Gaza contingents in place?" Jack asked.

"I've had people moving weapons into Gaza for the past two years," Strange answered.

"It doesn't take much to keep that pot boiling. My best operatives are in Egypt and Syria," he continued. "Syria is burning and it won't take more than a hot ash for them to explode."

"Set the trip wire!" Jack ordered knowing the distraction of Watergate and the unraveling cover up would provide the perfect smoke screen. He held the match that could set off a terrible conflagration. The Arabs, he knew, would lose. They couldn't fight their way out of a paper bag. Most of their equipment had been given to them by the Soviets. Half the time it wasn't operational, and spare parts were a nightmare to get. Their weapons were vastly outperformed by the U.S.-supplied equipment used by the Israeli army.

"It's nearly ready," Strange replied. "I can build up enough momentum over the next few months to force the Syrians and Egyptians to launch an attack in the fall. I'll send you updates, through the mail drops. The last digit in the phone number on the heading will be the key. When you decode Hebrew words, an attack is imminent." The information would be imbedded in business reports that had no meaning to an outsider.

It was their last meeting until late that year. Jack reached out his hand to Strange, who took it and shook it warmly. It was the first time they had ever done that. Then he was gone.

Jack had formed a germ of an idea during the meeting with Strange. He had concentrated his effort at building HOG by cultivating relationships with politicians who would take an occasional donation. Now he saw through the lens of the Watergate mess that he could do more. He could own these politicians.

Jack spent the summer watching as the country tried to recover from the Vietnam War. Nixon had already lost Agnew, his vice-president, to another scandal, and was in the process of violating rule one of problem management: when you're in a hole, stop digging. Watergate was beginning to get traction, and instead of coming clean at the outset, Nixon and company decided to stonewall.

Reports from the Middle East began to supplant news of Vietnam and were equally depressing to everyone—but Jack and Veronica.

Jack laughed as Strange infiltrated OPEC at the highest levels even though there was no need to do the cloak and dagger thing. Their presence at OPEC had assent from the oil ministers. Once a spook, always a spook. He never left anything to chance, especially where his life was concerned, and this was to be a deadly business. If the Israelis fathomed his mission, they would surely put him under a headstone.

Then it happened. The communiqué in early September. Jack decoded it and read the words in Hebrew: "Yom Kippur." The game was on. Jack contacted Cully and signaled him to cut production over the next month by 40 percent, and to stop drilling in all but the most mature fields. Production was already diminishing in those fields and would leave a large enough shortfall for HOG to begin ratcheting up prices as soon as the war started and the Arabs embargoed oil.

Later that day, Jack called on each of the CEOs of the major oil companies and relayed the message—in code—that they were to begin the slowdown and follow HOG's lead. Each assented, as they had promised to years earlier. Some tried to find out what was going to happen, others only smiled. He kept them all at arm's length, believing that plausible deniability was the best option for them, and for HOG. If the Feds ever investigated, the heads of the other oil companies would have the perfect out: they were just keeping up with the competition.

October was here and with it Yom Kippur. It finally started.

CHAPTER 27

Jack took a deep breath. He had been talking for hours, and it was now early in the afternoon. We were both scared, scarred, hungry and emotionally drained.

"Here, take this," I said, handing him some painkillers. The niceties, like having a nurse deliver meds on a cart were gone. "I'll scout up some food."

The hospital kitchen was overrun with staff and civilians milling about in shock. I found some muffins behind a counter and took a few bottles of water to wash them down with. Jack ate them both.

"How did Strange start a full-fledged conflict and disappear as if he had nothing to do with it?" I asked him.

"I'll get to that." Jack answered.

The stress of the day was wearing on Jack. He was seventy-eight years old and I had no idea if his heart would hold out. He was in pain, but I was beginning to realize that some of that pain couldn't be relieved by codeine. Confession might help, but he would carry this into eternity. One way or the other, he was desperate to tell me the whole sad story before he departed.

CHAPTER 28

Jack watched the news like a hawk on the morning of October 6, 1973. The war had started. On October 22, 1973, it ended just as abruptly. It was a stunning victory for the Israelis, but in addition to the loss of life and pride, the Syrians and Egyptians lost more territory. The prize for the Israelis in this bloody Crackerjack box was the Golan Heights. Still, it was an even bigger victory for American and international oil interests.

Jack chuckled at the thought of the Saudis, who were and are our "friends," as they "convinced" the other OPEC nations, right on cue, to cut back shipments to the western countries who supplied Israel with armaments. The announced reason was political, the unspoken one was financial.

He watched Veronica's plan being implemented almost perfectly. From early September to the beginning of November, oil production in domestic fields ground to a trickle. Oil processing at the refineries slowed to 40% of the norm for the late fall. It was a flawless execution by the oil business, and, moreover, of the American economy. It took only a short time for the price of gasoline in the U.S. to rise from $.25 to over $1.00 a gallon, with almost every gas station in the country out of gasoline at least one day a week. On the east coast, home heating oil became scarce overnight, rising from $.40 to over $1.40 a gallon, as reserves seemed to vanish down a dark hole in Staten Island. The shortages were the icing on the cake. Jack and the other oil executives knew that there was sufficient gasoline in reserve, but hiding these reserves through lost or falsified inventory reports made the embargo and the subsequent 3000% rise in imported crude oil prices, from $1.50 to over $30.00 a barrel, seem reasonable.

The gradual increase in OPEC oil shipments and the diminishing crude production at home, combined with the cover of Middle East turmoil, served to make what was a carefully orchestrated plan seem like a perfectly plausible coincidence.

Jack smiled at the Federal Government response to the crisis. They were AWOL. But then, one only had to remember that the Nixon administration, bogged down by scandal and taking a watch-and-see-what-we-can-get-out-of-this position, was very good at ignoring what was happening on their watch and, at padding their wallets by looking the other way at strategic moments.

HOG and every other oil company's gross profit margins from refining operations grew at the rate of seven dollars for every one dollar increase in the cost of a barrel of imported oil. Costs to refine oil rose, but disproportionately less. What was more significant to Jack was the discovery that international affairs could be manipulated so easily, and with impunity. It was a heady time as Jack realized that he could, in effect, rule the world by opening or closing a valve. It was all too simple. The country and the economy ran on oil. Whoever controlled that commodity controlled the economic future of America and in a very direct way the economic fortunes of rest of the world.

Veronica was elated, Cully was amazed, and Jack was very proud of his wife. Her germ of an idea had blossomed into the most significant act of larceny since John D. Rockefeller and the Robber Barons. She had done all the leg work and set up the liaison with OPEC, working behind the scenes to assure that all the players were on the team. Now it was Jack's turn to make sure that no one would try to derail them.

Jack wanted to secure the political support that would give the oil companies a free pass when public opinion turned against them. He saw that keeping things stirred up politically and economically would deflate any attempts to move against the oil industry. He reasoned that it's difficult to concentrate on causality when the economic carnivores were nipping at your hind end. He had no idea how right he was.

Jack promised the Republicans in the south support in the 1974 mid-term elections. The Democrats were at the GOP's heels over Nixon and the war and were definitely looking for scalps in the next election cycle.

Nixon was trapped in scandal, and the world was turned upside down. Vietnam was still a very hot topic, as the military began a strategic withdrawal that lead to us escaping like burglars caught in the act.

Jack said that Viet Nam was a losing proposition and when the area went communist as it would, it would take twenty years to sort everything out; but he also said that after the communists destroyed the economy, there would be opportunities for shadow companies to come in by the back door and make it financially attractive to which ever regime was in power to allow oil drilling.

⚓

Veronica was preparing for Cully's visit to New York for Thanksgiving. The holidays were coming and Strange and Jack met for a drink at the circular bar in Toots Shor's eatery. It was a popular place, with people coming and going after work and before the theater.

"What are you smiling about?" Jack asked Strange, as that was definitely out of character for him.

"I'm actually having fun," Strange answered perversely. "I haven't enjoyed anything as much since the big war."

"Here," Jack offered Strange a package wrapped in gay Christmas paper with ribbons and bows, "Veronica wrapped it. She thought it was for my secretary."

Strange laughed deeply. He had never received such an elegantly wrapped gift.

The package contained one thousand one-thousand-dollar bills. "This is only a small bonus. Expect one quarterly going forward."

After drinks, as they walked along Fifth Avenue, Jack asked Strange how he moved Syria and Egypt to attack Israel.

"I'm not sure it's wise to tell you," he answered, reluctant to share that kind of information with anyone. "But I trust you as much as I trust any man in a tight spot, so I'll give you the plain vanilla version. If you're ever questioned, you'll have enough information to make the questioner interested, but not enough to satisfy him or get yourself in Dutch."

"I appreciate your concern" Jack remarked naively.

"I'm not protecting you as much as I am covering my own ass." Strange replied.

"After you gave me the go ahead, I traveled to the Middle East and had my agents in the Arab world, who infiltrated the most anti-Israeli groups in Syria, Lebanon, Egypt, and Saudi Arabia, step up their efforts by feeding them money and munitions, and more importantly, information about Israeli plans for the occupied territories. Most of the information was of no real value, but it was always inflammatory. My agents kept the pot boiling and at the right time planted the story that Israel was going to make preemptive strikes in Egypt and Syria that reprised the strikes of the Six Day War."

"I'm amazed at the ease with which you do this," Jack said, "but go on."

"It didn't take long for this story to get traction in the Syrian and Egyptian military" Strange continued. "The generals put pressure on Nasser and Assad, who were skeptical, but didn't want the information to get to the public and risk an uprising. Then," he said, grinning at his own cunning, "at the right time, intelligence was passed that the Israelis would attack after Yom Kippur. That was all that was needed to light the fuse. The rest is history."

"I'm impressed at how you can play factions against each other and cause them to act with rumors and false intelligence," Jack commented. "I want to know if we can do something similar to keep the political fires lit at home. I want the public's attention off the oil companies and on issues about which they have little or no control."

"There is a way," Strange said thoughtfully. "As long as the Middle East is in turmoil, the price of oil will continue to escalate. If we continue to feed the conflicting factions money, arms, and reasons to fight, the situation there will occupy so much press time that everything else will be overshadowed. What isn't on the television isn't happening," Strange said with conviction.

"My resident spook is becoming a politician," Jack said laughing, "but how are you going to accomplish this without spilling the whole deal?"

"I've been working on a plan of my own for some time," Strange began. "The fabric of the Middle East is made of factions. On the one side are the sheikhs and the Shah. These men are absolute rulers who preside over their respective countries with an iron hand. On another side are the quasi-democracies. Both of these groups have one thing in common: They're under siege from the theocratic Muslims, who are trying to create Islamic states governed by Islamic law. Whether they are Sunni Muslims or Shi'ite Muslims, they're all constantly pulling at each other and are in a state of pandemonic equilibrium." Strange laughed at this novel turn of phrase.

"The wild card is Israel," he continued. "None of the players in the Arab world have much of a stomach for taking them on militarily. They know that the Israeli army and air force is equipped with the best armaments America can provide, and can take any of them out in an instant. They all hate Israel, perhaps even a little more than they hate each other. I believe," Strange went on, "that this witch's brew of conflicting ideologies, with billions of dollars at stake, can easily be manipulated with just a little tweaking."

"I agree," Jack said nodding.

"My thought," Strange said in a measured tone, "is to pass some money to the imams and mullahs who are railing against the Shah. I'd like to see how creating turmoil in Iran could affect the price of oil."

"While you're doing that, I have an idea about how to get an administration in the White House that might be sympathetic to oil and allow for some creative energy programs, like atomic, that would keep renewable energy off the grid until we've squeezed ever penny out of the petroleum dollar. There is a sizeable amount of research being done on solar and wind power, but much of it is over ten years out. Atomic energy is still the darling of the politicians and needs government support to get new plants on line. As long as this is out there, the public, which has the attention span of a gnat, will be placated.

"We'll meet again one week before Christmas," Jack said as they parted.

Walking home, he thought about finding political surrogates he could use to donate money to various candidates in the 1976 presidential election. He wanted someone who, unlike Johnson, a Texas oilman, would be more global and have more popular appeal. His thoughts wandered back to the Lake House and Reagan. He heard some rumblings that Reagan was going to seek the Republican nomination for president in 1976. But he knew that running in a general election against any Democrat would be difficult as the Nixon debacle just kept getting worse. He decided to watch the governor and test the political waters.

Veronica was waiting for him and he shared his thoughts with her.

"Money is the currency of politics and the first and best approach," she said. "Though I'm not sure how to make it look less like the quid pro quo it actually is."

"There are ways around that," Jack said. "There are political groups formed to promote causes. We would piggyback on them. Even with the changes introduced in '71 by the Federal Election Campaign law, Congress doesn't supervise groups that give campaign funds to them and these groups aren't going to turn down found money. The money can appear to come from an industry group no one thinks of as too political. I'll start on it tomorrow."

"The word around Wall Street is," Jack continued, "Watergate will be Nixon's undoing. House Republicans think the scandal will widen into the New Year. They're planning to ask Gerald Ford, the Speaker of the House, to convince Nixon to step down with the promise of a full pardon. That will put a lid on their mess and help them avoid getting completely swept away in the midterm elections."

"Can Ford win in 1976?" Veronica asked, thinking out loud. "If he can't, won't it be too soon after Watergate for them to risk putting someone like Reagan on the ticket?"

"I don't think Ford or Reagan can win in '76," Jack replied. "But 1980 poses the best opportunity for Reagan. Especially if we find a Democratic candidate in '76 who would be so over his head that the Washington establishment will chew him up and make him unelectable in 1980.

There are several Democrats who could fill that role. I've read about one who's looking into a potential run in 1976. He's the governor of Georgia, Jimmy Carter. My research tells me he'd be the best foil. He's honest and naïve enough to think he can swim against the Washington tide."

CHAPTER 29

"She's gone," Jack moaned disconsolately as he sat up with a painful jerk. The memory of that evening with Veronica, her beautiful gown, her perfume, the way her hair fell gently on her shoulders, and the grace of his vision of fifty-one years of marriage hit a nerve and he was crying. He described Veronica as his everything; wife, lover, and co-conspirator. She was his opposite; where Jack was rough around the edges, Veronica was smooth and polished. She was also, in every way, his intellectual equal.

Jack didn't care who saw him crying. What he created had swallowed whole everything he cared for. Veronica could not have survived the blasts, and if somehow she had, the lethal dose of radiation would take little time to end her life.

"Tell me about her," I asked sympathetically.

"I met her over fifty years ago," he said regaining his composure. "I was stunned when she walked into the room that first night. I was so taken aback by her beauty and poise, I forgot to let go of her hand after she offered it in greeting. More importantly, I forgot where I was and how I had gotten there. When Veronica took over for Cully and made the proposal that brought me into HOG, she could have asked me to sign up for the Foreign Legion and I would have walked to the nearest recruiting depot in Algiers."

"Then," he said smiling at the memory, "she took me to the veranda and kissed me as no other woman had ever done before.

She took care of the proposal and the wedding. I just grabbed on and tried not to fall off the most exciting ride of my life.

"She was a vision on our wedding day," Jack said as the memories came flooding back. "She outshone every woman at this very prestigious affair. We were married in the governor's mansion, and there were some astonishingly beautiful young women on the arms of some very old and wealthy Texas oilmen."

Jack spoke of their first years together. She had been his rock through orals and his doctoral dissertation at Baylor. But the tears came again as he spoke of her pregnancy and the birth of their son.

"She was my gift," Jack said in a voice full of gratitude. "I always felt that although it was a man's world, Veronica could wear their pants better than most of them. No matter what went on in my business life, she was my closest confidante and made sure that my scientific mind made good business decisions." Jack took a deep breath. The memory of Veronica was doubly painful for his complicity in her demise.

"She saw to our son's education. He possessed my scientific mind, and while Veronica nurtured his intellectual gifts she imparted her own grace and self-possession to her son. The boy was the best of both of us.

"She was as good at picking a wife for him as she was at picking me," he laughed as he choked back a tear. "She never told him who he was going to marry. She just put her choice in a room with Jack, Jr., and let nature take its course. She was even better at being a mother-in-law and a grandmother. When Jack the third was born, she was always there when she was needed. Her daughter-in-law didn't have to call. At other times, she would blend into the furnishings and wait until the next time her presence was required. It was much appreciated by young Jack and his wife.

"Her special grace was our most effective tool, especially after we entered the world of politics. She was active in the political arena throughout the eighties and early nineties charming money out of friends and business acquaintances for candidates who would help HOG financially and working against those who would injure it. After Clinton was elected, she took a break.

I asked Jack why Veronica would take a break from politics at such an exciting time.

"She smoked most of her adult life," he responded, "a habit I indulged in her though I didn't approve of it. She developed a cough and shortness of breath, our first clues that something was wrong. The news that she was in the beginning stage of emphysema was devastating. She had to change her lifestyle. Slowing down and giving up cigarettes wouldn't stop the inevitable, but it would extend the time before the disease would take her.

"She became less and less a public person," Jack went on sadly, "and spent much of her time helping raise her grandson."

Jack sat back and sighed deeply. He had come to the realization that among the millions of lives lost that day, Veronica was one of them, and it was his doing. His soul would be lost without her.

As I listened to him, I became less and less skeptical that this man had indeed set this cataclysmic event in motion.

CHAPTER 30

Cully arrived on Thanksgiving eve of 1973. Veronica could hardly contain herself and Jack was equally excited. They had not seen Cully since they had returned from the European gambit and they were looking forward to this wonderful reunion. Cully was exuberant about the shrinking supplies and escalating prices of gasoline and heating oil. Money was pouring in as the cost of crude oil from the Middle East, and their own crude, which sold on the open market, rose. The price of gasoline, heating oil, and their refined products was exploding.

"We have hit a gusher," he fairly shouted as they sat over a drink. "We're in big. I think it'll hit thirty dollars a barrel before we let loose again. I've been to so many luncheons this month with the boys from the oil companies that I can't even look at a chicken without gagging," he chuckled.

Jack tried to calm him with another cocktail, but Cully was on a roll, so they listened to him until he was too dry to talk any more and had to stop to take a drink.

Seizing the opportunity, Jack jumped in.

"We're going to back Reagan for president in 1980. We're not certain we can affect the 1976 presidential situation, but we're sure that '80 will be our year and we will own the White House."

Cully shook his head affirmatively. "I've favored what we've done because one company could point at another company as the reason for raising prices, and as long as we have a scapegoat,

I'm in for it. It could be dangerous" he said thinking as he spoke, "but then," he said smiling, "it could be the key to the future."

Jack sketched out his strategy in limited detail, knowing that while Cully could be trusted with the generalities of a plan, he was not good with too much knowledge. And, Jack knew that if it all came apart, the less Cully knew the better off he would be, especially if he were ever questioned by the authorities. Cully, a wily old fox himself, was never offended that Jack left some very obvious holes in everything he told him.

Jack was delighted at having his friend in New York and the visit was well spent filling in the general details of how they planned to proceed over the next few years. It was also an opportunity to make sure that Cully was reined in when it came to discussing how this all came about.

After a week of sightseeing and dining, Cully was safely back in Houston, and Christmas was fast approaching.

⚬⚬⚬

Strange was back from the Middle East with news and Jack was on his way to meet him in Greenwich Village. A few blocks north of the women's prison, at Tenth Street and Sixth Avenue, there was a delicatessen. The building above it was vacant and Strange had set up shop there.

When Jack got there, Strange was just putting away his electronic bug sweeping gear. Sandwiches and good cold beer were waiting.

"The word is" he handed Jack a beer as he spoke, "that the embargo will continue into March of 1974."

"That's good news," Jack mumbled as he ate his pastrami on rye. It was better than that. In five short months the price of oil would be changed forever upward. The plan was successful far beyond expectations.

"Have we done everything to keep the pressure on?"

"The trouble beginning in Iran," Strange reported, "is getting some traction, thanks to the money and weapons we're sending them. The Shah is shaky and his secret police are tightening the screws. The more pressure he applies, the worse his position becomes. The U.S. government is propping him up because of oil, but it will only take time and a push from the Iranian people, with a little help from us, to put the Shah out of business."

Jack mulled this over. "A dangerous situation in Iran will slow down shipments and send the market soaring. It's just a matter of picking the right moment."

Strange nodded his assent.

"We're going forward with our plan to get involved in presidential politics," Jack added. "We're going to get a friend to oil elected and keep the price pressure on through domestic energy policy.

Nixon and the Republicans are in trouble. Watergate has opened a serious can of worms. It seems less likely he'll make it through his term, and with the vice-president already gone, Gerald Ford will become president. He's a good man with a lot of support in the Republican Party, and he'll be hard to move out of the way in the primaries. It's just as well. The Democrats have plenty of fuel for their run at the White House, so waiting until 1980 for our candidate is a better plan."

Strange fell silent for a few moments and then he smiled. "Since we're sharing ideas," he began, "this is the perfect time for me to fill you in on a plan I've been developing for Iran. The events on the ground have exceeded my expectations and I've pushed ahead with some ideas."

What Strange began to unfold would not only guarantee turmoil in Iran and support their attempt to elect a friend to the White House, but it also had the potential to change history.

Smiling that very frightening smile of the cat who had cornered the rat, Strange said, "I have the apparatus in place to light the fuse that could push the Shah out, inflame the supporters of the mullahs and the ayatollah into an anti- American frenzy, and plant the idea that they could capture the biggest prize in Iran: the American Embassy."

Jack sat back in his chair and considered what Strange was promising he could deliver.

"How long could the Iranians hold the embassy before our military could mobilize and take it back?"

"They could hold the staff hostage," Strange said, "long enough to cause a major embarrassment to the president and set the stage for the 1980 election. As for a military response, there won't be one. There are several million disaffected Iranians who blame us for their problems. We'd have to fight them all with a burnt-out military short on men and morale."

"It will require precise planning and execution," Jack said in a cautionary tone, "but you wouldn't have told me about it if you couldn't do it."

Jack knew that he was into something that was not only dangerous, it was bordering on treason, but he had long since stopped troubling himself with legality or morality. He was too busy assuring the future to worry about anything but outcomes, so he put it out of his mind.

"Start to implement!" Jack almost shouted. "Do whatever is necessary, and have it ready to unfold in 1979.

There's a politician named Carter, the governor of Georgia, who's making noise as a potential candidate in 1976. With enough money thrown at the process, We'll get him elected. The professional politicians will marginalize him and leave him toothless, which will play into our hands. He'll be the perfect foil to hang this whole affair on and get Reagan elected in 1980."

Jack left with the agreement that they'd meet again in three months. The embargo would be ending and they would set the timing for this next phase of the plan.

Christmas came and with it a somewhat muted public celebration as consumers all over the country began to realize that their budgets were being busted initially by the cost of gasoline and heating oil, but subsequently by upward pricing pressure on virtually every product or service they purchased, most of which were dependent on some form of energy.

Salaries, which ranged from $6,000 to $12,000 for the average worker, were savaged. Not since the depression was the economy of the country in such upheaval. Nixon tried imposing price controls on some commodities, but the overall economy was taking its time making the correction forced on it by the ever escalating cost of oil. The cost of money was rising, putting more pressure on business, which passed increases along to the buying public, which led to higher prices for necessities—which, in turn, put more pressure on wage earners. The hole the public found itself in was growing deeper. People were forced to reach into savings and become two-income families to simply survive.

Veronica and Jack's Christmas was a season of great celebration. Christmas gifts were more lavish than usual. The party Veronica threw was grander than ever before. They were well known along Fifth Avenue as wealthy and sophisticated.

Their Christmas Eve dinner at the Four Seasons was lavish, followed by a stroll through Rockefeller Center and a nightcap at the Rainbow Room. It was a memorable evening.

"There are some new developments," Jack told Veronica as they strolled up Fifth Avenue toward home. "They're still in the formative stages but they will certainly keep the oil pot boiling. Iran is ripe for revolution and we can make it happen!"

"Can you really do that?" Veronica asked skeptically.

"I think we can push the radicals to the edge," Jack laughed, "with just a slight shove. They have an intense hatred for the U.S. and any opportunity to take a swipe at us should be attractive to them."

Veronica held his arm tightly and listened as he laid out the basics of Strange's plan for the Iranians and how the upheaval it would cause would push oil prices up to levels that could secure their position of enormous power and wealth. It was a very good Christmas indeed.

Strange returned to New York in April. The weather was turning warmer and the embargo was lifted. Oil prices were high and things couldn't be better. They met in Chinatown at the Wah Kee restaurant on Pell Street. It occupied an old brownstone with the upstairs for tourists and the basement, behind the kitchen, for regulars. Strange, in keeping with his m.o., entered through the rear door. Jack was in a private dining area that was sequestered from view. Here, over the best Chop Suey in New York, they set the timetable for one of the greatest embarrassments to the United States in its history.

"The structures are in place and secure. Money and arms will be easy to deliver. It won't take much. The Iranians are simmering and they don't look like they'll cool down anytime soon," Strange reported.

"Good. since our political and military support of the Shah won't change, no matter who is in the White House, we can play on that dislike for the U.S. The Iranians' memory of our assistance in overthrowing their democracy and returning the Shah to power is our biggest asset."

CHAPTER 31

I interrupted Jack's reverie with a resounding "HOLY SHIT".

"You and Strange were responsible for the attack on the embassy in Tehran? How did you do it and where did you get the set of balls to pull that off", I asked with both a trickle of disgust and a river of incredulity.

"It was relatively easy" Jack replied, as he started to relate the story of how Strange came to wield such influence in the Middle East.

"As the war in the north of France was winding down," Jack began, "Strange was sent south to the Italian border. Northern Italy was still occupied by the German Army with the help of Mussolini's Fascists. The allies had finally taken Rome and were looking to move further north while the D-Day push was moving east across France toward the Rhine. It was necessary to keep the Germans pinned down in Italy to prevent them from reinforcing the retreating German Army in France.

Strange crossed the Swiss border from France by train looking like a diplomat. He proceeded to the Free French Embassy where he was briefed on how he would move from the embassy to the countryside and on to Italy. He received his code words and location to meet the Italian partisans. Passing the roving patrol boats on Lago Maggiore was on him. He was moved out of the Embassy fairly easily as cars were moving in and out of the Embassy compound during the day, and hiding him in the boot of a sedan made him virtually invisible. Dressed as an Italian peasant, he crossed the alps near Ticino. He followed the valley south and found the boat hidden for him in Locarno. He rowed south on Lago Maggiore and as he approached the border he pulled to the shore and waited as the patrol boats passed every fifteen minutes. Then, as predicted by the weather experts the fog rolled in and silently he floated into Italy under a blanket so thick the patrol boats were forced to anchor. He crossed the lake and joined a group of Italian partisans in Varese and from there he was able to move freely.

The Germans could see that the tide of the war had turned inexorably against them and that their only hope was to reach the Fatherland in an attempt to help insure a stalemate which might lead to a truce and save Germany from total defeat. Strange and his cadre of battle hardened Italians were going to do everything in their power to prevent that from happening.

There was only one sure way out of Italy for the Germans; through the flats north of Venice, into Czechoslovakia, and north through Austria. There were many ways the partisans, now well supplied by the Allies, could make this sure way out into a very sore way out for the Germans.

Strange and his group moved to the hills overlooking the wine growing region of Friuli-Venezia Giulia where they were joined by additional groups of partisans. Here they remained attacking retreating German convoys until the final surrender of the German Army in May of 1945."

"The OSS," Jack continued, "the forerunner of the CIA, asked Strange to stay on in Rome and set up an operation to cover the Middle East. This was not going to be too difficult since the Middle East was teeming with people who spied for the Allies against the Germans. He spent several years vetting holdovers from the war and setting up his cover as a merchant who traded in rugs and antiquities through his branch locations in all the major cities of the fertile crescent and deep into Iran. He moved rugs, and many other products to all parts of the world. He staffed his operations with people who he recruited as spooks being careful to assure that each location knew nothing of anyone in other locations beyond that they were buyers who worked for Strange's importing business."

"How is that possible without being detected?" I asked naively.

"Over the years of buying in places like Syria and Iran," Jack went on, "Strange did favors for people on both sides. He was thought of, by the Shah's men, as a man of wealth and influence who could be counted on. He was equally known by the radicals for all the same reasons. Each side hid their relationship with Strange from the other to assure his continued cooperation and assistance.

Over time, the people he recruited and cultivated for his spy network branched out in pyramid type networks and recruited and cultivated groups of their own. In every case, the network was protected by the fact that each person in the network only knew the person who recruited them. If things got bad, damage to the group as a whole was minimized.

When we discussed the embassy gambit," Jack explained, "Strange already had the vehicle in place to make it happen. He passed money through his buying locations instructing his own network to see that this money reached the radicals in Tehran. His people, in turn passed money down their pyramids diluting the amount each person had to give to the radicals and avoiding any raised eyebrows. After the money was spread around, the networks passed the word that the embassy in Tehran would be a very good target."

"And that's all they had to do?" I asked incredulously.

"Yes!" Jack answered. "The history of the people of the Middle East taught Strange one important lesson. Like the proverbial elephant, Arabs and Persians alike never forget an injury. Favors, not so much, but if you insult them or harm them in any way, they will be your enemy forever. The U.S. did that to them in 1952."

All I could do was silently try to catch my breath and wonder how many more men like Strange were and are out there stirring the pot. I sat back as Jack continued his ever more incredible adventure.

CHAPTER 32

Jack sought out leaders in Democratic Party circles as the Summer of 1974 went and took Nixon with it. He observed a lack of direction there and used that weakness and his wealth to advantage. He gave these Democrats promises of support and money for their run at the White House in exchange for input, which could be read as approval, in the selection of a candidate. It took very little more than his signature on a check the size of a city block to convince them that Carter was in their best interests.

Jack spent much of his time talking with Cully about generic oil business, including production, drilled and capped wells, and prices. He kept discussions about politics to a minimum keeping anything he wouldn't want Cully to repeat out of the discussion.

Cully was very effective when it came to getting other oil company executives on board for one of their schemes, as long as HOG kept them out of the line of fire. So, it fell to him to enlist the oil companies in supporting Carter. It was always a pleasure for Cully to twist the arm of a competitor with some really old Kentucky sipping whiskey and a steak the size of a Brahma bull. He was very well suited for the work. He communicated to Jack that while some of them might have to swallow hard, they would all get on board. Cully hadn't steered them wrong thus far.

Jack was sending thousands of dollars through surrogates to campaign committees in Georgia, Washington and New York to help get Carter through the Democratic Party primaries. The

Watergate scandal and the defeat in Vietnam left the voters with a sour taste for Republicans. Getting Carter nominated would be the toughest part. Once there, it would not be difficult to push him over the finish the line. People were clamoring for change.

CHAPTER 33

In the Spring of 1975, Jack and Strange sat in a restaurant on the corner of 161st Street and River Avenue, across from the bleachers at Yankee Stadium, and discussed the progress of the Iranian gambit. Strange reported that the situation in Iran was static and contacts in country were in place and waiting for a signal. As long as the money and arms kept coming, they would stay that way.

Strange pointed out something of interest that was happening in Iraq. The Baath Party, a Sunni Muslim group, was taking control. They were favored by the British, and their leader, an engaging young man named Saddam Hussein, was someone to be watched. There was talk of him becoming president of Iraq.

"What do you know about him," Jack asked?

"He's a savage man, but very smart. The Iranian Shi'ite Muslims don't trust the Sunnis and there's talk of fighting. It could work for us."

"Do you think there's any chance it could affect our plans?"

"I don't think so," Strange answered thoughtfully, "but I'll watch it closely."

"I've made additional arrangements to fund your operations through a subsidiary company in the Caribbean. This will continue to keep the money offshore and untraceable while giving you another source of funds. I've deposited a substantial amount of money in a company account that will allow you to draw an additional half a million dollars a month. These are the numbers you'll need to draw down on the account. If I need to get to you," Jack said, "I'll use the mail drop, otherwise we'll lay low until I contact you."

———❧❧❧———

Veronica and Jack spent the remainder of 1975 and the beginning of 1976 counting money and using it to position Carter to win the Democratic Party nomination, and once done, working toward his election.

Jack watched as Reagan tried unsuccessfully to garner the Republican nomination, due in part to Jack's quiet sabotage of his campaign and in part to the reluctance of the Republicans to make much noise to unseat Gerry Ford as the Republican nominee. It did, however, set the table for 1980, especially if Ford lost to Carter, which he would with Jack's help.

Jack recalled election night 1976, as Veronica hosted a cocktail party for some friends and acquaintances. It was a somber evening for all but she and Jack.

Veronica used the occasion to start a movement among this group that was to contribute greatly to the election of Reagan. What her friends didn't know was that the field would be tilted in Reagan's favor.

———❧❧❧———

Jack was sitting up a little more comfortably. The talk of Veronica seemed to be an anesthetic for him. I asked him why he seemed to be moving through years very quickly and leaving out large chunks of history. His answer was simple. He told me that once the plan was operating successfully it took on a life of its own and there was no real need to do much more than count money and wait for the next opportunity to foment chaos and ratchet up the price of oil.

CHAPTER 34

Jack painted Jimmy Carter as a God-fearing, honorable man with some good ideas from outside the beltway. In fact, they were so good, and so naïve, that he pissed off nearly every bureaucracy and bureaucrat in Washington, not to mention Congress. His insistence on changing the way that bureaucratic Washington operated, and the strident attitude of his chief of staff doomed him to failure. He took on the federal government's budgeting process with an eye toward cutting waste and pork. The budgetary process which appeared to have been in place since the Revolutionary War, simply took last year's dollars and added more. Carter, through what he called Zero Based Budgeting, required federal agencies to start each budget year from zero and justify the need for funds for the upcoming year. He lost the bureaucracy, lost the Congress next, business followed, and it was soon apparent that he was going to fail miserably.

Carter did try some innovative ideas. Putting solar collecting panels on the roof of the White House and raising CAFÉ standards, the miles per gallon mandate to the car manufacturers, were both forward-looking ideas. They were a no-brainer to Jack and company, but did worry some of the other business leaders who went along with getting Carter elected.

Jack assured them that this was just a temporary bump and that these nuisances would last only as long as it took Reagan to get elected. But it would be a long four years.

The economy was equally uncooperative for Carter, and with the help of the financial institutions, stagflation, the merging of a stagnant economy and galloping inflation, pushed the prime rate, the rate of interest that banks borrow from the Federal Reserve, over 14%, which in turn pushed consumer interest rates up to alarming levels. Carter quickly lost the confidence of his party, and worse, the people. The table was set for 1980.

The last years of the 1970's where as bad as the previous seven. The country spent the decade in turmoil. The war in Vietnam took up the first three years and was all the news until it was joined by Watergate, the oil embargo, Nixon's disgrace, a terrible economy, and finally, under Carter, Iran.

Strange and Jack arrived simultaneously for their meeting at the Central Park Zoo. It was late in the summer of 1979 and they had not seen each other for some time. Communication through the mail drops kept them up to date but some things were best done without a paper trail.

"Can you get the Iranians to move by year's end?" Jack asked. "The winter doldrums will be deeper this year due to the economy. It would be the perfect start to the presidential election year".

"Yes, they're waiting for the word as we speak. Three months and done," Strange said.

———◈◈◈———

Jack characterized Strange as a man of his word and as such somehow he made it happen. He took the Iranian people's anger at the Shah for his ever-increasing despotism and cruelty, distrust and enmity of America for our role in the overthrow of their democratically elected government which returned the Shah to power in the 1950's, melded it with the fanatical religious zeal of the Islamic theocrats, and lit the fuse.

Strange placed some of his best operatives in student groups at the University in Tehran. These groups were fomenting revolution and the overthrow of the Shah. His operatives played nearly invisible roles and using information fed to them by other of Strange's operatives, they were able, quietly and unseen, to warn the students of impending raids by the Shah's secret police, spread rumor and innuendo about American moves to bolster the Shah, and, in general, fan the flames. Strange had operatives in the Shah's government, too; he rigged the game.

In November of 1979, the American Embassy in Tehran, along with the Iranian government was overrun by Iranian students and supporters of Islamic theocracy. The U.S. meddling in Iran, the Shah's disdain for his own people, the opportunity to seize power by the religious fanatics, mixed with a bit of incendiary material supplied by Strange, set the pot to boil over. U.S. embassy employees were taken hostage and paraded blindfolded in front of television cameras. Pictures of our national embarrassment were broadcast all over the world.

This affront to the U.S. by a nation perceived as camel jockeys was greeted by the American people with total cluelessness. The people had lost faith in the government and were at a loss to do anything other than rant. The Carter administration attempted to mount a rescue mission, but it failed miserably. This only added more fuel to the fire.

Strange, again strategically placed, was alerted to the small buildup of troops the Carter Administration sent to free the hostages, and planted information in the right places. This information was leaked to the Iranians, and the rescue attempt was over before it started along with Carter's presidency.

CHAPTER 35

J ack and Strange met again in Central Park in July of 1980. Jack told Strange about his excitement over the coming election campaign and though Reagan was holding his own in the polls, it wasn't a sure thing. There was the specter of Carter possibly securing the release of the hostages and stealing the election back from Reagan. He described how Reagan's closest advisors had approached him about an alternative strategy should Carter succeed in striking a deal to free the hostages. Reagan's people wondered if Jack had contacts on the inside who would be able to quietly make a deal with the Iranians to hold the hostages until after the election. Using the Iranian need for armaments to fight their war against Iraq as bait, could he make a deal to covertly supply them with Tow missiles in exchange for their cooperation?

Jack took only a few days to answer. Reagan's people could supply the munitions, but couldn't be directly involved in any part of the deal. There had to be plausible deniability for all concerned. He would handle it, but needed a person in the White House as liaison. His payback would be a few favors from the new administration. He wanted a moratorium on offshore oil drilling. It was the one piece of the oil equation, offshore drillers being a breed apart, that he could not control and the moratorium would make it a non-issue. Their answer was yes. The arrangements would be made.

At the beginning of this intrigue, Jack didn't know that the back end of the transaction was drug purchases to fund the very right-leaning death squads of the Contras in Central America that Strange had set up. Upon learning this, however, it didn't cause him more than a moment's hesitation.

"We need to get ahead of Carter's people," Jack told Strange as they walked through the park in the early evening, Strange confirmed that the Carter Administration had contacted the Iranians through back channels. He knew that Jack wanted it stopped.

"I've stopped it," Strange told Jack with finality.

"I'll let them know."

Arms shipments would be diverted from South America to the Middle East. This was going forward without a hiccup.

CHAPTER 36

Jack stopped his narrative for a moment and told me gravely, "I stepped over the line several times and there was no going back. It was one thing to foment war and destruction between other countries, but to cause the rescue mission to fail and subsequent deaths of American soldiers along with helping keep the Embassy hostages locked up was treason. I knew it, but I was ready to begin a new era of corporate control of the government of the United States."

I asked him what it was about Reagan that he found so attractive?

"Reagan was an actor who craved money and fame," Jack said simply. "He would do what he could to assure that he had both. His plan to stimulate the economy by lowering taxes was a ruse given to him by an "economist" named Laffer. Laffer came out of the University of Chicago business school. While he was not the only one in the Reagan administration who pushed this economic model, he was certainly one of the best known. It became known as "trickle-down economics". The theory posited that if taxes were lowered on the wealthiest, they, in turn, would invest those tax saving in businesses thus creating new jobs. It was nice on paper but the outcome, which saw us move from the largest creditor nation to the largest debtor nation, was devastating to all but the wealthiest. While the outcome was the beginning of a thirty year slide for the middle class, it was a bonanza for me and the top tier of Americans. Reagan also took a laissez-faire attitude toward government regulation, which became a license to steal for business throughout the economy. As a businessman, the Reagan years couldn't have been better.

I had engineered the election of 1980 which brought Ronald Reagan to the White House and with him economic and regulatory plans that would be a huge boon to HOG. As I said, it was a less than brilliant plan: reduce taxes on the wealthiest individuals and corporations with the idea that the beneficiaries would use the money for new investment and job creation. It was designed to fail and it did so admirably.

Unemployment was problematic when Reagan took office. When it shot up to 13% during the third year of his first term, and was linked with his inability to get those wealthy recipients of his tax breaks to stay home with their money, it was time to raise taxes. Reagan seeing the writing on the wall, began a series of what would be 11 tax increases which would save his presidency."

"A major part of Reagan's overall plan," Jack continued, "which coincided with my plan for corporate control of government, was the dissolution of the parts of the federal government that regulated many of the most important corporate functions. Reagan's people called it deregulation, and sold it as a cost-cutting device that would allow for business growth and ultimately more jobs and a stronger economy. I saw it as a license not only to steal, but to make the rules."

"So what happened," I asked Jack naively?

Laughing so hard it hurt, he asked me, "Where have you been for the last 30 years", trying to stifle his amusement because it really did hurt!

"Living underground to escape my demons" I answered.

"Sorry," Jack responded kindly, "You were in Vietnam?"

"Yes" I replied.

"Here's how it went." Jack continued. "New Year's 1981, arrived with a renewed hope that this President would bring much needed change and direction to a country seemingly adrift, especially to the average guy who had given his sweat and tears in Europe, Korea, and Vietnam. Hope was eternal. Reality sucked."

"The inauguration came, and so did the hostages. It was so perfect that it wasn't. But nobody complained. After the 70's, anything that made people feel better was embraced, whether it had an air of truth or the smell of a put up. The country spent the 80's adapting to cultural change, licking it wounds from the 60's and 70's and not paying attention.

America was transitioning from a nation that put men on the moon and brought them home safely through government sponsored programs to a nation that was told by it's president that it needed to duck when the government showed up to lend a hand. All the while the government under Reagan was passing billions of dollars to me and the wealthiest Americans and charging it to the people's credit card. It was utter simplicity. Keep government spending for defense and earmark programs at very high levels, lower taxes to starve out poverty programs, and borrow to cover the difference."

"Why was this allowed to happen?" I again asked.

"Historians who study the rise and fall of great powers" Jack explained, "tell us that the lynchpin that holds it all together is economics. Cultural issues may inflame differences, but they rarely take down an empire. The inability to maintain economic equilibrium is the eroding force in the fall of even the most powerful.

So also with the U.S. The onset of the conservative movement had begun in 1964 with Barry Goldwater, a true conservative, a "pay as you go Republican." The people in the Reagan White House were conservative in name only. They dressed in the garb of fiscally responsible representatives but this merely cloaked their neoconservative beliefs that business, not people, was the driving force in the U.S. and must be unfettered by regulations and regulators."

"Smaller government was their goal" Jack went on. "It was a simple process. Starve the beast by lowering taxes on the wealthiest, deregulate business and privatize government functions. The most significant example of this was the Saving & Loan debacle of the late 80's. Junk bonds, with interest rates as high as 13% and ratings as low a zzz, were sold to S&L institutions on the promise that they could resell them for more. Unfortunately, and to the detriment of the U.S. middle class taxpayer, this glorified Ponzi scheme fell apart when the buyers dried up and the S&L's were left with worthless paper and the taxpayers were left with the bill. People who wanted to know how this happened were told this was the "free market'. Where were the regulators? Shelved! When the dust settled taxpayers had to cover the bailout of the Savings & Loan institutions and in turn Reagan was forced to raise taxes in 1986. And what was the bill for all this? The tab turned out to be about four trillion dollars."

"Hog and the other oil companies stabilized oil prices and there was little movement for several years. People complained about the cost of gasoline, but it was more a residual whine than a demand that something be done. Another two or three years like this and the time would be right to ratchet up the prices again."

"I sound like a broken record," I said wryly, "but how did the people let this happen?"

"Reagan had one endearing charm," Jack said, "he could make feel good speeches. He kept the middle-class believing that the best days were yet to come, knowing all the while that the upward transfer of the nation's wealth was only just beginning."

"Reagan's term saw government oversight disappear in virtually every industry from the airlines to motor transport. The principle strike, a blow to the heart of the Constitution, was in the news arena. He saw to the repeal of the law that precluded consolidation of radio and print media within the same city. This law stood for decades and its repeal allowed these media outlets to fall into the hands of people who favored the neoconservative positions, effectively cutting off factual and in-depth coverage of issues that were of importance to the public at large. This allowed the administration and corporations to plunder the national treasury unnoticed. As more and more industries shed the shackles of government regulation, more and more money found its way into the pockets of lawmakers from both parties. The table was set for a fascist-style government."

"This was also the beginning of an era of warfare, and yet another economic boom for the oil industry. War was the other necessary ingredient to keep the people's focus off their pocketbooks and on the "enemy" foisted on them by whatever administration was in power. It was Orwell's *1984*, with life imitating art and a perfect ploy for the Republican administration and played into HOG's hand as well. Armies still ran on food and fuel."

CHAPTER 37

Jack's involvement in Reagan's run as president began in the shadow of a backroom deal to free the Embassy hostages. Reagan took it from there progressing through the air traffic controllers strike and firing, tax cuts for the top earners that depleted the Treasury, an attack on an island called Granada under the guise of freeing some American medical students from the oppression of the Cuban military and making Americans feel good about our military again, lots of really good speeches, and coming full circle back to Jack with Iran-Contra.

The end of Reagan's second term was approaching when the story of how the hostages were held until after the election was leaked to the press. Congressional Democrats, who were asleep for over six years, saw an opportunity to tarnish Reagan and elevate their chances in the 1988 presidential contest. They and the Reagan Administration settled on a sacrificial lamb, Jack's contact in the White House. The hearings made for very good morning television. The details were lurid and left the country with no doubt that someone in the administration played fast and loose with the hostages, while giving aid and comfort to our enemy, Iran!

In the end, the low level flunky who worked out the details of the arms for hostages trade was found culpable, but with the fix in, was exonerated on a technicality. Jack, somewhat relieved that this was over, knew that Reagan's Justice Department wouldn't pursue this any farther, regardless of the outcry from the Democrats.

Jack was busy arranging support for George Bush, the elder, as the election season of 1988 was approaching. Spending without the tax revenue to support it forced Reagan to raise taxes in 1986. Bush chose the mantra of "No New Taxes" to hold the Republican base and the independents in place. That suited Jack's purpose. The country was recovering from its collective nervous breakdown and was feeling a bit more positive, but the economy was still stagnant.

It was a good time for HOG and the other oil companies, who following HOGS lead, were making billions. Wisely, Jack left things alone in the Middle East while the Soviets embarked on the destruction of their empire. All through the years of the Cold War, they attempted to keep up with the U.S. in production of advanced weapon systems. These high-tech items cost a barrel of money and the Soviet economy was not nearly productive enough to keep apace of the U.S.

While the U.S. was building up Saddam Hussein in Iraq, the Russians were engaging in a losing struggle in Afghanistan that would take nearly ten years and leave them bankrupt.

Jack followed the Soviet incursion into Afghanistan for several years. Afghanistan was flush with untapped oil and mineral reserves that were of great value to HOG and the other American oil companies. The Soviets were intent on building a gas pipeline across the country and when they were unable to negotiate for the right of way, they decided to just take it. What they didn't bargain for was the tenacity of the Afghanis or the amount of support they garnered from around the Muslim world and the NATO countries. He believed that this war would have a short shelf life, but he soon saw that it would be long and costly to the Soviets. His interest grew exponentially. Jack saw the news from Afghanistan, the enmity between Islamic factions exhibited by the Iraqis and the Iranians, who spent much of the 1980's bombing and gassing each other in a horrific war, the rhetoric against Israel, and the pervasive hatred of virtually everything on the Muslim street as the stuff of continuing conflict and greater profits.

He supported the downfall of the Soviet empire, but was also aware that the groups who fought them in Afghanistan were dangerously single-minded fundamentalists who supported Muslim world domination by any means necessary. One such group, Al Qaeda, received support from the U.S. government, which supplied its leader, Osama bin Laden—a Saudi, whose family was close to Vice-President Bush—with money and weapons. Conservatives in Washington saw this as the best of all worlds: someone else fighting the Soviets, and draining their economy without bloodshed on the American side.

Jack arranged a meeting with Strange in New York. They were involved in intrigues for thirty years now and were trusted friends. Still, he didn't reveal Strange's existence to anyone. They convened their meeting at a bar in Bayside, a once-tiny hamlet on the north shore of Long Island, a short commuter train ride from Manhattan. McElroy's Tavern was a local haunt of the moderately upscale Long Island Railroad set. It had the longest bar in the city and served a fairly good dinner in the usually overcrowded and noisy restaurant.

Strange and Jack sat in McElroy's on a Tuesday evening planning their next foray into Middle East affairs guaranteeing a spike in oil prices. It was almost too easy. The U.S. government was propping up Saddam Hussein and giving him support in exchange for oil. The Russians, attempting to curry favor, gave him weaponry and support for his regime in the early days. Russian equipment was substandard and lacking spare parts. This was no matter to Hussein. His army, such as it was, was all he needed to keep a chokehold on the throat of Iraq. Politically, the Baath Party, populated by Sunni Arabs, who represented 20% of Iraq's population, was in control of the country. If you were a Sunni in Saddam's Iraq, life was fine as long as you kept quiet. If you were a Shi'ite, the other major sect, you were subject to hardship and apt to be tortured or killed if you protested the conditions.

There was a feeling in oil circles, and in the government, that Saddam was getting too cozy with the Russians. The "evil empire" was nearing its end and glasnost was the operative word in the late 1980's, but the Russians would emerge from the breakup of the USSR as a player. Jack knew that to maintain control in that part of the world, Saddam Hussein would have to be roped, tied, branded, corralled, and when under control, would provide the necessary pressure on Iran to keep things in the region in balance. Jack and Strange saw this as the next best opportunity to elevate oil prices and planned to make Saddam an issue and raise the Middle East pot to a roiling boil.

"He wants Kuwait," Jack said, more a statement than a question.

"Yes, it's a Shi'ite territory with oil," Strange replied, "and an ally of Iran during the war with Iraq. Some Iraqis look on Kuwait as a province of Iraq."

"Can you plant the seed that the U.S. might look the other way if he took Kuwait?" Jack queried.

"Saddam already believes the U.S. is only interested in his oil and wouldn't interfere," Strange answered.

"The neocons want Iraq. They may or may not stay out of it. No matter, it will keep the pot boiling either way."

The conversation turned to Afghanistan. Jack wanted Strange's opinion of the potential outcome and its effect on the Middle East.

"Afghanis are fierce fighters," Strange offered. "The Mujahedeen are savage and use terror tactics against the Soviets. They're religious radicals who will blow themselves up for Islam and should not to be taken lightly."

Strange agreed to keep a weather eye out for this group and see if they posed any threat to their plans. Strange and Jack were good at manipulating events, but neither of them saw it as anything more than protecting what they had built. Jack put any thought of the morality of their actions out of his mind, and it never entered Strange's.

CHAPTER 38

Jack helped engineer the election of George Bush. He was batting a thousand getting presidents elected. Money was now the currency of politics and when you threw enough in the right places, you controlled the outcome of any election. This philosophy works in the opposite direction as well. Enough money was contributed to the right Democrats to insure the nomination of Michael Dukakis. Dukakis, who lost big, did the rest.

Dukakis was an American of Greek extraction, and a politician who lacked the instincts of his opponent. He was fair game for the Republicans in the 1988 election, who 'Willie Hortoned' him while he "tanked" himself, literally.

Jack couldn't help being amused by the pictures giving credence to the adage that they are really worth a thousand words. Dukakis riding in an army tank looking like Mad Magazine's Alfred E. Neuman, with that 'what, me worry?' grin, was worth ten thousand. Add in the release for a furlough of a convicted murderer and rapist who committed another murder during this furlough, while Dukakis was governor, and the election contest was over before it started.

Jack was at home with Veronica the week after the election when the call came in. Cully was in the hospital.

"We're going to Houston," Jack said, trying to hide his concern. "Cully had a heart attack."

"How bad," Veronica asked as she packed their bags?

"He's stable, but they've found arterial blockage and as soon as they determine how extensive, he's going into surgery."

The flight to Houston on their private jet was several hours long and they arrived at the hospital as Cully was waking up in intensive care, still in a fog of anesthesia. He was pale and withdrawn for his seventy plus years and they could see through his gown that he was bandaged from the base of his throat to the top of his abdomen. His surgeon was there to issue post-operative orders and they were able to discuss Cully's prognosis.

"He'll be all right," the surgeon told them, "with rest, a good diet, and exercise. The recovery will take several months, and he cannot be allowed to work. The bypass was successful, but he must avoid excessive stress for the remainder of his life."

Veronica and Jack knew this was a death sentence for Cully. He was a wildcatter who knew only one thing, where to drill the next well. All the deals he'd made over Texas beef and Kentucky bourbon log jammed his arteries and put him in this position. Not being able to do this would be as good as putting him in the ground.

"How am I going to tell him?" Jack asked Veronica for some guidance.

"Leave that until later," Veronica advised. "Let's just get him back on his feet first."

It felt good to be back in Houston and he and Veronica spent the evening revisiting the places they enjoyed for the many years they lived there. After a quiet dinner in the hotel restaurant, they sought the comfort of their suite and some much needed rest. There was much to attend to tomorrow.

The night's rest was a tonic for both Veronica and Jack, and a good breakfast capped the morning. As they were leaving the hotel to go to the hospital, a limousine pulled up and a rather large man pushed them into the back seat of a Texas-sized Cadillac stretch limousine with impenetrable tinted windows. It was deja vu, complete with J. B. smiling like a Cheshire cat.

"You'll never grow up," Veronica laughed and hugged him. Jack just smiled.

J. B. flew all night to be with his father. He hadn't slept, but that was not unusual for this perpetual teenager. He was in Sumatra supervising a test well when the news reached him. He went to the hospital and found out from the charge nurse that Jack and Veronica were already there and where they could be reached.

"I'll be staying in Houston from now on," he told them. The implication was that he would be taking control of HOG.

"That will happen over my dead body—or J.B.'s," Jack whispered to himself angrily.

When they arrived at the hospital, Veronica went to Cully's room but Jack caught J. B. by the arm. "Come with me," he demanded, escorting him to the first unoccupied area he could find.

"These are the hard facts. HOG is a public company with a board of directors, of which I am the chairman. Cully has been CEO, but only in name. I've been running the company for over fifteen years, and I am not in any hurry to step aside. If you have a problem with that you can take it up with the board. Otherwise, you'll continue to do what you're paid handsomely to do."

J. B., not at all cowed, looked at him and smiled. "I know what you're up to and I'll do whatever the hell I please," he said with all the brass he could muster. "And if you don't like it, I'll take my story to the newspapers."

Jack left J. B. without saying another word and visited with Cully, who looked a bit better than he did the night before.

He was silent in the cab on the way back to the hotel. Veronica knew that there was trouble brewing with J.B., but she would wait to talk to him at the hotel. She had developed the healthy sense of paranoia that keeps conspirators silent in public.

"What does he want?" she asked, when they were safely in their room.

"The company!"

"He's joking." She almost laughed out loud. "What will you do, Jack?"

"I'll leave it to the board of directors," he said, lying to Veronica for the first time since they met. In truth, he signaled Strange to contact him at the hotel in Houston when he got the news about Cully. He was suspicious of J.B. since his father sent him to Indonesia, and planted a trusted employee to work at that site and keep tabs on him. This inside man reported that J. B. was skimming money from the company along with using his mouth more than his brain, bragging to anyone and everyone that when his father dropped dead he would control HOG. Now that it looked like his father might actually drop dead, it was his time to act.

The phone rang as Veronica was changing to go shopping. It was Strange.

"The hotel bar," he said.

"As soon as I put Veronica in a cab."

Ten minutes later Jack and Strange were sitting in the bar.

"Can you silence J.B?" Jack asked. "He's been skimming expense money and overcharging HOG for replacement parts bought locally. He has in excess of ten million dollars in an Indonesian bank vault that he's not about to leave behind."

"Yes," said Strange. "I'll make the arrangements. He'll have an unfortunate accident when he returns to Asia to close up his operation.

⸻ ❧ ⸻

Several days later, Veronica and Jack prepared to leave Houston with the assurance that Cully would be fine. He was up and feeling better and agreed, upon pain of death, literally, to follow the doctor's orders.

Jack watched with veiled amusement as J. B. swaggered into the HOG offices and was given a hero's welcome. He stayed there for several days, and to J.B.'s mind was getting everyone used to his style of running things. He left for Sumatra just after Thanksgiving. He was to be back just after New Year's Day, 1989.

Jack later learned from Strange that J. B. arrived in Indonesia a very tired but very self-satisfied man. He had the appearance of one who believed he was in control. On the plane back, he wrote down all he knew about HOG's conspiracies, planning to keep those papers as an insurance policy.

Making his way directly to the bank, he took along his oversized attaché case, which carried his papers, and an empty duffel bag to pack the money in. He was to take some time off before returning to Houston, and planned to spend the Christmas season in Europe. He would turn the operation over to his second-in-command and get out of this jungle in no more than two days. He was finally coming out of exile and would show them how it gets done.

J. B. finished his business in the bank and headed to his office to collect his personal belongings and destroy the paper trail that could expose his embezzlement. Walking into the building that housed the HOG operation in Sumatra, he was jumped by two men. It took only a few moments for J. B. to die.

The press reports, which were sketchy, told of an American oilman who was killed at a local office complex. Robbery was suspected. Jack smiled at the news, having become hardened to people who would destroy what he built, even if it was the son of his best friend.

CHAPTER 39

Jack described Bush's first year in the White House as more of the same. There was the usual clamor about gridlock in Congress and the economy. It was, however, a good year for HOG. Prices dropped a bit at the pump and the constant complaining about the high price of oil went silent.

Strange, now retired, was living in Rome and being paid handsomely to be Jack's eyes and ears abroad. He came to New York in the late fall of 1989 to meet with Jack at the fountain in Central Park. It was snowing as Jack turned into the park where 5th Avenue meets 59th Street. Approaching the fountain, he saw two men accost Strange. They had him, one on each arm, and were taking him toward a wooded area further into the park. It began to snow harder. Jack followed at a distance keeping them in sight but making not a sound on the soft snow. Strange and his kidnapers came to an underpass of one of the few roads that traverse the park. They stopped and the men made Strange kneel down with his back to them. Jack, coming quietly on this scene, drew the pistol that Strange had given him in Rome all those years ago and without hesitation fired two shots killing both of the kidnapers. Strange smiled as they took the identification of the men and made the scene look as if they had been robbed and murdered by one of the many drug addicts who frequented the park.

"These two are Russians" Strange fairly spat out the word, "they were probably sent by the KGB. They have been after me for some time. Fortunately, they are as inept as you are timely"

"We better move quickly" Jack said. "If those two were not here by accident, there may be more."

"I agree" Strange replied, "although, I recognize these two. They were likely working alone and settling a score from previous contacts I've had with them.

"Looks to me like it's two to nothing in your favor," Jack laughed.

"Anything but a shutout is a loss" Strange chuckled.

"What's happening in Iraq?" Jack queried as they hustled away towards 5th Avenue.

"I've baited the hook and Saddam has taken it. But the region is becoming even more fanatical. The Israelis have a nuclear weapon. The Iranians are determined to get one.

The defeat of the Soviet Union has given the Islamic fundamentalists a stronghold in Afghanistan, anyone spoiling for a fight can find one. It's becoming critically dangerous over there."

"If history holds true," Jack said smiling, "there will be a spike in oil prices as the Saudis, who use any excuse to raise prices, will demand to be protected from the Iraqis, as they slow down production. Futures markets will heat up, and traders, sensing a disruption in production or shipments, thanks to Kuwait's strategic location on the Persian Gulf, will pay higher and higher prices until the frenzy ends."

"I agree with your assessment."

"When do you think it will happen?" Jack asked.

"Not until next summer, Saddam wants to solidify his position in the north. He'll ask the U.S. government for their take on a move like this. My CIA contacts tell me that Bush will ignore him."

"I'm here in New York to do some much delayed site seeing, but I better be on my way back to Rome, I'll signal you if I hear anything. This incident confirms it. I've noticed some increased interest in my activities from a source I haven't been able to place until now. It's still may be nothing, but…" his voice trailed off as he took his leave.

---o/o/o---

Jack and Strange knew that Saddam was going to attack Kuwait, but neither Strange nor Jack could have imagined what would play out as a result.

Jack received a call from Strange at midnight the 1st of August 1990.

"Tomorrow!" was all he said.

Strange's agents passed the word that Saddam was about to move against Kuwait. The beginning of what would be the end of life as Jack and Strange knew it had started.

CHAPTER 40

Jack lurched up and howled in pain. He needed more pain killer to keep him going. He was crying, less because his leg hurt than for what he had done. He was at the point in the tale that laid the blame right at his feet. His thoughts were turning the thumbscrews tight, and he was suffering the severe agony of remorse. This time he couldn't put it out of his mind.

He took two codeine tablets from me and rested quietly for a few minutes.

"I must call Veronica, she's at home with her nurse. She doesn't like being seen in public in her state."

Jack sounded delusional. He knew Veronica was dead, but his pain and remorse were getting the better of him. I played along hoping not make his condition any worse.

"Phone service was knocked out by the explosions, there are massive power failures, and cell phone service is out, too," I told him trying to bolster his sinking emotions. He sat there with tears in his eyes wondering where his family was and if any of them were alive.

The ER was still busy. It was nearly five o'clock in the afternoon and the wounded kept showing up. The burn victims were the worst. The hospital was running short of everything including morphine. The scene was best described as agony on a scale of 10 to the tenth power.

The generators were working since early that morning and there was a fear that they would run out of fuel and lights long before they ran out of patients. It was chaos and it was all Jack's doing.

After the pills kicked in, he continued with his story.

CHAPTER 41

Jack was well aware that George Bush was a close personal friend of the Saudi Arabian royal house and shared business interests there. When the Saudis took exception to Saddam's attack on Kuwait and expressed concerns that if Saddam was bold enough to go after Kuwait, they were next, Bush listened closely. Their argument, that if Saudi Arabia fell there would be chaos in the Middle East, the possibility of all-out war, and the total cut-off of oil production, resonated in the administration. This theory was further embellished by the neocons, with a push from some less than accurate photo shopped reports of an Iraqi troop buildup at the Saudi border.

Jack saw that there was another wrinkle in this scenario that factored into the equation. Saddam was reportedly trying to build a nuclear program; it followed that if Israel had the bomb, so would Iraq. In the always volatile Middle East, additional players with nuclear capability were not an option the U.S. would allow. While the U.S. supplied Saddam with nerve gas, biological agents, and delivery technology, it had no desire to see the Butcher of Baghdad with a nuclear device.

Jack supported the Bush notion that building a coalition of world powers spearheaded by the U.S. for the purpose of liberating Kuwait would leave Saddam surrounded by most of the free world and a number of the Arab states and effectively control him. Bush, however, felt himself being boxed in by the neocons in his administration who wanted not only to throw Saddam out of

Kuwait, but also to take all of Iraq. Defeating Saddam, who was outmanned and outgunned, would not be a problem, but taking him out would. Bush understood that removing Saddam would require rebuilding a fractured Iraq. It would take time, lives, and treasure and be politically dangerous.

The neocons and their friends in the intelligence services using the same photo-shopped satellite photos, helped Bush convince a broad coalition of countries that Saddam was in fact massing his troops on the Saudi border, even though it wasn't true. This tidbit was used as additional justification for invading Iraq. Jack logged this in. He was now certain that those in power would do anything, fabricate any story, to achieve their objective of nation building; accountability to anyone be damned.

The Gulf War began on January 17, 1991, and lasted about a hundred days. Saddam's army was quickly decimated. Losses of Iraqi soldiers numbered into the high tens of thousands with some estimates at one hundred thousand killed or missing in action. Allied losses, numbering in the hundreds, were minimal for the scale of the operation.

Jack smiled all the way to the bank as Saddam agreed to a cease-fire and accepted all terms dictated by the coalition. It was a huge victory, whose major offshoot was another spike in the cost of oil and a subsequent rise in the price of gasoline and heating oil. The only down side to this victory, Jack observed, was Bush's refusal to go to Baghdad and take out Saddam, which infuriated the neocons. He watched as the American Enterprise Institute and its offshoot, the Project for a New American Century, both neocon operations that believed taking what was necessary for American survival was justified under any circumstances, abandoned Bush. This left Poppy Bush high and dry. His administration had no love for the neocons and their rigid pragmatism and they thought him too moderate to lead the change that was occurring in the Republican Party. The party of Lincoln was shifting inexorably to the right. The new conservatives were promising smaller government, fewer business regulations, lower taxes, and an unspoken guarantee of corporate control of the government.

Jack saw that Bush was in trouble. The cost of the war combined with the residual effects of the economic policies of the Reagan White House left Bush a budgetary crisis. He had few options to balance the budget but to raise taxes and lose the neocons putting himself out of office after only one term. The loss of the White House was all the ammunition these new conservatives needed to take firm control of the Republican Party.

Jack was wary of the ideas that these men brought to the table. They were scary. They saw the Soviet Union bow out as a world power in 1991, and knew that China was years away from reaching its full potential. They never forgot the treatment of Nixon during the Watergate hearings or his subsequent resignation. They believed in the ultimate power of the presidency and in reshaping the world in the American image. The window was open for them to effectively control world affairs. Their conspiracy would begin when they took over Congress, as they did in 1994.

CHAPTER 42

Jack met Bill Clinton, the former governor of Arkansas, at some political occasion or other, and he, like many others, was charmed by this young man's good looks, Rhodes Scholar intellect, and southern drawl. He was also taken by his ability to bend whichever way the wind blew.

Clinton was a Democrat, but he could wear a Republican suit if the outcome fit his purpose. Jack, seeing an opportunity to manipulate the White House to his continuing advantage, decided to throw whatever money and influence he could behind him and get him elected.

Jack called Clinton a lightning rod. You either loved him or hated him, and, in either case, passionately. Jack liked him and saw his divisiveness as an additional smokescreen to hide behind. He was hated by the neocons who huddled together, and not unlike Jack and Strange, formulated a plan not only to make more and more money, but to co-opt the political process and impose their ideology on the country.

They found sympathetic ears among businessmen, Jack observed, who came to the same conclusion that Jack had arrived at 12 years earlier, that is, business could run the government. These businessmen supported the neocons in congressional races and would back them in efforts to control domestic affairs. It was to be a bloodless coup, at least domestically, put in place by the White House and congress, in conjunction with a sympathetic press. It would make the corporations wealthy and empower them to write their own legislation, pushing the country closer to corporate control. This new group would carry the mail for HOG and the others and cast the last phase of the plan irrevocably in stone.

Jack said many times that corporate control of America was coming; now it was here. Business cooperation with the neocons from the Nixon White House would give these political operatives a free hand to not only to finish off Saddam Hussein but to rewrite the map of the Middle East. This group believed that democracy would be the catalyst that would put out the fires that burned in the Middle East, even if that democracy was forced on them and was only an illusion. They saw oil as the way forward for the foreseeable future and they were going to control it no matter who it rightfully belonged to.

These men were also determined to get a neocon in the White House, and with a neocon Congress and Senate, put their plans in motion. What the oldline Republicans who went along with this group didn't know was that in going along, they had given over their party.

In an effort to blunt this takeover by the neocons, Jack and Veronica lent their support to Clinton and with their experience and influence got him elected. A Democrat in the White House would keep these men at bay, at least for a while.

Clinton's first year was nothing to brag about. Jack shuddered as an attack on the World Trade Center brought bin Laden onto the radar. He knew the ferocity of this man. Terror had come to the American shore.

Jack watched as the Contract with America swept the Republicans into the House of Representatives in 1994. The Gingrich-led party was true to its word, but Clinton, in a brilliant political move, stole their thunder and produced a balanced budget. It wasn't much of a feat, since he knew this was what the House would send him. He just managed to take the credit for it and piss off these ultra-conservatives, who began a vendetta against him. There were some additional economic moves, free trade agreements, that didn't seem like much at the time, but would add credibility to Jack's feeling that corporate America was driving the bus and the American worker would no longer be allowed on board.

The midterm elections in 1994 were a watershed moment. Congressional control shifted to the neocon Republicans for the first time in nearly forty years. Part one of their plan was an enormous success. Part two would be more difficult, but their bitter hatred of Clinton was a driving force that would not be stalled.

Jack knew that Whitewater, a Republican attempt to taint Clinton, would turn out to be nothing more than an expensive farce. The GOP however, was encouraged that they could disrupt the Administration, and pushed harder. Clinton, meanwhile, didn't make it very difficult for them. His sweet tooth for sweet young things, and often some not so sweet, gave them their opening. The Jones case, a hangover from his days as governor of Arkansas, was festering. The Special Counsel appointed during Whitewater was extended. The witch hunt was on.

There was a wrinkle, Jack noted. The economy was hot and growing. Interest rates were falling and the stock market was surging. The balanced budget which produced a surplus and reduced the national debt gave the middle class a much needed shot in the arm and carried Clinton into the White House for a second term. The Republicans would have four more years to plot their takeover.

In 1998, the middle of Clinton's second term, Jack was worried. He called Strange in Rome and arranged to meet him at the Pantheon, where it had all started.

A few days later Jack sat at a table opposite Strange in the Piazza della Rotunda.

"How are you?" Jack asked a now seventy-three-year-old Strange. "You look well."

"I'm fine. The pulse of this city keeps me alive. But you didn't come all this way to see if I'm still kicking," he said smiling. "What's on your mind?"

"As you know," Jack began, "Clinton got caught with his pants unzipped and as a parting shot after the midterms, the House is moving to impeach. The Senate won't find him guilty, but it's not the verdict that matters. Clinton is emasculated. If there is a threat, and your reports indicate that bin Laden is more than just an idle one, Clinton will be powerless to act. Rumor has it that he had bin Laden in his sights several times, but was unable to pull the trigger. The wag the dog scenario has Clinton's hands tied and its carte blanche for the neocon Republican movement. They'll make hay while Clinton lays low. What he did for a piece of ass has left the door open for the march toward the unthinkable."

"What do you mean?" Strange asked.

"They're going to try to take out Saddam. After this administration is over, the neocons will run someone for the White House who will play ball."

"But how can they guarantee they'll win the White House?"

"That's the easy part. They'll rig the election if they have to."

"So they take the White House and have the congress," Strange said. "How will they justify attacking Iraq? What do you base this supposition on?"

"That's the scary part, another Pearl Harbor! The American Enterprise Institute's Project for the New American Century, spells out the need for another attack on America, a second Pearl Harbor, as justification for what they believe should be American foreign policy, which is, hit first, answer questions later."

"Do you really think they would do something that depraved?" Strange bit his lip and shook his head, "Attack their own country?" He answered his own question sardonically. "I've seen most everything in my life, why not that."

"They may not be that over the top," Jack replied, "but they may not attempt to stop something from happening. Keep your ear to the ground, we need to stay as far ahead of them as possible."

"I'll do everything I can."

With that they parted and Jack returned to New York. He continued to follow the neocons closely as they wasted no time lining up the team for 2000. The candidate was academic. The vice president and the cabinet would be the players. At the behest of the soon to be vice president Cheney, they would pull the strings. He was a man known for his humorless approach to issues. He called it his way and condoned no discussion.

Jack knew that to accomplish their end, the Republicans needed a patsy; someone with name recognition who was easily controllable and lacked the brainpower to think quickly or on his own. They found him in Texas, the son of the former president. George W. Bush was an extremely likeable guy who would have been a fabulous frat brother. He could party better than most and Jack thought he was like a young J.B. The sense that he was too rich and too lazy to be smart was as appropriate for him as it was for the late J. B. Johnson.

The one who scared Jack was Cheney. He was tied at the hip with a concrete company that had grand designs and a corporate ethic that made the Borgias smile. He was in and out of Republican administrations for over twenty years and believed that military power would serve where others thought diplomacy better.

Jack saw a mirror image of himself in Cheney. They shared what Jack characterized as the delusion of the wealthy and powerful, that is, the grandiose idea that what they think should be done, will be done, by God, because it's the right thing to do and because it protects what they hold to be worthwhile protecting—generally their own wealth.

There was another thing that worried Jack. The Republican administration was running on a platform of Reagan's trickle-down economics and was planning to reduce taxes for the wealthiest 1% of citizens and throw a bone to everyone else. He read this as dangerous. Just as in the Reagan administration, this would be detrimental to the middle class. The success of HOG through all these years relied on the middle class grousing all the way to the pump as HOG smiled all the way to the bank. This had the look of a blatant attempt to destroy the working class segment of the economy and eliminate them as a political entity.

Jack worried that the threat of terror here at home was increasing. The American airbase in Saudi Arabia inflamed bin Laden, who was operating terrorist training camps in Afghanistan and Pakistan. This made Jack edgy. He knew how easy it was to rile up the Arabs for some money. How much more excited would they get for religious reasons, and bin Laden had already tried once.

He also felt there was little left in the Middle East but conflict and terror. He despaired at trying to influence the neocons, believing that when they got into the White House, they would carry gasoline to the fire, and once in power, they needed only the appearance of something big to light it. Jack knew that what he started was beginning to spin out of control. He was genuinely fearful that these men were so full of hubris that they could cause the spark that would set fire to the entire Middle East. He was beginning to have feelings of regret.

CHAPTER 43

S trange called Jack in early August 2001. He was still living the good life of an seventy-six-year-old, well-to-do Roman. His health was quite good, and except for an occasional bout with agida from too much good eating, he was as sharp as ever.

"Bin Laden is planning something big," he said, an uncharacteristic edge to his voice. "The real spooks out there in the cold are on high alert. They've been trying to get word to the Americans, but are receiving no response. The information I have and the lack of response from the American government both worry me greatly."

"Any ideas about what bin Laden might be planning?"

"I'm not sure," Strange said, "but I believe that the lack of chatter coming from Al-Qaeda, bin Laden's organization, is a bad thing. It could be very bad. Intelligence types in the White House and other agencies have been trying to get the National Security Advisor to make the president at least face the possibility of an attack in the U.S. The word is, without much success."

It would come out some years later that there was a PDB, presidential daily briefing, in August 2001 that warned of an attempt by Al Qaeda to attack targets in the U.S. This was summarily dismissed by President Bush.

CHAPTER 44

9/11 had come to New York and with it a savage attack on the greatest city in the world. One of such ferocity, that it took the leaders of the country days to calculate the magnitude of the event.

Strange was right, bin Laden was planning something so bold that the White House couldn't imagine, didn't want to imagine, or, being aware of it, chose to do nothing to stop it.

Jack watched the aftermath and the news coverage, taking great interest in this tragedy as he felt some responsibility for it, if only indirectly. The airbase in Saudi Arabia was bin Laden's excuse for the attack, but Jack had his own ideas. He became a news junkie. His pulse raced a little faster every time he heard the signal on the TV that meant a regular program was being interrupted for a special news bulletin. He pored over news accounts of the hijacking of each plane, the course that each pilot took to his target, and the response of the government. Piecing each of these elements together, he realized that there was no response from the government. NORAD was silent. No fighter jets scrambled, no air raid sirens sounded, and no mention of the hijackings on the early morning news. He found this puzzling and disturbing.

The planes that bin Laden's men flew into the Twin Towers and the Pentagon were heading west. Jack traced their flight paths and saw that they made significant turns, taking them off their flight paths. He studied NORAD's published policies, and discovered that if something like this occurs, air traffic control signals the offending aircraft that they are off course and gives them a new heading to take them back to their original flight plan. If the aircraft doesn't respond, the air traffic controller responsible for the aircraft notifies his next in command and appropriate steps are taken to try to establish contact with the errant aircraft. If this fails, NORAD is notified. When four aircraft are in this mode, all hell should break loose. It didn't! NORAD should have scrambled F-16's to intercept these planes. It didn't! With his own experience fixing events, Jack could only surmise that this was allowed to happen.

The days after the attack were chaotic if you watched the television. Like sharks in a feeding frenzy, network news reporters were on this story like there was blood in the water. Jack was to take Veronica to Europe for a few weeks that fall. Her health was failing and she loved Rome and Paris when the leaves were turning and the tourists were gone, but the trip was delayed for several days as all commercial and private aircraft were grounded. All except the planes, arranged by the White House, that took bin Laden's family members from the U.S. to WHERE???

Jack thought the whole scene lacked the finesse of one of Strange's operations. The attack wasn't stopped, leaving him to believe the administration needed it to justify some other plan. Jack was appalled at the thought that the administration allowed an attack on American soil of this magnitude and even more appalled at the thought of what would come next: Iraq.

CHAPTER 45

Jack was at Ground Zero when the president showed up in New York and, in an uncharacteristic move, galvanized the country promising that the perpetrators would be caught, dead or alive. He sent the military to Afghanistan with world support. It was a heady time for this cowboy from Maine. He did all the right things, made all the right alliances, and even said the right things. Jack was astounded at how much support the U.S. was receiving from the world, but he was wary. Years spent fomenting international crisis left Jack cynical about accidental incidents, believing that all international problems, flare-ups, and conflicts had something in common, someone who started them and someone who profited from them. He believed this was the case here, but just couldn't put his finger on it yet.

Jack called Strange and told him that the trip would be delayed several days. He was anxious to see his friend and get the latest scuttlebutt and unpublished news of the world. Strange told him that there was much happening that would be best discussed in person. They would meet in Rome. The flight ban was lifted a few days later and Veronica and Jack were on their way. They kept an apartment in Rome, it was a city they had grown to love.

They arrived in Rome tired but exhilarated. New York was chaotic. 9/11 was as fresh on day five as it was on the morning of the attack. It was good to be away from it.

After unpacking, Veronica took a nap. Her emphysema was beginning to worsen. Jack called Strange before lunch and they met in a restaurant across from Jack's apartment. It was a bittersweet reunion as they both reflected on what they had done. Even Strange felt some remorse, though his feeling was based on his belief that morons ran the government. Had they just ignored Saddam in 1991, he thought, none of this would have happened.

"What do you think will happen now?" Jack asked him. "Will the U.S. get bin Laden? Will these threats subside, or is the genie out of the bottle?"

Strange's eyes grew steely and cold, a sight Jack remembered from the first time they were together on the submarine.

"The U.S. is going to move against Iraq," he said with solemnity.

"Well, I said they needed another Pearl Harbor, and I guess they got it. I know this group in the White House feature themselves as gunslingers, but I can't fathom how they can build support to go after Iraq, when it was not involved in this terrible tragedy, and there are far greater dangers in the world."

"You're getting old," Strange laughed, "and so am I. There are lots of questions about this attack, but don't look for answers. The men who staff this administration and let this happen have their motives. They'll use it to draw a line from bin Laden to Saddam. The administration will build up Saddam's defunct nuclear, biological, and chemical weapons programs into a nuclear program that is seeking to become world class. The word on the street is that any information showing Iraqi attempts to purchase components for weaponry would be handsomely rewarded. If this weaponry looks like it might be nuclear, the reward will be doubled. Spooks all over the world are falling over each other trying to find a connection. We're talking millions of dollars."

"I started this to preserve something worthwhile for my family," Jack said wearily, looking for some way to exonerate himself. "I didn't want to destabilize the world." He was feeling a depression overtaking him that he hadn't felt in his adult life. The law of unintended consequences was throwing the book at him.

"There are communiqués going back and forth between North Korea and Iran, China and Syria, Russia and anybody who'll listen," Strange went on. "Nuclear is the word. The axis of evil has sized up the White House and found it comical. The arms race part two is on for real. The only problem is that the administration has neither the tools nor the will to address it. They are hard on their target: Iraq."

Jack sat back in his chair and sipped a Montepulciano D'Abruzzo. "I'm fearful for the future," he said with resignation. "Can we undo what we've started?"

"Yes! We can get them out of the White House!" Strange said, his voice ice cold. "Do you want them taken out?" He said this slowly, his head slightly tilted in a way that suggested he would have leveled the white house with all hands in it if Jack had given the nod.

Jack mulled this over for a moment. "Something needs to be done," he answered, agreeing with Strange's assessment, "but even if the president was shot by a Chinese albino in broad daylight on a busy street, the spin machine would make the man an Iraqi with ties to Saddam's secret police. Besides that," he sighed, "removing the president, who is currently popular at home, will leave the vice president in power and increase the drumbeat for war. If you take out both of them, that leaves the Speaker of the House in charge, and he's no better."

Strange half-heartedly agreed. "The word on the wire is that these guys were after Iraq from the beginning of their administration. They needed an excuse and they got it, even if it wasn't an Iraqi operation. Problematically, all the intelligence assessments agree that taking Iraq will open the biggest can of worms ever seen.

On the surface, Iraq is a secular state, run by the Baathist party, who are Sunni Muslims. They are more religious than the Shi'ites, but they are in the minority. The Kurds in the north have been rebellious for years which brought down Saddam's ire on them and with it a lot of death. Fracturing this unholy alliance would sic the Shi'ites on the Sunnis and Kurds. The

Kurds, because of their geographic location, would be relatively safe, but the Sunnis, who would get help from the Saudis, who are also Sunni, and the Shi'ites, who would get help from Iran, which is predominately Shi'ite, would be at each other's throats in short order. All chatter points to an operation lacking the size in manpower to prevent the destabilization of the country and incurring a long term investment in men, machinery, and money. The hubris of this group could leave us with a second Vietnam. If they don't throw the kitchen sink at Iraq, and the word out there is they won't, this will be a major league snafu."

"This is depressing," Jack said. "We have much more to discuss over the next weeks" he said as they took leave of each other.

CHAPTER 46

Jack and Veronica spent the winter of 2001-2002, in Rome and with the first hint of spring in the trees, sat with Strange, who had by now met Veronica, in the dining room of their Roman apartment while Strange regaled her with stories of his CIA gambits. He was less guarded in his old age and more given to revisiting the past like it was something to hold on to if he was to live longer.

"There's more news," he finally said. The discussion turned somber as talk centered on the situation in the Middle East. "While the administration is focusing on selling a war with Iraq, the war in Afghanistan is slowing down. The Taliban have retreated into the mountains near Pakistan, where their sympathizers have given them shelter and support. It's rumored in CIA circles that the U.S. Army had bin Laden trapped at some place called Tora Bora," Strange said shaking his head. "The trap was sprung on three sides. They just needed to close the door and they'd have the man who caused so much destruction. Somehow, the order came down to let the Pakistanis do it. They didn't and bin Laden escaped."

Jack was incensed. These men in the White House were without souls. It seemed like they just let bin Laden go.

"Rumbles from my old contacts," Strange went on, "who speak to me out of courtesy, are pointing to plans being made in Iran to disrupt any attempt to form a coalition government in Iraq, after the inevitable attack by the U.S. Iran, would infiltrate the Shi'ite mosques in Iraq. With eighty percent of the Arab population of Iraq Shi'ite, this will hardly be a difficult task. The message coming down from Iran to the Iraqi Shi'ites is to lay low, let the Americans in, and then create an untenable position that will bog the U.S. down for months or years.

Iraq could be a huge win," Strange continued, "if the Americans come in with a five hundred thousand-man force. Anything less and they'll never control it."

"I've been told by a friend," Jack shared with Veronica and Strange, "someone close to Cheney, that the vice president expects oil to top a hundred dollars a barrel and gasoline to be over four dollars a gallon by the 2008 election. This friend didn't have a handle on why, but a reasonable guess is it has something to do with Iraq."

"Did I ever tell you about my synthetic oil project?" Jack asked Strange, trying to find anything to change the subject.

"No, what is it?"

"During the Second World War, German scientists were working on developing synthetic oil to fill the gap in war fuel we were creating by bombing their oil pipelines and production facilities. My motivation was the knowledge that at some time in the future we would pump the last barrel out of the ground. The country that could create a synthetic substitute would control the finances of the world."

"I've been thinking about going to New York and pushing some political friends to propose legislation that would require the government to fund this type of alternative energy project."

"Be careful, Jack," Strange sat up in alarm. "The word is that anyone who goes against the administration will be publicly humiliated or worse, just disappear. Stay out of this issue, and make sure to provide protection for the people working on this project," Strange insisted.

"Okay, I'll post around the clock security."

"Good," Strange smiled. "Anything that even hints that it will derail the attack on Iraq will be removed. These people have decided what they want to do and will do whatever is necessary to see that it happens.

I have a friend in the Italian security service," Strange continued, "who told me that someone in the administration cooked the books about a shipment of yellow cake uranium Saddam was supposed to have contracted for in the late 1990's. He heard that there were official documents, but Italian security people knew they were a forgery. Still the U.S. government is going to use this as evidence against Saddam."

"Whew" Jack whistled. "How will they get away with this kind of chicanery? I know that the government is making unsubstantiated allegations that are being carried by a co-opted press, but how can they sell this story?"

"By the time anyone could discredit it, the Army would be in Baghdad," Strange said in disgust.

Jack sat back. Dinner had been excellent and the long pull he took on the Louis XIV Cognac was even better. He looked across the table at Strange and then at Veronica.

"It's been a great run," He said smiling as he rose from the table.

"Goodnight, my friend" he said to Strange as he took Veronica's arm and led she and Strange out to the street in front of the apartment and saw him into the waiting car. He was convinced that the end of their run was in near.

Later, in the apartment, he called Jack Junior and told him to put the synthetic oil project on permanent hold, gather up the test data, degauss all the computers and make it disappear. He'd explain why when they got back to New York.

Veronica put her arms around him and hugged tightly. "You know," she told him in soft consoling tones, "these forty-eight years have been wonderful and I'm proud of all your accomplishments. You've cared for your family and your employees, and no matter what happens going forward, that can't be erased."

Jack thought to himself that he'd give anything if it could. What he had put in motion might well by the undoing of all that he had built!

Before he left for New York, Jack made Strange promise that he would visit for the Christmas holidays.

CHAPTER 47

As the war drums got louder and louder, Jack saw that there was a taste for blood in the American mouth and it needed a scapegoat to satiate it. Saddam was the target and anyone who spoke up against this was shouted down and suffered severe economic consequences.

In Strange's conversations with Jack, he described the scene at the Pentagon as chaotic; intelligence reports were coming in from everywhere and much of the information was nebulous enough to fit any scenario dreamed up by the administration. The administration used the rest of 2002 to built their case for attacking Iraq.

The fall of 2002 came and the city mourned 9/11; briefly. New York is not a place to mire itself in pity. The pace and the vibrancy of the city dictates that life goes on in quick time. That doesn't mean it doesn't hold a grudge. The chip on New York's shoulder was two towers big.

Thanksgiving was over and Christmas was approaching. Jack had asked Cully to come to New York for the holidays, but Cully's Doctors put that trip off-limits. Cully wasn't thriving and had taken to spending his time in south Texas near the Rio Grande Valley, where it was warm most of the year.

Jack arranged for the company jet to pick up Strange in Rome. He would arrive in a week. He was anxious to congratulate him on his call of the Niger yellow cake uranium. The British White

Paper of late September laid it out exactly as Strange predicted. It was almost funny. Jack had seen political shenanigans and helped some of them along in his career, but nothing this patently corrupt. There was a war coming, everyone knew it, and no one seemed to want to stop it.

He was spending more and more time at home with Veronica. Jack Junior possessed his father's scientific mind and his mother's political savvy. He was doing a terrific job managing HOG so Jack felt comfortable staying home and assisting with Veronica's care. He did spend a considerable time walking around Central Park and down Fifth Avenue to 48th Street and the ice rink at Rockefeller Center. He always felt like a kid in a toy store at Christmas time in New York. The city was decked out in lights and glitter and the mood was positively joyful.

A week later as the lights of the City signaled the onset of evening, Strange was ushered into the living room. It had been several years since he was in New York at the holidays and marveled at the decorations in the city. He was looking older still but steady on his feet and sharp as ever.

Jack poured a sherry for each of them and the talk came around to the impending war.

"As I speculated they are going to try to do this on the cheap," Strange told him. "My sources say that the administration thinks that the Iraqi army is their only problem and they don't think much of them. They couldn't be more wrong."

They sat quietly for a moment and then Jack spoke. "I can think of a dozen reasons for eliminating Saddam, but there are easier ways than full frontal war. Now it seems, from what you are saying, they will play directly into the Iranians hands by doing this half-assed!

"In the Middle East," Strange said, "the enemy of my enemy is my friend, no matter that I have been fighting with him for decades. The Iranians hate the Iraqis, but they are joined at the hip religiously, and the Iranians hate the U.S. above all else."

Veronica entered the room. She was feeling better and looked as good as she had in some time. She forgot her manners for a moment and walked to Jack and hugged him tightly, then moved gracefully to greet Strange.

"Sherry?" Jack asked as Veronica greeted Strange with a hug.

"No sherry for me," she said. "I've selected a very special bottle of Champagne for dinner."

When the dinner bell rang they moved to the dining area, which overlooked Central Park. Dinner was served and the conversation, which centered on the war, as it did in most American households, was lively.

"I wish we could find a way to derail this juggernaut," Veronica said. "It will devastate Iraq and set the table for total chaos in the Middle East."

"I'm afraid it is inevitable," Strange said sadly.

"Congratulations," Jack said smiling at Strange, "your prediction was right on target."

"I've more news," Strange announced. "Iran is shipping arms and explosives across the frontier between Iran and Iraq in anticipation of the invasion. They are banking on the administration targeting Baghdad and ignoring the small settlements and towns along the way. There are Shi'ite militias in these towns that will form the basis of an insurgency. There is talk of Al-Qaeda trying to get a foothold with the Sunnis, but the Sunnis won't have any of that.

The Pentagon is at war with itself," Strange continued. "There is a good deal of infighting going on. The administration will send less than two hundred thousand soldiers to Iraq. Generals who see this as a potential disaster and speak their minds are being forced into retirement. Those who don't speak know that they'd get the gate if they did."

Jack called a halt to the conversation as it was time for dessert and coffee. There would be more time over the next few days to discuss the world situation. Now was the time for reconnecting with his friend. There were smiles all around as Tiramisu and espresso were served.

CHAPTER 48

C hristmas was peaceful for the Duncan family. Jack Junior, his family, Strange, and a rejuvenated Veronica making home and hearth a respite from the news of the day, which was Iraq 24/7. Jack's thoughts, however were ever more filled with remorse and foreboding, and as the New Year came and went, he and Veronica were alone again.

On the evening of the State of the Union message, Veronica and Jack settled in to watch the president. By Jack's reckoning, it was a fairly good speech for a president who often had difficulty being coherent. That is, until he uttered the sixteen words about Saddam's purported attempt to buy yellow cake uranium from Niger. Jack was outraged. This was a blatant lie, and every security service, along with the president's national security advisor, knew it.

Jack and Veronica had set in motion an evil—and this government compounded it—that would haunt America for decades. They started something that in days past, when the country was run by sane people, would have had a very short half-life. With the group in power today, what they did would soon be catastrophic.

Jack retreated to his study after the speech and called Strange who was watching the speech, as was most of Europe and the Middle East.

"There is no truth in the statement about yellow cake uranium," Strange told Jack, "and the headlines in the Italian papers will say so. Italian security circles already have. This is a hoax and a bad one. Too bad the American press is co-opted and the people are too much in shock from September eleventh to question the president."

"March," Jack said gravely, believing that the President would wait no longer than thirty days to make his move.

"Most likely," Strange answered, and hung up the phone.

They both knew that war was inevitable.

CHAPTER 49

One month later, Jack and most of the world sat glued to the television. It happened exactly as Strange and Jack imagined. The bombs falling on Baghdad looked like the fourth of July. Shock and awe, the reporters were calling it, from the administration playbook.

Veronica came into the room and turned off the television. She too was feeling uneasy about where their meddling in Middle Eastern affairs had led.

"I think we should move back to Houston," she told Jack.

"I'm worried that this attack on Iraq might inflame the Muslim world, which has a seemingly endless supply of suicide bombers."

"You needn't worry," he told her. "We are completely safe in Manhattan."

It was the lack of conviction in his voice that worried Veronica even more.

Jack nearly had a stroke from laughing so hard when the President, in May, 2003, declared 'Mission Accomplished" in Iraq. Seventy percent of the American public, including Jack, were a tad more skeptical as the insurgency and civil war started to take its toll on American soldiers and then Iraqi civilians. The U.S. was getting bogged down and our troops were bearing the brunt of it.

After a year and a half of watching the Iraq situation deteriorate into looting, insurrection, and disappearing pallets full of millions in hundred dollar bills, Jack sat out the election of

2004. Senator John Kerry made a less than stellar run at Bush for the presidency. He came up as empty as his rhetoric.

Kerry, who in Jack's judgment was too bland, was a decorated Vietnam War combatant assailed by groups of Republican operatives on his war record. He uncharacteristically folded his tent and went home without a fight. The administration now had another four years to work its magic on the American economy and continue to line the pockets of HOG and the other oil companies.

The war in Afghanistan in the meantime was an orphan. The initial gains made in 2002, up to the beginning of our foray into Iraq, were all but wiped out. It became a holding action, and not unlike Iraq, a money pit. To the military suppliers and the oil companies, it was also a gold mine.

The news in 2005 and 2006, covered very little else but the war in Iraq with its soaring body count, there was a devastating hurricane named Katrina that nearly destroyed New Orleans, the prison at Guantanamo Bay in Cuba, where the government was holding "enemy combatants" and torturing them, and growing unemployment. American deaths were in the thousands and Iraqi civilians, from 2005 into 2007 were dying at the alarming rate of thirty to fifty per day. Suicide bombings, improvised explosive devices, kidnapping, torture, and assassinations were the order of the day, and the oil that was to gush from Iraq's wells to pay for the war was barely a trickle.

The topping on this inedible sundae of dismay, which had large scoops of the financial effect of two wars and unfunded tax cuts, with a syrup of plain vanilla mismanagement of the economy, was an inevitable recession. By the end of 2007, the economy was tanking and job losses were growing proportionately. The republicans were scrambling to try and save themselves from the debacle that would be the election the following November.

CHAPTER 50

Jack and Strange were in contact almost daily with Strange providing Jack the best inside information he could glean from sources that were keeping low to stay out of the administration's line of sight.

Jack's proximity to Wall Street and the denizens of that hell hole gave him an inside track on matters economic. They passed on insider information about the markets. He passed on inside information about oil. It was an unholy alliance at best, but it worked well for both sides.

As 2007 ended, Jack placed a call to Strange. "There are rumblings coming out of the street," Jack said, "that some very large institutions are holding significant amounts of paper based on mortgages of questionable value. The markets could get dicey within the year. You might consider liquidating any holdings you have while the market is still strong."

"Thanks for the heads up" Strange replied. "I'm glad you called, if you hadn't I was going to call you. I'm losing contacts," he told Jack. "The old guard of professional operatives is being pushed aside for younger, less experienced players who support the administration's position and twist information to suit that purpose. I'm also worried about the situation in South Lebanon. Hezbollah, and the conflict with Israel, has the Arab population up in arms. Bush's lack of a diplomatic effort, along with some huge public relations gaffs by the Israeli military, has inflamed the Islamic world.

If the U.S. has any standing left after the Iraq invasion and its subsequent mishandling, it has been eroded completely by the undisguised support Bush gave the Israelis, supplying them with cluster bombs which are designed to inflict maximum casualties on combatants, but seemed to find mostly civilians."

"There's change coming" Jack stated with emphasis. "The people are restless and tired of the rhetoric. The war in Iraq and the quiet war in Afghanistan have Americans worn out. The neocons are in an unfavorable position and look like losers this election cycle. We need to mend fences with some important allies in some strategic parts of the world."

"What are you going to do about it, Jack" Strange quizzed.

"Other than send contributions, very little. The Republicans will run the same tired candidates for the nomination and McCain will get it. How he plans on getting the right wing to support him is the only question to be answered. The Democrats will try someone new and this time I think he or she will win.

The Clintons will be in the field and there is a young Black man from Illinois who is causing some stirring on the left. One way or the other it will be a Democratic White House with a good chance for a Democratic House and Senate.

There is much to discuss which will best be done face to face"

"Are you still coming for Easter" Strange asked? "It is still one of the most beautiful times of the year in Rome"

"Veronica and I wouldn't miss it. We see you in a few months."

CHAPTER 51

Jack and Veronica were recovering from the excitement that was Christmas and New Years in New York. Veronica's emphysema was advancing and she was tired and lay down to take a nap. As Jack was settling down to read some business reports, the bellman called the apartment. He informed Jack that Mr. Strange and another man wanted to see him. Jack told him to send them right up.

At three o'clock that afternoon, while Veronica was napping, Strange arrived with a young man who bore a strong resemblance to him.

"This must be your contact at the Italian security apparatus" Jack posited, smiling.

"This is my son, Gianni," Strange answered with uncharacteristic pride. "He is Section Chief of the Rome Bureau."

"Buon Giorno, Senor Duncan".

"Buon Giorno, Gianni, benvenuto."

Strange laughed so hard at Jack's Italian pronunciation that he had to sit down.

"Stick to English" was all he could get out as he caught his breath. "We have much to discuss and much to plan.

"I brought Gianni here because he has received some very distressing information about the worldwide banking system. They have taken a page out of our playbook and the news you passed to me about bad paper is about to turn into a trillion dollar rip off."

"The banks have done as you said, Jack. They have sold worthless paper, these credit default swaps, with the help of the rating agencies, to some very unsuspecting buyers under the guise of grade A investments. When the bottom falls out some investment houses and banks will be gone. The banks will raise the alarm that the end of the world is coming, cry disaster and look for bailouts from all the world governments. It could amount to trillions of dollars.

"I suspected as much" Jack said, "but there is more isn't there?"

"You are right Mr. Duncan" Gianni answered. "The Iraq situation is cooling and there will be movement to bring troops home. But, Afghanistan is going the other way. It will soon be made public that a mineral find in the north of Afghanistan has a potential value of over several trillion dollars. The U.S. government will not surrender that much wealth to either the Chinese or the Russians and certainly not to the Afghans.

The Afghani government, which is in the pocket of anyone who will pay it, is negotiating with the Taliban and the representatives of Al-Qaeda. They believe that playing all sides against the U.S. will neuter the military and cause the Americans to go home with their tails dragging leaving them to reap the lion's share of these mineral deposits. It's a no lose strategy for them because they are the only government that Afghanistan has.

As you are no doubt aware, unemployment in your country is beginning to be a concern. As the American economy goes, so goes Europe and the world."

"I am in agreement with your assessment" Jack said, "but there is more to this or you would not have traveled here and blown your cover in the process."

"Sadly yes," Gianni replied. "The funny business that you and my father have engaged in for so many years is serious, but taken by itself, it is only a bump in the road. If the bankers have their way, they will recover and go right back to the schemes and money games that are bringing us to the edge right now. The second time will be catastrophic and possibly lead to destruction of the world economy and the collapse of many governments with the rampant chaos and devastation which will include famine, civil wars, and possibly world war.

"You are not exactly the harbinger of good tidings, Gianni," Jack commented, "but much of what you said has every possibility of happening. The question is how do we prevent this from occurring?"

"It would serve no purpose to announce this to the news media" Gianni replied. "They are not journalists anymore, they are stenographers taking dictation from their masters. We are, for now, to only sit and wait and hope."

"I have to agree", echoed Strange. "The sky is falling doesn't get much attention these days."

"What do you suggest, Mr. Duncan," Gianni asked?

"There is little that we can do," Jack replied. "What these men have set in motion will have to play itself out. There will be hardships for the under classes, but the economy will recover and the national debt will climb. That's not the worst that can happen. The offshoot of all this chaos will embolden enemies of the American government, bin Laden in particular, to think that we are weak and accessible. Our problem is to assess who is coming after us and I think you know who."

"What do you mean?" Gianni queried.

"The weakness in the economy will embolden all of the middle east players. I think it has already. This whole thing could unravel," Jack said, his voice giving away the knot in his gut.

"Yes," Strange said with the kind of emphasis intended to slow down the impending panic. "We're all in a bind, but this is the time to take a deep breath, not to exhale. We are fortunate that we know we are up against it and that what ever comes next will not happen immediately. That gives us the time to make the appropriate moves to protect what we have and to move against those who are a threat."

"You are right in you assessment, Mr. Duncan," Gianni said, "the real threat is bin Laden. The missed opportunity to destroy him has only made him stronger in the eyes of the Muslim world. His hatred for America will manifest itself in something far worse than 9/11. When it is set in motion, I'm afraid we will be unable to stop it."

"Again you seem to know more than you are saying," Jack remarked. "What's out there that bin Laden can bring to bear that is worse than what he has done?"

Gianni looked at his father as if to ask permission to continue.

"I'll fill in the blanks," Strange volunteered. "The U.S. Government has repeatedly denied the existence of atomic bombs that can fit into a suitcase. They don't want it out there that they have the technology. And they certainly don't want it known that the plans were stolen by the Russians. The Russians, in turn, don't want it known that they had their scientists build several of these suitcase bombs. And, they really don't want it known that these scientists lost or sold the bombs to the Russian mob."

"This sounds too much like the Keystone Kops to be true." Jack said shaking his head. "How could this have happened?"

"Seriously, Jack!" Strange chided, "these are the same people who might have stopped 9/11 and couldn't. They are as inept as they are brazen."

"The Russian mob has put out feelers to interested parties. Their asking price is $500 million per bomb," Gianni confirmed. "There are no reports of anyone taking them up on the offer as yet, but sooner than later someone, bin Laden most likely, will step up to the line."

"Why isn't the U.S. bidding on this?" Jack asked.

"If they did," Strange offered, "the administration would have to admit that they lost the technology in the first place. It would destroy the Republican Party if they ever breathed a word of this.

Gianni and I will monitor the situation through our networks in the Middle East. If we can change the trajectory of this disaster, we will."

CHAPTER 52

Jack, Strange, and Gianni kept in contact over the next two months following leads, pressing their own networks for information, and in general coming up empty in their search for the suitcase bombs. Jack provided the necessary finances to run this operation and there was ample frustration to go around.

Jack called Strange in late February to compare notes. Strange told him that there was a noticeable lack of chatter coming from bin Laden's group. This was worrisome and followed the pattern of the 9/11 attack.

"Do you think something is in the wind?"

"Yes," Strange answered. "There is no word of the suitcase bombs which can only mean they have been sold and are on there way to the target which is most likely somewhere in the States."

"It won't be Washington," Jack responded, "if it is bin Laden, he will try to hit New York again. He wants panic and anger and he'll find them both there."

"You're right!" Strange agreed. "It will be New York and on a significant day. I'll keep as close to it as possible.

Are you still coming to Rome for Easter?"

"We are making plans to bring the whole family and look forward to seeing you and Gianni then."

CHAPTER 53

Jack's telephoned Strange early on Wednesday morning of Holy Week.

"Have you heard any more about bin Laden?" Jack asked, unable to hide the worry in his voice.

Strange didn't speak for a moment. When he finally did, Jack turned pale.

"I'm glad you called as I was just about to call you. There's an unconfirmed rumor from some trusted Arab operatives that Al-Qaeda has moved the suitcase bombs into the U.S."

"I've passed this on to the few friends I have left in Washington, they're trying to verify the information but are stymied by lack of cooperation from the administration's CIA people. They think they have Al-Qaeda under a microscope, and Homeland Security has the foolish notion that they have security as tight as a drum."

"When do you think the plot would play out?" Jack asked Strange.

"This Easter, and most likely Easter Sunday," Strange replied. "The Muslims have the notion that Afghanistan and Iraq are a crusade against them and would likely hit back on the most solemn Christian holiday."

"Strange, Easter is only 4 days away!" Jack cried. "What can we do? We have to warn the people of New York. This will …" his voice trailed off.

"Get hold of Schumer and Clinton," Strange said. "Get them to warn the president to shut down the New York and New Jersey ports and all entrances to Manhattan. I've heard that they'll trying to smuggle the bombs through one of them."

CHAPTER 54

Jack began to sweat at the memory of Easter Week. He was visibly shaken by his recollection. I found a towel and some cold water and put it on his forehead until he was settled again.

Holy Thursday morning, the day after he spoke with Strange, he was making the final preparations to fly his family to Italy on Good Friday.

He explained that he had received several calls but there was no one on the other end. He knew intuitively that it was Strange calling from Italy. He tried several times to return the calls but to no avail. That he could not make contact raised his heart rate and left him with a disquieting feeling that perhaps trouble was coming sooner than expected.

Jack also continued to try to reach Schumer and Clinton, without success. Local phone service was no better than long distance but it didn't matter. The government was shut down for the weekend. He knew an horrific event was coming on a high holy day of Christianity and he was powerless to get anyone's attention or stop it.

I later learned that Strange tried to call Jack Holy Thursday morning and throughout much of the day to tell him to get his family out of New York now, and now didn't mean tomorrow. Strange's alert to Jack of the rumored attack on New York on Easter Sunday was no rumor at all. It was confirmed by his most trusted agents in the Middle East. The attack would, however, be on Good Friday, not Easter Sunday.

Strange also called his son, Gianni, to confirm the rumor. Gianni's sources in the Middle East were very reliable in the past and they too had information that nuclear devices were on their way to New York and would arrive on Friday. Italian intelligence was still not well received in Washington because of their exposure of the Niger yellow cake uranium presidential faux pas and so their information was considered suspect and ignored. Strange, attempting to stave off the unthinkable flew to Washington, on Holy Thursday, in a private plane owned by the Italian Secret Service. He took his information to as many intelligence agencies as he could. He went to the CIA first, but his friends there were on holiday and all that he could do was to leave messages. He went to the FBI and Defense Intelligence Agency. He even tried National Security Agency, but in every case they refused to believe him and rudely told him where to put his information.

Finally he received a call from the CIA at his hotel.

"Jonathan," Strange said to his longtime friend and CIA source, "they're going to blow up New York!"

"How can you be so sure?"

"You know my sources," Strange said to his friend, "my contact is in the government of an Axis of Evil country. He knows that Arabs or Muslims are about to blow the shit out of Manhattan and that the administration is doing denial. They think they have security covered. My contacts in Iran and Syria believe that if this insanity plays out, the U.S. will take out its anger on all Moslem countries, including them.

My contact can't talk directly to the U.S but feels if he can help stop this from happening he might avoid having his country nuked in retaliation."

"What are you going to do," Jonathan asked?

"Go to New York," Strange answered. "I can't raise my friends there by cell phone or landline. The best I can do is camp out along Interstate 95 and hope like hell that I can spot the devices.

I was told they would be in utility vans with a New York power company logo. The giveaway would be Virginia license plates on the vans."

"Long distance and cell phone service is down," Jonathan asked?

"Yes!" Strange replied emphatically.

"That's bad. I need to look into that. In the meantime, I'm sending a car and a driver to your hotel. The best place to wait is at the last rest stop south of exit 14 on the New Jersey turnpike. Everyone going into the tunnel or to the bridge to Manhattan passes that way."

"Thanks," Strange said.

Strange met his driver, Bob, in the hotel at 6:00P.M. Bob was briefed on the critical nature of the assignment and directed by Jonathan to follow Strange's orders to the letter.

"Head north on I-95," Strange instructed.

Bob found the quickest way out of Washington as Strange continued to call Jack without success.

"Trying to call New York?" Bob asked Strange. "Jonathan told me there was a problem."

"Yes," Strange replied. "I hope that I can raise my friend and have him call the mayor, but this damned Italian cell phone won't work."

"Here," Bob offered, "try mine."

"Thanks," Strange said dialing Jack's number. "This one doesn't work either. It rings and then it shuts down."

Strange and his CIA driver made the trip up the turnpike in good time, stopping at the service area where Jonathan indicated they should wait, while trying to call anyone they thought would listen, but with no success. It was frustrating.

Strange was watching the road as the first light of morning appeared in the eastern sky and just as sudden as the sunrise he jumped to his feet and started toward the door.

"Let's go," he shouted at Bob who came running behind him. "It's the vans!"

Three Con Edison utility vans with Virginia plates were stopped at the far end of the service plaza. They parked in such a way that their windows were side by side They sat for a only a minutes as if they were going over their mission one last time and then started northward again.

"Bob," Strange ordered, "don't lose them. If we can't get anyone on the phone, then we'll have to take them out ourselves."

Bob took the entrance ramp to the turnpike at breakneck speed. He knew the importance of the mission and wasn't going to fail because of faint-heartedness. A few minutes into the chase, the standard issue two-way radio in the car crackled.

"We've got company," Bob said sounding somewhat relieved. "That's Jonathan's car coming up behind us and traveling fast. He's got two other cars with him."

Bob was very good at tailing a subject without being seen, but the men who planned this provided for every contingency. When Jonathan and his cadre caught up to us, they made a move three abreast across the turnpike to overtake the vans and force them off the road by any means necessary. A little more than ten miles from the Holland Tunnel exit on the New Jersey Turnpike, three vehicles that were in front of and apace of the vans slowed down and allowed the vans to pass while keeping any vehicles that were behind the vans from gaining on them. It was perfect. They went slow enough to allow the vans, now traveling at over 100 mph, to pull away and out of sight.

Jonathan, in the shotgun seat, opened fire and the other two cars with him followed suit. The three blocking vehicles began to weave back and forth across the turnpike making it impossible to pass them.

Strange was nearly apoplectic as Bob first tried one way then another to squeeze through this moving roadblock. This was taking forever and the people in New York City would see eternity up close if they couldn't get through.

Suddenly, the closest blocker was gone. Jonathan hit his gas tank and the resultant explosion caused the car to veer to the right and fly off the road landing in a ball of flame. The second one was easier. One of Jonathan's cadre caught it in the left rear tire sending the car careening up against the median guard rail and back across the turnpike and into the base of a concrete overpass. The last blocker's car took the next exit off the turnpike with two of the CIA cars in hot pursuit. It took Jonathon's men a little over five precious minutes of this dangerous ballet to leave the track open for Strange and his driver to pull past them and follow the vans. They were almost 10 miles behind. Bob pushed his government cruiser to the limit. By the time they had them in sight again one of the vans was missing.

"They've split up," Strange said in disgust. "One of them is heading further north to the Lincoln Tunnel or the George Washington Bridge."

"What do you want me to do?" Bob asked.

"Stay with the two you can see. Maybe we can stop one of them" Strange answered. "We're less than 3 miles from the Holland Tunnel exit off the turnpike and about 10 miles from the Tunnel." The road was fairly straight so doing over 100 mph was not too hard to negotiate. He had a bead on the vans and was gaining.

"There's a pistol in the glove box," he told Strange. Strange didn't need any more instruction than that. He was very familiar with the 9mm. Glock he was holding in his hand.

"Extra clips?" he asked as he rolled down his window.

"Under the seat," Bob replied.

Strange secured the extra clips, chambered a round, and opened up at the van. He was aiming at the tires and fighting the wind and the motion of the car over bumps in the road made hitting a moving target tricky. He emptied the entire clip at the closest van. Miraculously, he hit the back tire and the van careened off the road and burst into flames. They still had to get the one they up front.

Bob was gaining on the van but he could see the toll booth up ahead. The van blew through it at full speed. A minute later Bob and Strange did likewise.

"Step on it," he shouted to Bob, his voice ringing with panic. "It's got to be here. We have to stop that van now!"

Bob was driving at breakneck speed, but the road turned into the city streets of Hoboken, New Jersey and at this hour on Good Friday there was little traffic to impede the van. They made up as much ground as possible but the van blew through the tunnel toll booth in an EZ Pass lane and sped into the tunnel. The chase was over.

Strange looked up as the first light of morning hit the skyscrapers of southern Manhattan, it was 7:50 a.m. and he knew in his heart that the deed was done and there was no way of stopping it. He knew the catastrophe that was about take place.

"Get the hell out of here and fast," he yelled at Bob.

Bob took the first side street to the left and tracked back to the road to the turnpike towards Washington. Jonathan, who was a short distance behind them, saw them and followed. They were on a different mission now, a mission to save themselves. Out of Hoboken and back on the turnpike extension in less than two minutes, they blew through the turnpike toll booth at over ninety mph. They were five minutes out of Hoboken and back on the turnpike going as fast as their government issue vehicles could travel when they heard it. It was in the distance, but far louder than anything either of them ever heard. Strange looked back toward New York City and what he saw made the hair on the nape of his neck stand straight up.

"They've hit the George Washington Bridge!" He needed to say nothing else.

Five minutes later, they heard the sound again, this time much closer, but they were fifteen miles away from the tunnel and moving fast. The wooded area of northern New Jersey would help muffle the blast wind and allow them to make good their escape.

CHAPTER 55

The pain in Jack's leg had subsided somewhat during the almost eight hours he sat in the ER with me. The pain in his heart grew with each new person that was stretchered in with catastrophic burns, wounds from flying glass, or radiation burns.

There were secondary explosions that shook buildings but were not close enough to present any danger to the people in the ER. At least that's what we thought. As it turned out, the winds from New Jersey died down. They shifted in a northeasterly direction delaying the inevitable for the already devastated inhabitants of Manhattan; a bath in a chlorine cloud. The terrorists didn't settle for simply making the statement that they could place nuclear devices anywhere they chose, but they wanted to put an exclamation point on the damage they had already done. They placed explosives at the chemical plants that dotted the Jersey shore opposite Manhattan and set them to go off an hour after the nuclear devices. The effect was horrible. People on the New Jersey side of the Hudson were dying where they stood in the streets.

The later news reports and video would show an eerie scene as the cold air held the chlorine cloud low over the water as it all swept across the Hudson river like a gossamer predator creeping ever so slowly upon its prey. The cloud hit lower Manhattan first and like the leaves hitting the wall in Clement Moore's Christmas poem, rose from the heat of the fires from the second explosion. For some first responders and those who survived the nuclear explosion it was an exquisitely painful death. The only saving grace, if there was any to be found this day, was that some of the people who died from the chlorine were spared longer and more painful deaths.

There was one piece of good fortune. The winds again began to blow cold and hard. The effect was to dissipate the chlorine cloud before it could cross the entire island of Manhattan.

Jack didn't know, nor did anyone else in the ER, that they were spared from additional tragedy by these winds of chance. But Jack was still disconsolate. He was sobbing quietly. He told me his story as he remembered it and took blame for his actions in a very Catholic way. He confessed his sins and for his penance, he was mourning the loss of his world.

The influx into the ER began to slow down as the late afternoon sun began to sink behind what was left of the west side of Manhattan. The Doctors who were at it all day took Jack to an X-ray machine that was drawing power from the backup generators. They photographed his leg, shot him full of local anesthetic, reset the breaks as best they could, splinted and wrapped the leg, and rolled him back to our little room. They gave him a strong sedative and he slept.

I watched him for a few moments. The lines in his face softened and he was truly at peace for a few moments in his private, yet sadly public, hell. I found my way to the cafeteria, which was nearly stripped bare. There was coffee brewing. Sometimes, in the middle of the most terrifying crisis, the little things are what bring us back to our reality. The smell and taste of coffee was all that was real at that moment.

Doctors and nurses who worked over sixteen hours without a break, sat drinking coffee in small clusters and talked softly and grimly about what had happened and what would be, no pun intended, the fallout of the day's tragic events. I asked if I could join them and was welcomed as a fellow traveler.

As I listened to their conversations, I began to understand what fate lay in store for me and millions more New Yorkers. The radiation levels they monitored with their blue badges from the X-ray department were off the charts. The bombs were dirty and would, over time, kill all of the people who passed through the ER that day. The deaths would be slow and painful. Cancers from the radiation would eat away at their bodies and ultimately reach their brains. It was a death sentence with no reprieve.

As I walked back to the ER, I was angry. I hadn't done anything to anyone that would invite such a payback. No vendettas, no unfinished business, no hard feelings. Why had someone come to hate me so much, that he would want to take my life, and that of several million other New Yorkers? I was angry at Jack and our government too. What was it that was so important that they would risk the loss of one life? Money? Power? Fame? It seemed that all these things were quite worthless in the bright light of the aftermath of their pursuit.

I sat by Jack for the next several hours. The noise level in the streets surrounding the hospital was increasing as FEMA first responders and Hasmat emergency service vehicles began to enter Manhattan. Staten Island was spared from fallout and lost only a few hundred people to the chlorine gas. Brooklyn was less lucky as the early fallout made it across the East River, but the wind shift pushed much of the fallout northward into Queens. The Bronx was spared as the offshore breezes carried the fallout and the remnants of the chlorine out into the Long Island Sound and the Atlantic Ocean. Manhattan had borne the brunt of the attacks. Over two million souls departed in the blink of an eye and many hundreds of thousands more were irradiated and doomed to die a very painful and slow death.

CHAPTER 56

Several months had passed and it was August in southern New Jersey. All of Manhattan along with parts of Brooklyn and Queens were totally evacuated and would be deserted for the foreseeable future. Jack's story had now become mine.

I had finally managed to connect with Strange, who came to see his friend.

Jack, whose cancers moved quickly through his body barely looked up at Strange, but managed a smile and a raise of the hand in recognition. Strange, now eighty-three, understood. He withdrew and sat with me for a short time without speaking.

"Jack told me the entire story," I said, "up to my meeting him in Pennsylvania Station.

"I tried to warn him and the city," Strange said sadly, as he related what happened that terrible day. He looked at Jack and a tear fell from his eye.

"Why were you and your friends the only ones following these people?" I asked?

He looked as if he was trying to swallow back the bile that was rising in his throat.

"They simply didn't care," he said. "They didn't want it known that they were unable to recover what they lost," he went on in a tone that spit acrimony. "With the change in the Congress last election cycle, they were hunkered down in the White House."

"The government was in denial," he went on. "There was no one listening.

"Have you seen his son," Strange asked, more to ease his own tension than curiosity about Jack, Jr.

"He was here last week. He came to see his father, but spent considerable time trying to find his wife, son, and mother. I told him what I saw at the station, but could give no assurances whether Jack III was dead or alive. His wife would have been on the George Washington Bridge at the time of the first blast."

"As for Veronica, I've checked all the hospitals and rescue and recovery services that are helping account for survivors. She was not directly in the blast zone, but was likely killed by the shock waves that were so powerful they took down Penn Station and the buildings around it, and would have hit the west facing buildings along 5th Avenue like a sledgehammer. The building she was in was leveled.

Jack Junior was hollowed out when he left me," I said. "He mumbled something about business to attend to and I haven't heard from him since."

Strange reported one additional piece of shocking news, Jack III was alive. No one knew that he survived and Strange managed to spirit him out of the country.

"Why would you need to get him out of the country," I asked unable to grasp the gravity in Strange's tone.

"For the same reason that I must move you to safety. We are all in danger," Strange said in a matter of fact tone. "There are people who do not want this story told. What they know about you is that you helped Jack after the explosions and whether or not he told you anything is a chance they won't take. Things are hot and I must get you out of here."

Strange suspected that he was being followed while he was here and that he, and his son, Gianni were in danger if they were found in the U.S. He couldn't come again so he made arrangements to move Jack and I.

I wasn't prepared for the lengths he would go to assure our safety. It seemed like he barely raised his hand and three men in scrubs came quickly with a gurney for Jack and a wheelchair for me. We were loaded into an ambulance which screamed out of the sanitarium with siren blazing and lights flashing.

Jack's admiration for the amount of planning that Strange put into an operation was well placed, but even though Jack had described all of the capers he knew of, this one was more than I could imagine.

We left the sanitarium and headed south and west toward the county hospital. The ambulance pulled into the ER dock where a second gurney and an operative in a wheelchair that were already in the ambulance were off-loaded. They were hurried into the ER and never stopped, leaving by the front door as quickly as they entered the back. They were hustled into a waiting hearse with the gurney completely covered by a sheet. To the casual observer it was nothing more than disposing of a dead body, to someone following it was a poor attempt at a getaway, which was exactly what Strange had planned.

From the "in" door of the ER to the hearse took no more than a dozen seconds and they were off again behind tinted windows to where I had no idea. We, in the meantime, simply drove away from the hospital with lights flashing as if we were on another mission of mercy.

CHAPTER 57

Several hours and many miles later, we arrived at Atlantic City International Airport. The ambulance sped past the main terminal and toward the FBO and a private hangar where Gianni and his Italian Security Service Gulfstream jet were waiting. In the time it took to move Jack and I onto the plane and fire up the engines, we were on our way over the Atlantic.

As we settled in, Strange saw that I had questions. How did Jack III survive? Where were we going? How were we going to keep the government from eliminating us.

"On the morning of the explosions," Strange began, "Jack III was not at Penn Station. I knew that Jack Sr. was going there to meet him and as we sat in the rest stop on the turnpike, I tried calling him numerous times only to hear clicks on the other end. Fortunately, it had the desired effect. He was running late and would miss the early morning train from State College and would have to drive into the city. But I think that the rest of the story might be better told by Gianni who debriefed Jack on the plane over the Atlantic."

"Jack was traumatized" Gianni began, "but he told me this story"

He was not in the station on Good Friday. He had been delayed by a series of frantic and inaudible phone calls. He didn't recognize the phone number in the display on his cell phone, but they were so insistent that he tried several times to return the call. He was not accustomed to receiving calls at 2:00 a.m. and not in this way. This had him on edge. He was already running late when the first call came in. He had spent the evening before finishing a report he had been asked to do by his grandfather. It was his first assignment with his new employer, Houston Oil and Gas, since his graduation. He was irritated when he awoke to find his printer had jammed and he had to reset the print job and start it over.

The suspicious phone calls made it even more frustrating. He was late and it looked like he would miss his train. He moved as quickly as he could but the interruptions were too much. He hadn't wanted to drive into the City, but it looked as if he would have to if he was to be close to on time. He would call his grandfather later in the morning, but it was time to get on the road.

The drive across Pennsylvania on Interstate 80 in the very early morning was somewhat lonely with the exception of a few long haul truckers, there were few cars on the road. He hitched on to the back of an 18 wheeler, and except for some wind swirl from the truck he was flying. By 6:00 a.m. he was crossing into New Jersey. He was tired but elated that he might not be too late.

Then it happened, up ahead he saw the flashing lights and traffic building. An accident in the median strip had the state troopers closing the left lane and filtering traffic, which was beginning to build with the onset of the morning rush hour, into one lane. He slowed to 20 MPH and saw all the time he made up in Pennsylvania dissipate in New Jersey.

He used the slow down to call his grandfather who would be up and around by this hour. His cell phone was fully charged, but there was no response from his grandfather in New York. No ring. No answer.

The slow down became a traffic stop as an ambulance arrived at the scene and the injured were treated, stabilized, and transported. After 40 minutes, the traffic began to flow again. It was nearly 7:00 a.m. and Jack tried again to call his grandfather but to no avail.

He was an hour and a half out of New York and hungry. He pulled off the Interstate at the first restaurant he spied along the way. He would have breakfast and call his grandfather.

The morning breakfast crowd was heavy with golfers. It was, he remembered, Good Friday, the unofficial opening of the golf season in the east. Even so, he noted that these must have been die-hards as it was bitter cold for an April morning. At 7:50 a.m. Jack climbed back into the driver's seat of his vintage Austin-Healey. He reset his radio to a New York news station and drove back onto the Interstate. He had yet to reach his grandfather or his mother who was traveling the very same road only miles ahead and likely on the George Washington Bridge by now.

The news station was full of the normal local stuff that makes up a morning radio broadcast. The weather was what he guessed it to be; clear and very cold with winds out of the northwest at a brisk 12 miles per hour. It was 7:55 a.m. and the announcer was segwaying into the traffic reports when the road under jack's car began to shake. The radio went silent though it was not the first thing he noticed. It was the blinding flash of light ahead of him and the ferocious wind that pushed his small car sideways down the highway that had his undivided attention.

Regaining control, he turned onto the median strip and headed back west. He knew exactly what had happened and wanted to be as far away from the center of this blast as possible. He had just witnessed an atomic blast. It needed no further explanation than that. It was get the hell out of there as fast as wheels could take him, and hope he was far enough away to avoid the electrical interference that could short circuit his car.

The Austin-Healey must have had the same feeling because it fairly flew westward back into Pennsylvania. He stopped in Stroudsburg to get his bearings and try to get a fix on what had happened. He searched the radio dial and found a Philadelphia station that was reporting that something had happened in New York, but not exactly what it was.

He found a diner and sat down with a cup of coffee to collect his thoughts. His grandfather had told him that in a pinch he was to call the number on the card he had given him and say the word 'wolf'. He did just that and sat and waited.

The TV in the diner had gone to a news conference at the White House. The president was addressing the nation and giving them the bad news. New York had been nuked. No questions taken by the president and no answers to the same question asked 300,000,000 times: how?

His first thoughts were for his family. His mother, grandmother, and grandfather were all in or around the blast area. He knew enough about radioactivity to understand that they were dead. Even if the original blast didn't get them, the fallout would.

When his cell phone rang it so startled him that he almost spilled his coffee. It was an international phone number on the display. He answered it immediately. It was Strange. He had gotten Jack's message. He explained that he had been trying to call Jack's grandfather all night but phone service was out. It took him six tries to finally get through to young Jack.

Jack was nearly hyperventilating as he related what he had seen that morning. He wanted Strange's help in finding his family. Strange told him that would have to wait. He was to get into his car and go to an address in Washington as soon as possible. His life could well depend on it.

The phone went dead as he quickly paid his tab and moved toward his car. He decided that he would stay away from the main roads in and out of NYC as the emergency services would probably tie them up indefinitely. He headed south on Pennsylvania 611 through Easton and Philly. Once in Philly he would cut west and south through Virginia avoiding the tunnels around Baltimore.

The drive was uneventful and took his mind off the tragedy he had witnessed that morning. He was trying to piece together the full meaning of Strange's dictum to him about getting to Washington ASAP because his life depended upon it. He knew little of Strange's relationship to his grandfather other than Strange represented HOG in Europe. He had been to his grandfather's for holidays when Strange had visited and had listened to the chatter about conditions in the Middle East and Europe, but he had no idea what it was that Strange actually did or how he would know that Jack was in danger.

Strange took over the story from here. "Jack arrived in Washington at 3:00 in the afternoon," he began, "and with little difficulty found the house that I had directed him to. As he approached it, the garage door opened and Gianni waved him into it. It was a one of many CIA safe houses.

Once in the garage, Jack was directed through the kitchen of the house into a sitting room located in the center of the house with only interior walls and no windows. There Jack met me for the second time."

"What happened then?" I asked, wanting to know more of this cloak and dagger action.

"After very brief pleasantries," Strange began, "the conversation turned to the reality on the ground. I explained to him that New York had been nuked by a 'terrorist' cell from Virginia. The bombs were smuggled into a little used harbor that wasn't on the Homeland Security radar and sources in Iran, Syria and Lebanon said that it was a put up job ala 9/11. They were worried that if such an attack took place the US might retaliate in kind anywhere and everywhere in the Middle East. Their information was specific and pointed to a so-called terrorist cell in Virginia that had been infiltrated by agents of the DIA, but had been off-limits to the CIA and NSA. I flew to Washington to try to rouse some old friends in the CIA to take a look at the information, but they were totally in the dark and skeptical. They were good enough to give me a driver and cell phones. The driver worked but the phones were useless.

I told Jack about the chase up the Jersey turnpike," he continued, "and how several unmarked vehicles were in the just the right place at just the right time to intercept him and simply block his pursuit by creating an artificial traffic jam at highway speeds."

"Jack wanted to know why I felt that he was in danger," Strange went on.

"I gave him the short version of my involvement with Jack's grandfather and our plan to create and control events to our benefit and how, the government, after losing the suitcase nuke technology saw an opportunity to turn a serious breach of security into an excuse to take out Iran ala 9/11 and Iraq. But they had to eliminate anyone who knew of the suitcase bombs. He understood. Missing the train created a glitch in their plan, but only a minor one. They would clean up the loose ends later."

"How did you get away?" I asked impatiently.

"We stayed in the safe house for a few more hours. The government agencies friendly to the administration would be on the look out for us and there would be no reprieve if we were caught. The CIA was at odds with the administration" Strange continued, "but my friends there could only give temporary shelter and limited cover. They arranged a plane from a small airfield in Virginia. We used it as a decoy. Gianni had his own plane, which belonged to the Italian government, waiting at National Airport.

Our plan was to send two cars from the safe house to the airfield in Virginia. Jack, Gianni, and I would go blackout and wait until dark, and neutralize the remaining agents who were staking out our position."

"The decoy cars pulled out of the garage of the safe house at 6:30 in the evening," Strange went on, "and as expected, they were followed by three unmarked sedans. The decoy cars made no pretense of the direction they were going. They drove as if they didn't expect to be tailed. They made it easy for the chase cars to keep up. The first part of the escape plan went off with a hitch.

We went blackout and sat quietly for about 45 minutes. The fading twilight of early spring made visibility very difficult. What the CIA agents on stake out didn't know, was the house behind the safe house was connected by tunnel and that a car was waiting in its garage. We had put out several street lights on the escape house street making it almost total darkness. I sent Gianni out of the safe house. Five minutes later Jack and I moved into the tunnel between the safe house and the escape house. It was difficult going in the dark, but we managed to reach the escape house. We waited for a several minutes more before moving to the garage. As we entered the darkness, Gianni hurried us along with a smile in his voice. He had neutralized the remaining agents permanently, and was eager to get to the airport and out of U.S. jurisdiction. We drove away from the escape house and headed to the private hangar at National Airport."

"What happened to the operatives who went to the airport in Virginia?" I asked.

"They arrived at the airport and 'discovered' that they were being followed. After a brief bit of gun play, they took off on a carefully planned route into the Virginia countryside and disappeared giving the impression that we were still in the country."

"Did you encounter any trouble at National Airport?"

"No," Strange answered. "The Airport was beginning its normal evening slow down. The number of flights in and out diminished as night progressed in an effort to cut down noise in the surrounding neighborhoods. The evening rush to New York and Boston was over and the parking area was emptying. Gianni chose an area in long term parking that would afford the most cover for the car. It would take several weeks before anyone noticed the vehicle had been abandoned and several more days to discover that it was an unmarked CIA vehicle. By then we would be far away in the Italian Alps.

We moved furtively through the hangar area to the last hangar on the flight line. The main doors were open but the hangar was dark. Gianni moved sidewise down the wall flanking the aircraft, a light went on in the cockpit of the jet. Gianni sent a beam of light into the cockpit window and the pilot who was watching him approach, opened the aircraft door and walked down the three steps to the hangar floor. He and Gianni had arranged signals to be certain no one had been able to compromise their escape. All was right.

Jack and I moved quickly into the belly of the craft and took seats behind windows that were blacked out from the inside. As soon as we were settled in, the jet engines started and shortly, we began to roll forward and down to the end of the runway. We were second in line for takeoff and in less than ten minutes were airborne and heading out over the Atlantic. I made sandwiches for Jack and Gianni and then we slept.

The pilot woke me when we were 2 hours out of Italy. The smell of fresh coffee I made woke Jack and Gianni. We had a full plate to chew on."

"Jack was like his grandfather," Strange went on, "quick and agile of mind with the plodding thoroughness of an engineer. He wanted to know if I thought any of his family survived. I told him that they were most likely killed in the blast or soon to be dead from radiation poisoning. He took it with little emotion. He was rested and clearer in his mind of what would need to be done. He told me that he was in for the ride and wanted to play his part in finding and dealing with the people who did this. He just couldn't get to the who or how."

"Gianni," I asked, "as an Italian citizen, what's your take on all this?"

"I cannot comprehend" Gianni replied, "the magnitude of the evil I have been a witness to and the depravity of people who could even think about doing something this heinous."

"I still don't understand why these people would want us dead," I said as Strange took a second to reflect on what Gianni had just related. "Whatever we could possible accuse them of could never be proven?"

"The simple accusation that the bombs were American technology and the government couldn't protect it," Strange began, "would open an embarrassing can of worms for the administration. The Russians, who stole the plans and built the bombs, won't admit to ever having the technology because they don't want to be seen as inept and/or corrupt enough to lose or sell the bombs to the Russian mob. The mob won't admit anything about anything and the terrorists won't finger the mob."

"That leaves us" I said finally understanding the fix we were in. "We're the only ones who could and would make the accusation."

CHAPTER 58

Several hours later and miles closer to an uncertain destination, I was somewhat refreshed by sleep and fresh coffee. As the sun was coming up through the plane's windows, I was still marveling at the efficiency with which Strange had moved Jack and I out of harm's way, but I wanted to know more about what happened to Jack III.

"That was easy," I said, "you made that look like child's play!"

"What was easy?" Strange quizzed with a definite edge to his voice. "Three CIA agents who probably knew nothing of us died at the safe house and had the plan backfired, we might all be dead too. We are in danger", Strange said emphatically, "we have to land in Italy and avoid being seen or we will be compromised and eliminated."

"Sorry," I said weakly.

"That's all right", Gianni said in a conciliatory tone, "Jack thought the same thing after we got him out of the country."

"What happened?"

"We landed in Milano," Gianni answered. "and in the privacy of a blacked out government hangar Jack, dressed in the coveralls of a serviceman, was loaded on to a utility van on its way to make service calls in Bellagio, on Lake Como. Silvana Mille, one of my most trusted agents, was already in the van. She was to brief Jack on weaponry and how to find their destination should they get separated. I came along as the driver.

The road to Bellagio" Gianni continued, "was about 110 kilometers under normal conditions. These weren't normal. I needed to know if we were spotted in Milano. I set out on SS36, a main artery going north towards Bellagio. 55 kilometers later, I exited without warning at Nibionno, drove west a few kilometers and at Lurago d'Erba, turned onto S41. It was a good road but winding and hilly with plenty of places to set a trap which had become necessary. At the turn in Lurago, I noticed a large sedan with four men in suits behind us. Silvana had seen them too and pointed to Longono al Segrino on her map. It was the perfect place. The road formed a very tight 'S' and would require the sedan to slow down. This would allow the van to gain some ground on the north road out of the town. The landscape became wooded there and at the north end of Lago Segrino there was an opening in the trees. We would stop there and take up positions at the edge of the forest."

"Don't stop now," I said, "I want to know how you set up your field of fire" the combat veteran in me coming out, "and if young Jack is as steel nerved as his grandfather."

"We left the van in the center of the opening," Gianni began solemnly, "the tree line formed a bowl behind us. Our field of fire was at 4, 6, and 8, on the clock. We had AK47's with 30 round clips and Glock 9mm. with 15 round clips."

"Nice!" I commented. "Did they take the bait?"

"Five minutes after we got into position" Gianni went on, "they drove right up to the back of the van. All four of them got out and drew weapons. That was the signal. Jack turned out to have a steel spine and a really good eye. He took out the two men by the driver's side door with two quick shots. Silvana took care of the one on the passenger side and I got the driver trying to get back to the sedan. Five seconds and 4 shots."

"Who were they?" I asked.

"My best guess is contractors." Gianni replied.

"What about the noise?" I pressed.

"No noise. Silencers." He answered.

"What happened next?" I asked, anxious to hear more of this story.

"Nothing" Gianni answered smiling. "We proceeded to Bellagio without incident and I drove the van back to Milano."

"Where did Jack and Silvana go?" I wanted him to fill in the rest of the story.

"The same place we are going" Strange chimed in, "the high ground."

CHAPTER 59

The morning sun reflected off of the reddish tan roofs of Milano as we made our final approach into Linate Aeroporte. Strange made a final check of our planned exit from the airport and all the contingencies he had put in place should we be followed. It had been many years since I took up a weapon, but a warrior never forgets, he just gets a little slower.

The plane nestled softly to the ground and wound its way to the far end of the airfield. Once safely inside the blackout hangar, Jack and I were moved into a waiting ambulance. Gianni served as our guide and Strange rode shotgun. We traced young Jack and Silvana's route north along SS36 but never left the highway until we reached a point south of Bellagio where the road forked. We went right towards Lecco and Ospidale di Lecco, a beautiful and very modern hospital.

Strange, dressed in the white coat of a Doctor with a stethoscope around his neck, led the way. Jack and I were wheeled into a private suite that Strange had arranged in advance. We gave the appearance of the rich and famous being brought in for special treatment, a scene not unfamiliar to Lake Como, and then disappeared down the private elevator into an underground garage where Gianni had parked his utility van. In less than 15 minutes we were back on the road heading north to the high ground. But that's another story.

CPSIA information can be obtained at www.ICGtesting.com
Printed in the USA
LVOW11s2344300114

371762LV00013B/249/P